Old
Testament
Exegesis

D0078091

SOCIETY OF BIBLICAL LITERATURE
Resources for Biblical Study

Edited by

Marvin A. Sweeney

Number 39

OLD TESTAMENT EXEGESIS
A Guide to the Methodology

by
Odil Hannes Steck

translated by
James D. Nogalski

NCMC
BS
1174.2
·B3713
1998

3894 8421

OLD TESTAMENT EXEGESIS

A Guide to the Methodology

by
Odil Hannes Steck

translated by
James D. Nogalski

SCHOLARS PRESS
Atlanta, Georgia

OLD TESTAMENT EXEGESIS
A Guide to the Methodology
Second Edition

by
Odil Hannes Steck
translated by
James D. Nogalski

Copyright © 1998 by the Society of Biblical Literature

All rights reserved. No part of this work may be reproduced or transmitted in any form or by any means, electronic or mechanical, including photocopying and recording, or by means of any information storage or retrieval system, except as may be expressly permitted by the 1976 Copyright Act or in writing from the publisher. Requests for permission should be addressed in writing to the Rights and Permissions Office, Scholars Press, P.O. Box 15399, Atlanta, GA 30333-0399, USA.

Library of Congress Cataloging-in-Publication Data

Steck, Odil Hannes.
    [Exegesis des Alten Testaments. English]
    Old Testament exegesis : a guide to the methodology / by Odil
Hannes Steck ; translated by James D. Nogalski. — 2nd ed.
      p.   cm. — (Resources for biblical study ; no. 39)
    Includes bibliographical references.
    ISBN 0-7885-0465-7 (pbk. : alk. paper)
    1. Bible. O.T.—Criticism, interpretation, etc.—Methodology.
I. Title. II. Series.
BS1174.2.B3713 1998
221.6'01—dc21   98-20955

Printed in the United States of America
on acid-free paper

The growing precision of our understanding should enhance, and not diminish our sense of wonder.

Alfred Brendel, pianist

Contents

Preface to the English Edition

This guide to the methodology of Old Testament exegesis has been used in the German speaking world for 25 years. In 1989 (for the 12th edition), it was thoroughly revised and expanded. The 13th edition from 1993 is now presented in English translation. This book is not an introduction to self-study, but presumes an academic setting (advanced seminar, etc.) in which the principles of this methodology can be illustrated to the student. Examples illustrating the various points of the methodology can be found in the footnotes of this workbook.

Changes have been undertaken for the benefit of English readers regarding the bibliographic references in the German edition. Where translations of German works exist in English, these are mentioned (even if they are not translations of the most recent edition of that work). In addition, more recent publications treating certain subjects have been added to the English version of this guide.

With the aid of scientific exegesis, this manual shows one how to approach the *historical* meaning of Old Testament texts during the period of their productive formation. This meaning is the *original* meaning of an Old Testament text within the transmission realm of the Old Testament. This meaning must be processed because it is the foundational meaning. This meaning is constitutive for the formulation and the context of an Old Testament text. For this reason, this workbook places particular emphasis upon two aspects: (1) Historical exegesis must proceed from the *existing* text and the final context rather than from diachronic hypotheses. (2) The complexity of the Old Testament, in its existing form, however, forces one to *diachronic* exegesis. It does so because the origin of the formulation (!) can only be understood as arising in a particular time in Ancient Israel. The procedures of §6 and §10 demonstrate that exegetically historical work must ultimately arrive at the shape of the text and the context as it exists in the Old Testament.

The subject of this guide is not the application of Old Testament texts or alternative methods for understanding the Old Testament. These alternative methods include reader response criticism, deconstruction, feminist, material-ist, and psychological approaches (see J.Ch. Exum and D.J.A. Clines, eds. The New Literary Criticism and the Hebrew Bible, JSOT.S 143, Sheffield, 1993; and below, p. -). This guide concentrates on historical exegetical methods.

I wish to thank the translator, Prof. Dr. James Nogalski, and all those who have helped him for their concerted efforts in making this guide accessible to the English speaking world. Special mention should be made for the help of Prof. Drs. Pamela J. Scalise and Mark E. Seifrid, as well as Ruth Funk, Peter Schwagmeier, and Konrad Schmid, who compared drafts of this manuscript with the German. Finally, the Old Testament Colloquium of The Southern Baptist Theological Seminary and Prof. Dr. Steven Tuell read the English translation and offered helpful corrections and insights at key junctures.

In addition, I wish to thank the Society of Biblical Literature, Scholars Press, and Neukirchener Verlag for helping to make this translation possible. Finally, I wish to mention Prof. Dr. Marvin Sweeney for his careful reading as editor of the series Reources for Biblical Study.

Zurich, May 1995
Odil Hannes Steck

Preface

Dear Reader,

You should work with this book. Perhaps you have already thumbed through it, and glanced through portions. The first impression was probably: it's all so complicated, so difficult. Don't worry. This book will not confuse you, but will help to clarify your thoughts.

I can picture the situation. A short text lies before you from the Old Testament—in Hebrew. You must exegete it. You desire to comprehend this text, but how should you proceed? In the grasp of this text, do *we* say what we want to hear, or does *it* tell us what we should hear? One must ask the question self-critically, because an ancient text cannot defend itself. It has long outlived its author who could protect it. It needs your help. This book can accompany you as you become an attorney, mediator, and defender of the text, in order that it can speak *its* message, and come to life for us. What is necessary for this task?

Understanding the words presumes knowledge. This is certainly the case among living people, but even more so for an ancient text. This book would like to show you how one acquires such knowledge. The historical tool, developed over generations, will be delivered to you as precisely and exactly as we use it today. Its service to you, and to the text, is to find the knowledge necessary for understanding, by means of the clarification of very simple questions.

Your text has been variously transmitted in the ancient manuscripts. How did it read originally? §3 of this book will help you with this question.

Copyrights did not yet exist in antiquity. Even in a short text, statements from various times can stand next to one another. That is no deficiency. It is the richness of an ancient text. To take the text seriously means to distinguish the statements in the text, to separate that which was once separated, and also to listen separately to each of the voices in the text from various times as portions of various literary works of the Old Testament to which they once belonged. But one may not forget the return trip, the trip from the separation

back again to the unity, to the harmony of the voices in the text as it stands
before us. That is the path by which God has been manifested in the course of
the text's development. §§4–6 will teach you how to distinguish various biblical witnesses in your text; to hear them separately; and then to hear them again
together.

But now on to the goal of understanding, what is it that these voices want
to say?

Whoever speaks prudently, formulates precisely. Therefore, understanding primarily means to listen to the language; to perceive how something is
said—and how it is not said. If your text is formed according to a common
pattern, then it provides insight into what it wants to say, like birth announcements and menus in our time. §7 seeks to prepare the way for the question of
the linguistic shape of your text.

A text intends much more than just what is there. When contemporaries with the same level of knowledge interchange linguistically, they can
also understand one another through allusions, associations, and connotations.
We are not contemporaries with ancient Israel. We must inquire into those
things connected with a text which are left unspoken. §8 formulates the question of the text's intellectual connotations. §9 treats the question of the expressed, historically concrete associations from the time of formulation, including the date, author, and the addressee of your text.

These are simple, necessary questions. They help partially clarify how one
can experience what the text has to say, and how it lived during the time when
it was formulated and transmitted in Ancient Israel. The goal and culmination
of all exegesis is to determine and to trace the contents of the text's statements
in order to become its attorney, as far as those of us from a later time are able
to do. §10 will make it easier for you to reach this goal.

The questions are simple, even though the path to elucidation in this book
is not quite as simple because of the great antiquity of the texts, the manner of
their transmission, and the foreign, unfamiliar world which one encounters
therein. This difficulty is also related to the current status of the tool which we
must lay before you in all its refinement and precision. Anyone standing at the
beginning of one's study does not master it in the initial encounter. However,
when using this book, one can concentrate on that which is most important in
every section. Teaching sessions, particularly introductory exegesis courses,
will help you concentrate on that which is most important. They will also help
you to grow with this book. It is so written that even at the end of one's study
(in exams, master's work, or even doctoral work), it can still serve as an orientation and as stimulation in the methodological questions of Old Testament
exegesis. Last but not least, please remember that this book has all types of
Old Testament texts in view, but not every text asks all of the questions explicated in this book.

Even the print type of this workbook will meet you half-way, in order that
you can find your way through the whole thing. As you will see, one must dif-

ferentiate between the larger (serif) and the smaller (sans serif) print. As you know, even the "small print" is important, but in our case secondary, namely to be used for closer scrutiny, for explication and differentiation. The shaded sidebars are a second help. They emphasize in print the concrete procedural directions for the individual methods.

In exegetical work with this book I wish you joy, courage, concentration, and through it all, the discovery of how rich a biblical text is, and how rich it can still make us.

Foreword to the 12th Edition

A decade lies between the 8th edition of this book, which Hermann Barth and I undertook, and the currently revised 12th edition. A revision has thus become necessary in light of the literature references alone. At the same time one must consider numerous changes in the specific development of the discussion, at least briefly and selectively. Greater engagement and expansions have been undertaken in §1, in order to facilitate entry and orientation, and in §6, in order to properly convey the blossoming of the redaction-historical questions in recent years. Further, there is an introduction to the inter-related methodological steps of §§4–6 and §§7–9 respectively. Finally, the formulation of concrete procedural directions for the individual methods should facilitate the practical utilization of the workbook. A number of places have been shortened in order to keep the size and cost of a student book manageable. Above all, extensive dialogue with other methodological positions has been reduced. It is sufficient if our position from the 8th edition is documented.

The overall structure and, to a large extent, even the formulation of the workbook, have not been changed for the 12th edition. Feedback from assistants and students indicates these elements have proven effective in practical terms to those who use the book. Reasons of continuity in the essential outlook enable this, and reasons of cost require it.

Dr. Hermann Barth asked me to undertake and to be responsible for the revision by myself. For some time, he has not been involved in academic education, but in the pastorate. He is now employed by the Evangelical Church of Germany in Hanover. With a heavy heart I now follow his request to take his name off of the title page of the workbook. In continuing thankfulness and affiliation I emphasize the extensive contribution which he provided in the preparation and formation of this book during an extraordinarily fruitful and pleasant collaboration. His contribution remains preserved directly or indirectly even in this new edition.

The *purpose* of this workbook remains unchanged. In this regard, what we said in the foreword of the 8th edition can only be repeated. The workbook, "now as before, proceeds from the supposition that the goal of the discipline of Old Testament studies not only includes the acquisition of certain factual knowledge, but also includes the adoption of exegetical methods for determining the original meaning of Old Testament transmissions. Only thus can one achieve discernment with the results of research and instruction in procedure which transcends mere reception.

Therefore, as before, the workbook is conceived primarily for use by teacher and student as a synopsis of the individual methods: their definition, their procedural steps, and their significance for the total historical understanding of an Old Testament text. This is done without detriment to the book's claim of contributing to the present discussion of method in Old Testament research. With this decision about the purpose, the book does not wish to be, indeed cannot be, an introduction to self-study. Rather, it is designed for use in academic instruction. It is related to, indeed dependent upon, the processes of the demonstration and utilization of the methods which take place there. It would like to provide a written basis for this position.

For the moment, if we disregard the workbook's approach and the adoption of its perspectives concerning the purpose of Old Testament research, the following reasons present themselves for using the book during one's course of study and occupational practice:

1. As a workbook, its primary function lies in classroom sessions and the processes of exegetical education. Specifically, it is used to accompany the student in several areas: beginning exegesis courses and papers; demonstrating and practicing a transparent process in exegetical lectures and seminars; advanced seminar papers and exegesis papers in the discipline of Old Testament.

2. As for the purpose, we envision that using this book during one's education will aid the user in acquiring basic exegetical capabilities. Among these capabilities, we include the mastery of the approaches and the paths toward solutions which are essential for exegetically determining meaning. Relatedly, the capabilities include the competency to determine which results the specific methodological approach to the problem produces when determining exegetical meaning. Learning and practicing these capabilities aids discernment when preparing Old Testament texts exegetically and when sifting through commentaries, etc.

3. In the exegetical practice of pastors and teachers of religion, it is important that one master the basic capabilities acquired in one's study. This

mastery protects one from undiscerning surrender to available secondary literature, and aids one in the critical use of this literature. It also enables one to pursue exegetical questions reasonably as they arise in practice. Because of the preparation time available, the workbook itself no longer serves, in its entirety, as a guide in many theological vocations. Therefore, the basic capabilities acquired with its help during one's study become even more important. Naturally, one can freely consult the workbook for information and as a reminder, even in one's practice."

My heartfelt thanks go to the Zurich assistants, Dr. R.G. Kratz and E. Bosshard, who have allowed me to learn from their teaching experiences with the workbook, and who have aided me with advice and deed in the revision. Heartfelt thanks also go to Dr. H. Barth, who provided me with critical insights for the revision, and to Brigitta Rotach, who helped me with the editorial work, and who, together with students Nicole Charmillot and Martin Riwar, very conscientiously helped me correct the galleys. I am no less grateful to Mrs. R. Funk for all her care in typing the manuscript, and to *Neukirchener Verlag* for their determined effort to produce a clear and economical teaching book for students.

I hope this book, even in its revised form, aids the understanding and the awe of the Old Testament.[1]

Zurich, November 1988
Odil Hannes Steck

---

[1] The motto of the book is taken from A. Brendel, *Musical Thoughts and Afterthoughts* (Princeton University Press, 1976), 37.

Translator's Preface to the English Version,

second printing

Comments from students and colleagues who have utilized this work in English underscore its usefulness and usability within classroom settings. These comments have been overwhelmingly positive, attesting to the validity of a historical exegetical introduction which both defines the methodological components and teaches students how to utilize them for themselves. Moreover, Steck's presentation illustrates how these components relate to one another, and many have expressed appreciation for this integration.

The feedback has also indicated that the scope of this work must be given due consideration within the didactic process, as Professor Steck states. Advanced students who have used this work have commented that it has helped them to put the pieces together. Rather than seeing the exegetical components as an eclectic assortment which only "specialists" of the various components can "do," Steck's introduction illustrates for them how the perspective provided by each methodological lens adds depth to the whole.

The workbook, while concise in its format, contains more information than a beginning student can possibly absorb within the confines of a typical course introducing the exegetical process. Left to themselves, beginning students will struggle to comprehend this work. Certain measures can, however, help insure that beginning students benefit from the book at a level appropriate to their present skill. Beginning students should concentrate upon the larger (serif) type and especially the summaries beside the shaded sidebars. Those teaching beginning students can help by integrating the book's presentation into the class itself. Two approaches have worked well in this regard.

The class can process Gen 28:10–22 since chapter 11 uses this text to illustrate the method. Or, one can lead the class through the various methodological observations in class as they relate to another text. Both approaches help beginning students comprehend the methods by illustrating them on a familiar text.

This second printing has corrected several typographical errors, and in response to feedback, the entire book has been reformatted with larger type to make it more reader friendly.

Lombard, IL, 1998
James D. Nogalski

Part One

Introduction

Anyone studying theology because of the desire to address the people and the questions of our time may be puzzled when looking at the syllabus of an introductory course on Old Testament exegesis at the beginning of the course and when considering the table of contents of this guide to the methodology. The direction of the work on biblical texts runs backwards. The biblical texts are not brought ever nearer to our present time in their authoritative significance for a Christian's faith, doctrine, and life. Instead, they are distanced further and further from today, and placed in the situation of their origin, which lies well in the past. Do these two movements not cancel themselves out? No— a necessary connection exists between the two.

The *goal* of all theological work is to bring the biblical word of God to life, and to give it dynamic and relevant expression for humanity today. The *task* of all theological work is to make sure, in this process of conveying the material, that the word of the biblical God remains that which confronts and which speaks what humans by themselves do not always know or desire. Within the framework of Christian theology, *Old Testament exegesis* also has a concern for determining the goal and task introduced in this workbook.

Exegesis has a subservient, but at the same time an undeniable role. Why? The biblical word of God in the Old Testament received its formulation in a certain time and through human witnesses with linguistic and experiential horizons which are more than two thousand years older than ours. If the formulations of these ancient texts are to become understandable, then one must ask about their meanings when these formulations arose and when they circulated inside the Old Testament. Therefore, Old Testament exegesis necessarily inquires into the past for the *original meaning* of the text. The inquiry of Old Testament exegesis into the original historical meaning has fundamental significance if these ancient texts are to be protected from the caprice to which we of today honorably, dishonorably, or unknowingly subject them in order to hear what we want to hear from them. It also has fundamental significance if the texts are to be allowed to speak their own message, in contrast to all later recipients. These statements are true even though, for us today, the inquiry is only a first step on the path of conveying the word of God toward which all theological disciplines must work together responsibly. Our workbook stands within this framework. It seeks to introduce one constituent task of the biblical speaking about God in the present, but it is a *fundamental* and *indispensable* approach. This approach asks about the original meaning which maintains the outlook, character, and richness of an Old Testament text against any patronizing treatment of the biblical message through a later message. All use of the Old Testament today, for theology and the church, must be measured against this approach. No less so, the frequently misused and painful reception history of the Old Testament during two millennia must be measured against it.

One could object, especially in the case of the Bible, that it is primarily the reader who actively contributes to the meaning of the text. The objection contains something valid, but at the same time something dangerous. It is undisputable that a reader productively cooperates in the perception of the text's dimensions of meaning which exceed the original author's intention. Nevertheless, the meaning originally given, particularly with biblical texts, must be protected over against reader associations about the text, in order that a hermeneutically responsible reception remains on the text's path of meaning, and does not allow the recipient to control the text. Should the historical association disappear, then so would the outlook of the biblical text for today, and it would be fatally replaced by the subjective, arbitrary reflections of "the text in me." Therefore, the principal task of exegesis is to protect the text's outlook.

§1 Foundation and Overview

A. THE TASK OF OLD TESTAMENT EXEGESIS

Old Testament exegesis is the endeavor to determine the historical, scientific, and documentable meaning of texts which have been transmitted in the Old Testament. Exegesis, therefore, confronts the *task* of determining the meaning and the intention of statements in the encountered text. It does so within the text's historical sphere of origin, and in the different phases of its Old Testament development, so that today the text manifests its historical character.

Exegesis is a *scientific* procedure to the degree that its understanding of a text is grounded exclusively upon knowledge and arguments whose appropriateness to the subject can be evaluated (approvingly or disapprovingly) by others, and whose rationale can be substantiated. Exegesis certainly does not maintain its scientific character by orienting itself to the experimental and empirical sciences, and by binding itself to their ideal of an ever more precise objective knowledge. Exegesis would then have to limit itself to the analysis and description of the linguistic surface of the texts. However, texts are a formal outgrowth of life events yet they supersede that life linguistically. Therefore, by means of a dynamic process, exegesis must understand texts as an event in which the following elements lead to the existing linguistic expression, including their "unspoken horizon of meaning," (H.-G. Gadamer[1]). This process includes the historical and social conditions, intellectual conceptions, experiences, impulses, the author's conceptual purpose, and the character of the

---

[1] Quoted literature will only be cited with an abbreviated title if the complete bibliographical reference can be taken from the Literature section (D) of the current chapter, or relatedly, in the case of literature on methodology, the introduction to the Old Testament, and theology of the Old Testament (sections H,G, and N in chapter two).

addressee. Exegesis can be evaluated against its subject matter only if it can provide an intersubjectively grounded account of the historical life which terminates linguistically in the text. Scientific exegesis does not, therefore, consider the text as a defenseless object which submits itself to the superior grasp of the scholar. Rather, it considers the text as a living entity which appears in relationship to life. The fundamental attitudes of scientific exegesis are therefore attention, the readiness to learn, the capacity to encounter, and the recognition of limits in relationship to the text as something other, or something foreign.[2]

To the extent that scientific exegesis relates to the *historical* determination of the text's meaning, in the period of its productive formation, it is limited to determining the original meaning inside the transmission realm of the Old Testament. As noted above, its direction of understanding is thereby differentiated from the event of a modern bible reader's personally encountered understanding. The individuality and depth of a bible reader's understanding has been determined essentially by experiences of the present. Scientific exegesis brings the text itself into direct relationship with those experiences. Scientific historical exegesis does not depreciate this directly applied understanding, but is able to clarify and to enrich it through the manifestation of the original meaning of the text: (1) by correcting arbitrary, subjective exploitation of the text; (2) by indicating the central subject matter of the text; and (3) by exposing the text's particular impulses which the present needs. Scientific historical exegesis is thereby an attorney for the original meaning of the text, providing the fundamental contribution for the clarification and enrichment of applied understanding. Naturally, applied understanding requires still more extensive theological help. Clarifications of meaning beyond Old Testament exegesis are necessary to the extent that an Old Testament text receives aspects of meaning which are expanded or modified through the witness of the New Testament and through far-reaching changes in the experience of reality. These clarifications take place in the theological realms of the New Testament, Church History, the history of dogma, and the history of theology. Also, they take place through dogmatic theology, ethics, and practical theology, in relationship to the form, validity, and obligation of the expanded or modified meaning of the text in the face of the present experi-

---

2 In addition, Kaiser, *Exegetical Method*, 40f, says correctly: "Scholarship requires that we give reasons for our judgments and avoid unfounded assertions; that we make clear our dependence on the work of others; that we specify the degree of probability of our results; that we present unsettled or presently insoluble or newly arisen problems for what they are and, if circumstances permit, give the reasons why we have not gone into them or given answers." In light of exegesis performed both orally and in written form, one should emphasize that in addition to the supporting arguments of an opinion, one should undeniably include a reasoned deliberation that excludes possible alternatives, in one's scientific inter-subjectively interpreted rationale (the principle of the exclusion of the opposite).

ence of reality. Only after these clarifications, in which theology has its undeniable task, can and should one turn back again to a higher plane. Specifically, one should be led by the content, through theological responsibility, to an applied understanding of the text for today as the goal of the totality. Then, no limits are placed before the vision of bringing the message of the biblical text productively into play for humanity in the present time, whether in the form of the traditional sermon, role plays, or bible dramas.

Also, scientific historical exegesis is always *critical* exegesis. Its execution necessarily includes critically recognizing one's own, or alien, presuppositions concerning the understanding of the text (above all as they come to light in B II 1). It also includes the necessity of recognizing any preconceptions imposed by exegetical tradition or by constellations from the history of research, by which everyone admittedly remains influenced. Once recognized, critical exegesis must control the preconceptions by relying upon the original meaning of the text. At the same time, the critique is directed at the text itself. This statement does not mean arrogant criticism of the text, rather it means an attitude of methodological doubt, which leads to a distinctive historical formation of judgment on various perceptions, approaches, and conclusions in the face of a text's character. It also interrogates the text's claim of truth in its historical situation.

B. IMAGINATION AND METHODOLOGICAL DIRECTION DURING EXEGETICAL WORK

I. The Value and Limits of Methodological Direction

Scientifically established exegetical work is methodologically transparent work. Nevertheless, it is not exhausted by the correct application and evaluation of the methodological steps for a given text. The process of determining the historical meaning of the text in its life situation is much more complex. Therefore, the value and limits of the methodological steps must be more closely determined.

Anyone utilizing methodological introductions must be conscious of the fact that the individual *methods* derive from an arsenal of elementary questions about the historical understanding of a text. These questions were already mentioned in the preface and include the following: The transmission of the text in the ancient manuscripts is not consistent; what is the original wording (see §3)?; The Old Testament writings have frequently grown by means of a protracted transmission process; how far do the oldest parameters reach, and what are later expansions and contexts (see §§4–6)?; Every linguistic utterance participates in the intellectual world of its author; what patterns of speech and concepts does the text presuppose (see §§7–8)?; In the same manner, every text participates in the historical and socio-historical realities of its time; how can one determine the text's historical realm, including that of its author and addressees (see §9)? The methods which are correspondingly elaborated (text criticism, literary criticism, the transmission-historical and redaction-historical approaches; the form critical and tradition historical approaches; and the determination of the historical setting) then constitute the development of an intellectual path where these questions will find answers. By its questions and by weighing observations and arguments, the description of methods pays attention to insights and possibilities which have proven effective on many individual texts. In its preliminary sketch, the description of methods presupposes images of expectation and the anticipation of results as suggested by the current state of exegetical science. But therein lies the problem of methodological exegetical work. Utilizing methods which depend upon the state of research and which anticipate results must neither patronize the texts, nor allow the texts to provide answers only according to the manner of the questions. The text does not have to subjugate itself to the current state of the description of methods. Rather, the utilization of the methods must remain steadfast to the data of the text.

But what access does historical exegesis have to the data of the text except the access of questions, observations, and argumentation guided by the methods? Here, the exegete's imagination plays a decisive role in looking at the selected text, by employing fantasy in the desire to understand a text historically. This fantasy is not obstructed and not yet rigidly controlled by methodological instructions. On the basis of the original hermeneutical unity between the text and today's reader, one's *fantasy* and *imagination* must thereby move in two directions during constant reading and reflection.

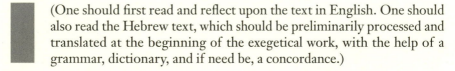

(One should first read and reflect upon the text in English. One should also read the Hebrew text, which should be preliminarily processed and translated at the beginning of the exegetical work, with the help of a grammar, dictionary, and if need be, a concordance.)

On the one hand, the exegete envisions how the text offers itself as a component *of today's world*, and on the other hand, the exegete envisions how the meaning and the setting of the text in *its own historical context* are manifested.

II. The Employment of Fantasy and Imagination

1. The Conception of the Text as a Component of Today's World

Before entering into an understanding of the text as a historical entity, the exegete should employ fantasy and imagination in order to imagine the text as a component of *today's* world, and to grasp those impressions and effects which the text might exert today on the exegete and on others (possible conversation partners, even for a sermon or lecture). These impressions and effects influence any historical understanding today, primarily subconsciously, and they represent a hermeneutical unity between text and reader, which must certainly be regained in an applied understanding after the exegetical historical interpretation. Employing fantasy and imagination helps to make one cognizant of these impressions and effects. It also helps to keep their influence active, but at the same time under control.

A series of simple questions can stimulate the power of conceptualization. The exegete poses these questions to himself/herself and to others when specifically considering the text. These include:

- What feelings, reactions, and associations does the text call forth in me? (For example: innate/foreign; my text/not my text; inviting/repulsive; happy/sad; illuminating/vague)
- What does the text say to me that is new, and in which life situation does it address me?
- What is important to me thematically, and in view of the statements of the text, to what do I not relate?
- What do I recognize as familiar?
- What stands out to me?
- What do I miss?
- What do I not understand?
- What disturbs me, or stimulates disagreement? (For example, as a "learned" Christian, as a woman, as a man, as a democratic person to whom absolute royal power is a thing of the past, as a person who wants to find himself/herself, as an engaged citizen who intercedes on behalf of universal human rights, and who takes offence at the "cruelty" of the Old Testament.)
- What dawns on me regarding specific statements?
- What do I think about when reading? Given the desire to understand, what do I draw upon for comparison?
- To which people, in which life situation, could I show the text as an enriching, illuminating word of God?

The answers to these questions will turn out very differently for various exegetes because, when fantasizing, these questions largely employ active and knowledgeable awareness of the present, life experience, knowledge of people, self-awareness, and education. Yet the goal of this line of questioning is by no means uniformity. Rather, the goal is to make one conscious of a realistic life-like situating of the text in one's own time which shall again take effect after one's exegetical-theological investigation has been clarified.

The development of text dimensions that present themselves alongside the historical-exegetical investigation (but, as we claim, not independent of it), is today the subject of multiple endeavors, which are themselves also systematized. An overview is given in the periodical installment entitled, "Zugänge zur Bibel," *EvTh* 45 (1985): 469–560; English readers consult J.C. Exum and D.J.A. Clines (eds.), *The New Literary Criticism and the Hebrew Bible*, JSOT.S 143, Sheffield, 1993. An example in connection with historical exegesis is the essay by H. Utzschneider, "Das hermeneutische Problem der Uneindeutigkeit biblischer Texte—dargestellt an Text und Rezeption der Erzählung von Jakob am Jabbok (Gen 32,23–33), *EvTh* 48 (1988): 182–198. Compare the recent work: U.H.J. Körtner, *Der inspirierte Leser. Zentrale Aspekte biblischer Hermeneutik*, Göttingen, 1994.

2. Conceiving the Text as a Component of Its Own Historical World

For this line of questioning, which cannot be overestimated, the goal is to achieve a comprehensive *historical* conception of the historical arena, origin, intention, meaning and effect of the text in its time, through the employment of fantasy and imagination prior to and alongside the methodological work. The preceding endeavor of portraying the text as a component of the present world now sharpens the vision for the portrayal of the text in its historical character. Moreover, at this point in the working procedure, one is certainly not concerned with exact, unchangeable insights. Rather, one is concerned with observations and impressions that present themselves when one looks at length into the Hebrew text (which has been preliminarily translated and with which one has become familiar) with tranquility and with the greatest possible precision.

Even the power of historical conceptualization can be aroused by a series of elementary questions. They march in continuous oscillation between observations upon the text concerning the effort of achieving an understanding of the factors of origin, and the imagination of a total picture of historical understanding. This larger picture encompasses an image of the intention, meaning, and effect of the text, and it sees the text as a life-event of its time.

I. Imagination from Text Observations

Text observations are the alpha and omega of this stage of the work, when they are directed toward the formal as well as the material flow of the text. The observations serve to acquaint one well with the text to be treated in its original language, and to draw attention to its distinctiveness. They also provide the first possibility for creative exegetical discoveries prior to the work which will be guided by the methods and the secondary literature, where these discoveries can then be substantiated, examined, and explained.

1. Freely Roaming Observations on the Text

The following working procedure is recommended as the starting point:

First, one should translate one's text over and over again until one is utterly familiar with it. Then, using freely roaming observations, one should note everything in the text which strikes one as a historical phenomenon.

2. Observations on the Linguistic Shape of the Text

Only then does a phase of *directed* observation follow. Essentially, these observations constitute pure *text observations regarding the linguistic shape*, which even the beginner should be able to list with the knowledge of Hebrew already acquired.

a. Observations from Sentence to Sentence

First, one proceeds through the text, not verse by verse, but sentence by sentence (compare also H. Schweizer, *Biblische Texte verstehen*, see §2H, p. 37ff; B. Willmes, *Bibelauslegung*, see §2).

> The linguistic observations are especially directed toward the *type* of sentence from which the text is composed, toward the manner of prominent *connectors* between the sentences, and toward the character of the *succession of sentences* in the text (aspects which are the result of the continuity or the change in the types of sentences and the tense).

In detail, the approach is elucidated thus:

- How far does the first sentence extend (in terms of content and grammar)?
- How is the sentence constructed (sentence parts and their position; the type of sentence such as: nominal sentence, verbal sentence, inverted verbal sentence, main clause, or dependent clause; and the tense)?
  What does this type of sentence construction express for the content? (subject/object, accent, action/condition, temporal condition)
  Which of the exegete's expectations of content does this linguistic shape correct?
- Do the same for sentences two, three, etc., until the end of the text.
- Along with this procedure, one should pay attention to the manner in which the new sentence is related to the previous sentence or sentences.
  Is the sentence attached to the previous sentence(s) or not? (Are all linguistic and material references missing?) And what type of possible connection exists?
  Does a dependency exist upon the previous sentence or not, in the sense of a parallel or subsidiary ordering (the relationship of the main clause and dependent clauses, relative sentences, infinitive constructions), and if so what function does the dependency express?
  Is there a continuation or change of subject, object, type of sentence, tense, or temporal condition?
  How far do the series of connected sentences extend, and when does an interruption take place? (In certain situations this is an important clue to the structure!)
  Do the individual sentences offer any relationships which point beyond the text under investigation and show that it belongs in a larger literary context?

In the succession of sentences, do repeated principal words, catchwords, or word pairs manifest themselves in explainable positions?

What do these observations inside the succession of sentences signify for the content?

b. Observations on the Text as a Whole

The observations acquired regarding the succession of sentences leads to the next step of the work, namely observations on the *entirety of the treated text*. How is the text *structured*, according to agreement between formal and content observations? One must observe the linguistically recorded macro-organization in the main paragraphs and the micro-organization in the subsidiary paragraphs, as well as their finer syntactical organization in the construction of the individual sentences and in the relationships/correspondences between the sentences and the sentence parts.

In detail, the following questions can provide direction:

- Are there Hebrew organizational markers (for example, *lākēn*, *hinnēh*, *wě'attāh*, independent personal pronouns, interrogative pronouns)?
  Are there additional turning points in the flow (changes of scene, action, location, persons, speech formulas)?
  Is there one foundational stylistic pattern which conveys the entire organization (for example, seven imperatives in Ps 100, some with *kî*; the "we" and the "non-we" in Ps 46)?
  Do relationships between the beginning and end determine the total organization of the text (framing inclusio)?
  Are there symmetries in the sequence of the organizational components (for example, according to the pattern ABAB or ABBA)?
  What do the succession of the sentence type or tense in the text provide for its organization? Which essential perspectives are thereby recorded (principal statements, subordinate statements, conditions, the progression of movement/action, and the relative and absolute aspects of time)?
- To what extent are the individual sections under observation essential parts or non-essential parts of the whole?
  In its present linguistic shape, is there a perspective in which the text appears as a harmonized succession of statements?
  Can one find a dominant substantive statement that fashions the flow of the text and determines the organization? Do introduction, climax, change, or statement of purpose play a role in the organization of the text?
- How are the individual sections under observation in the text structured by themselves?
  Even within this smaller framework, do correspondences, word relationships, or subject relationships manifest themselves (such as inclusios, or

parallel formulations in sentences, in words, or in contradictory statements)?

• Which elements of the statement in an individual section stand in relationship, formally and materially, to that which precedes and follows?

It is recommended that one *write the Hebrew text* one time according to the observations gained concerning the macrostructure and the microstructure in order that its construction also becomes *graphically* visible.

By way of example, in Ps 100, the seven imperative statements, which include verses 1b–5, then stand under one another in seven rows. In Ps 46, one can write the five chains of statements (46:2–4,5–7,8,9–11,12) so that their nominal statements, as well as the developmental statements and further developmental statements dependent upon them, likewise stand under one another. Observable agreements in syntax and use of tense then play an important role. Also, one should graphically accentuate the symmetrical construction of Isa 1:21–26 in its two segments (1:21–23,24–26) by drawing in the brackets of inclusion: 1:21a (A); 1:21b (B); 1:22 (C); 1:23 (D); 1:24 (D’); 1:25aβb (C’); 1:26a (B’); 1:26b (A’). At the same time, the special position of 1:25aα stands out.

3. Further Text Observations

Finally, it is important that every exegetical worker gives careful consideration to *two points*:

First: In its own time, did the text appear as an understandable, inherently completed statement, or must the context be taken with it (relationship of the text to the immediate/wider context)?

Second: What remains unclear concerning all these text observations, or relatedly, with the translation, which must be clarified via additional information?

At this point, it is profitable for the experienced exegete—but not for the beginner who would here be overburdened—to elucidate the text further with *various specific observations*.

• To what extent does the immediate context help to delineate the lexical breadth of meaning for the words?

• What types of words fashion the text (for example, action verbs or verbs of circumstance, abstract or concrete substantives)?

• What stylistic devices appear in the text? What could be their material intention?

• What means does the text employ in order to offer its material statements (for example, concrete or abstract substantives, images, comparisons, metaphors)?

• What conceptions are awakened by real, concrete sequences or by linguistic images (metaphors) in the text? What should the listener/

reader see before one's own inner eye because it is expressed or intended? And what should one not see because the formulation points in another direction and excludes certain associations? Most of the severely neglected observations which challenge the exegete's historical (!) fantasy, are to be made here regarding the desired clarity of the text.

- Within the thematic framework of the text, what would also be conceivable or expected, but is not spoken? Are statements missing because they were considered self-evident at that time, or were they deliberately omitted?

II. Imagination of the Realities of the Origin of the Text

- In which situation did the text originate (time, locality, institutional framework, and instrumental events; the person who speaks the text; the persons who hear it)?
- Which experiences could stand in the background of the speaker and hearer/reader? Which experientially guided designations were provided? Which experiences were addressed in the text directly or indirectly?

III. Imagination of the Intention, Meaning, and Effect of the Text

- What precisely compelled the speaker to formulate this text in light of the realities of origin?
- What does the speaker want to effect in that historical locality when the text is heard (for example, insight, action)?
- How do the material statements, in their particular form and relation in the text, hang together with the realities of origin?
- What do the material statements of the text, and their form and respect, have in common with other statements in the Old Testament? What attracts attention as a surprising new accent?
- Which experience of reality of its time does the text desire to clarify and influence? Which unmistakable experiences, intrusions, and perspectives of reality are bound with the statements of God in the text?
- Which view of humanity or Israel in its time and world does the text open?
- In light of the material statements, what contrasting statements or supplements does the Old Testament offer elsewhere?
- What effect did the text actually have in the realm of ancient Israel for the short-term (with the first hearing) or for the long-term (with its wider transmission)? Does the actual effect deviate from the intention of the speaker, and what could be the experiential reasons for such?

Even with questions like these, the answers of different exegetes will deviate from one another both prior to and after the methodologically guided, scientific investigation of the text. This deviation is connected with the fact that, at any given time, two essential factors come into play in varying degrees: the exegete's prior knowledge and the ability for historical intuition.

(1) *Prior knowledge* helps to decrease a text's historical strangeness and resistance on the level of material cognizance. Simultaneously, it essentially determines the number of possibilities available for comparison and association.

This statement is certainly true for the extremely important area of general knowledge, hence of education in the broadest sense. On a large scale, it maintains the perspectives of understanding, analogies, comparisons, and contrasts for ascertaining the text's historical character. For example: A. von Menzel's presentation of the court of Frederick the Great enables one to see the scene in 1 Sam 20:24f as Saul's "round table" (G. von Rad), and to recognize the modest royal household; knowledge of the constitutional entity and the democratic formation of intention within the constitutional organs of our time sharpens the view of the king's function in the royal psalms; one may compare the night visions of Zechariah with the night poems of N. Lenau, or psalms of lamentation with the protest songs of B. Dylan, and the lament poems of N. Sachs, etc.

It is naturally self-evident that specialized prior knowledge in the area of the Old Testament prepares historical and textual materials for substantiation, deepening, and shaping through historical observations and imagination. In the process of imagination, this specialized prior knowledge can be expanded, where necessary, by examination of reference works.

(2) The *ability to conceive historically* is an indispensable presupposition if the text is to step forth from the medium of letters and paper, and become visible as a life-event in its time. To present the realities of the text's origin clearly by means of the controlled employment of historical fantasy is just as important as the attempt to situate the material statements, animately and tangibly, in their original historical field of relationship, and to reproduce the realities and events named in the text itself by means of the power of conceptualization.

One must note emphatically that this imaginative progression through the text, relating to the realities of origin, intention, meaning, and the effect on its historical world, is not completed just once *prior to* the methodologically directed exegetical work. Rather, this progression continuously and productively accompanies and limits these elements as a part of the exegetical work.

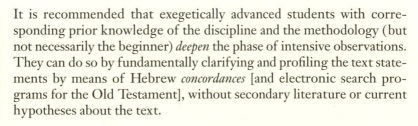

It is recommended that exegetically advanced students with corresponding prior knowledge of the discipline and the methodology (but not necessarily the beginner) *deepen* the phase of intensive observations. They can do so by fundamentally clarifying and profiling the text statements by means of Hebrew *concordances* [and electronic search programs for the Old Testament], without secondary literature or current hypotheses about the text.

Several things will bring the exegete further clarification and, above all, will bring directed questions for the further exegetical processing of the text in every methodological field. These include: parallel and deviating examples regarding the use of words and the syntactical form; ferreting out contrasting concepts, recurring semantic fields, and corresponding formulations, whether these appear in the immediate context, in the same book, or in specialized languages such as wisdom, cult, law, and prophecy. Instead of these elements, the beginner can pursue the important words in the corresponding articles of theological dictionaries. The beginner should not, however, be distracted by the abundance of material offered in the dictionaries, nor by the opinions presented there. From the outset, the beginner should not avoid the act of clarifying and discovering the text to be treated.

III. Results

Very diverse impressions and elements will come to light in the imaginative, holistic act of understanding a text when one employs fantasy, intuition, observation, and the capacity of association. Some of these must even be abandoned as incorrect based upon methodologically guided examination. Still, this imaginative act provides three *opportunities* which are indispensable for an adequate historical meaning. First, it limits the methodological constriction which results from a dependency upon the current state of research by the text's imaginative and discernible characteristics. Second, the imaginative act provides a holistic view of the text as a historical life-event, a perspective which is all too easily lost under the partial aspects of the individual methods. It is, however, precisely that perspective which must then be taken up and administered in the interpretation as a substantiated historically determined meaning, by utilizing the results of the methodical operation. Third, the imaginative act provides the articulated relationship between text and interpreter that attains its goal in a theologically substantiated applied understanding of the text.

Thus, exegetical work is completed by reciprocally limiting and enriching historical imagination and methodically directed questions. This reciprocity must be kept in view, even though the task of more closely characterizing the methodological steps dominates in that which follows.

C. OVERVIEW OF THE METHODS OF OLD TESTAMENT EXEGESIS

I. The Stock of Methods

The stock and description of the exegetical *methods*, as already mentioned, are dependent upon the current state of exegetical science and its insights into the formation of Old Testament texts. It is thus necessary that the existing methods constantly be further developed. Also, new methodological questions arise from new attention to the text. At present, new approaches have appeared in several areas: in the field of linguistic structural analysis; in the investigation of effective history as the harvesting of a text's power of meaning which is no longer familiar; or in the particularly debated psycho-analytical text interpretation. In addition, approaches arise today in which the bewilderment of the exegete is brought emphatically into play. One may mention so-called "feminist" and "socio-historical" exegesis. We will come back to these at the end of this section.

The manual lying before you concentrates on the fundamental, proven, and methodologically elaborated approaches: text-criticism, literary criticism, the transmission-historical and redaction-historical approaches, the form-critical and tradition-historical approaches, and, of course, determining the historical setting. These various methodological steps are constituent questions of historical understanding, and they each aim at particular aspects of the text. They are thus nothing more than preparatory work for the central exegetical task: *interpreting* the text's historically determined meaning. This act of interpretation, which is frequently called detailed or contextual exegesis, does not exist as a sequence of procedures which are guided by the constituent methodological questions. With its historical focus, which the text itself conveys, the interpretation aims more toward a conception of the entire text as a linguistic utterance of life in its time. It uses all individual insights synthesized from the methodologically fragmentary procedures. The results of this historically determined meaning of the text are finally brought into operation by attempting a precise English *translation* of the text.

II. Grouping the Methods

Each of the methodological approaches takes its reference from certain Old Testament text markers. A historical perspective on these realities of the text should also be attempted within the framework of the descriptions of the individual methods. An initial orientation can already be provided, to the extent that the methodological questions allow themselves to be divided into *two groups* relative to the direction of questioning and the reference point in the texts.

1. One group of methods is governed by the question of the evolution of the text: text-criticism, literary-criticism, transmission-historical approach and the redaction-historical approach relate to the fact that, as a rule, the text at hand has not arisen in a single stroke. Rather, in its text history, the text has undergone a multi-stage development from its original oral form up to and including its manuscript transmission, an evolution which the methodological approaches ascertain and clarify.

2. The second group of methods is governed by the question of the presuppositions of a text, or relatedly, its ascertained textual stages. The form-critical and tradition-historical approaches, as well as the question of the historical setting, relate to the fact that the form of the text, at *every* stage of its development, has been determined by stipulations and components which are presupposed by the author: the peculiarity of the language spoken by the author, the preset genres of human speech in the author's cultural world, the conceptions and thought structures of the author's intellectual world, the contemporary historical realities, social realities, and the historical setting of the addressee of author's utterance.

Both groups of methods likewise allow themselves to be depicted in a graphic display as follows.

1. The Question of the Evolution of a Text

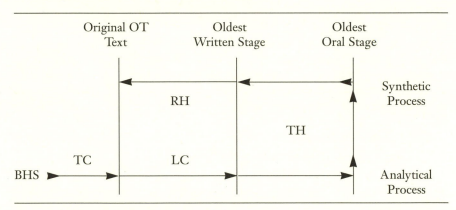

BHS = *Biblia Hebraica Stuttgartensia;* TC = Text Criticism; LC = Literary Criticism;
TH = Transmission History; RH = Redaction History

The evolution of an Old Testament text allows itself to be portrayed as a growth process which falls into three larger phases: (1) delivery and evolution in *oral* transmission up to its first written record; (2) delivery and evolution in *written* transmission up to the completion of the productive formation of Old Testament tradition, at least until the attainment of the canonical validity of the text; and related to this approach, (3) the delivery and development of the text history in the *manuscripts,* up to its presentation in *Biblia Hebraica.* Exegesis attempts, first of all, to peel away the various layers in an *analytical* process, by working backwards, in order to trace the development of the text in its historical course *synthetically,* and thereby to trace the influencing powers and the governing markers.

2. The Question of the Presuppositions of a Text and Its Stages

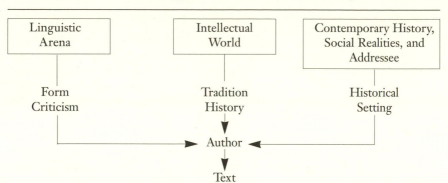

The diagram illustrates simply how language, culturally preexisting genres, the intellectual world, as well as contemporary historical and social realities, are embodied in *one* particular text (or relatedly, in *each* stage of its development). In the three areas, inquiry (containing and encompassing many individual texts) can and must also be made into the history of linguistic-structural characteristics the history of a concept or an entire conceptual arena, and into the history of the political and social realities in the larger historical context.

III. Interdependence of the Methods

The grouping of the methods undertaken in the previous section represents a reflection of the relationship of their content to one another, and in *this* regard, it has led to a division into two areas of questioning. That does not mean, however, that the *execution* of exegetical work should be determined by a corresponding partition. Rather, the intermingling of the methodological steps, oscillating between expansion and correction, is indispensable. Simultaneously, this intermingling means that the question about the text's presuppositions should be asked for each stage of its development. The changes of a text, or text complex during their oral or written transmission, do not make themselves known without determining each different historical setting or the linguistic patterns and theological streams affecting the text. The interdependence of the methods reaches even further, and connects *all* of the methodological steps to an over-arching system of correlation, as will be explained at length in the detailed presentation of the methods.[3]

3 One hears repeatedly of the experience that time is not sufficient in a two-hour introductory exegesis course to offer initial text observations, presentations, and practice which are equally

IV. Characterizing the Individual Methods[4]

1. Text Criticism

The task of text criticism is to confirm the "original text of the Old Testament" ("Original Text", "original wording") by critically sorting the Hebrew text transmission as well as the ancient translations. "Original text" means that text form which exists in the Old Testament at the conclusion of the process of productive, written formation.

2. Literary Criticism

Literary criticism investigates individual texts and larger text complexes at the stage of the written, fixed formulation of the wording. It therefore asks about:

a.   the literary integrity of a text;
b.   its larger literary context (in cases where the text is literarily integrated) or its larger literary contexts (in cases where the text exists from two or more literary layers or where it has been incorporated as an integrated text into a larger context, a context which also continued to develop).

---

weighted for every step of Old Testament exegesis. If the time frame of the course cannot be expanded, the following suggestion could be considered.

The *progression* of the introductory course, and then relatedly the writing of the exegesis paper are *concentrated* upon the following steps, subsequent to an initial translation of the text (§1 B I):

1. an observation phase according to §1 B II;
2. deciphering the text-critical apparatus of BHS (§3 B II 1a);
3. an analytical (§4) and a synthetic literary-critical stage limited to a given text and its immediate context (from §6 Redaction History, p. 78);
4. form criticism (*Formgeschichte*) related to the linguistic shape, structure, and, if necessary, the form (*Gattung*) of a text (§7 B II,III);
5. tradition history relative to the intellectual background of concepts, word ensembles, and images in the text formulations (§8);
6. an interpretation (§10) with the incorporation of the clarification of the historical setting of the text (§9);
7. definitive translation of the text (§10 F).

In the introductory phase, the more difficult and overtaxing questions and decisions regarding text criticism (§3), transmission history (§5), and redaction history (§6), can be briefly presented and explained in the progression of the introductory course. A more precise presentation and practice, demanded by text complexes, must follow in other places of study, namely within the frame of exegetical lectures and seminars (for which this workbook is also conceived).

4 This workbook will follow the "*Journal of Biblical Literature* Instructions for Contributors" in: *AAR/SBL 1993 Membership Directory and Handbook*, Atlanta, 1993, p.383–400, for the abbreviations for biblical books, Hebrew transcription, and significant resources. Abbreviations used for some German works may not be present in this resource. In that case, abbreviations will follow the abbreviations in *Die Religion in Geschichte und Gegenwart*. K. Galling, ed. 6 vols., plus index. Tübingen, ³1957–1965.

3. The Transmission-historical Approach

Transmission history concerns the oral transmission of an individual passage, or relatedly a larger complex. Concentrating upon the oral transmission distinguishes transmission history from literary criticism. Proceeding analytically, transmission history inquires behind the oldest written setting of a text, back to its oral origin.

A synthetic process then reverses the direction of questioning, and attempts to depict the historical process and the context of the text's development from its first recognizable oral form to the oldest written setting. Transmission history accentuates the operative historical factors and intentions of the statements.

4. The Redaction-historical Approach

Redaction history continues the synthetic aspect of transmission history, except in the arena of written transmission. It thereby traces the history of a text from its first written form through its expansion (or commentary) by additions, and through its incorporation into larger complexes, up to its final setting in the present literary context. It determines the historical factors and intentions of the statements operative in this history.

5. The Form-historical Approach

Form criticism works out the linguistic genre of a particular text (no matter what size) for each of its ascertained stages of growth. In its course, form criticism investigates the linguistic formation of the text. It also determines the genres which the text incorporates and utilizes, as well as their life setting. Form criticism aims at a methodologically appropriate understanding of the construction and the intention of the statement in the encountered text. It performs this task to the degree that one can recognize the distinctive character of the linguistic shape, including the choice of genre. This shape provides the perspective from which the content is viewed and the intention for which it is formulated.

In this context, form criticism necessarily inquires beyond the individual texts to the construction elements and the formative models of the language used by the Old Testament authors. Further, it ascertains the history of the genres and pursues their formulations in various texts.

6. The Tradition-historical Approach

For each developmental step, tradition history seeks a text's particular characteristic based upon intellectual, theological, or religio-historical contexts. In addition, tradition history determines the thought structures, material, concepts, or conceptual complexes, as well as their deviations, which are presupposed by the text, taken up into the text, or assimilated by its author. Parallel to the inquiry into individual texts, yet superseding it, tradition history also considers the intellectual, theological, and religio-historical contexts themselves. In particular it considers the history of the various concepts and their coexistence within the framework of a larger profiled conception.

7. Determining the Historical Situation

The goal of this approach is to identify the time of composition and, if possible, the author and addressees of the text (or its individual layers). Then this approach seeks to highlight more precisely the contemporary historical and social realities in the environment of the text's origin.

In the following, all of these constituent methodological questions will necessarily be presented ideally, one after another. In the practice of exegetical work, however, they achieve application through continuous interrelation and mutual expansion.

V. Concerning the Question of the Expansion of the Stock of Methods

The primary stock of methodological approaches described above, which this workbook wants to introduce, has been designed for the principal exegetical question concerning the original meaning of the texts at the time of their origin. These approaches were not decreed by exegetes, but were occasioned by the biblical subject matter itself, and they are directed very simply toward that which one must clarify if one wishes to see a text in its original setting: toward the formative relationships of a text, and toward the intended substance of its statements when it was formulated. Even for the current revision of the workbook, there is essentially nothing to change regarding the stock of methods.

Despite all the differences in execution, unanimity exists between this methodological book and those by G. Fohrer and H. Schweizer (cf. §2H), in that the Old Testament text should speak in its own words and outlook, with the help of reasoned and intersubjectively controllable explanations. Indeed, Old Testament exegesis is a constituent task of understanding. By keeping one's own presuppositions in check, one should come as close as possible to the original historical meaning in which the text should be understood within the sphere of the Old Testament itself. Now as before, this workbook is more cautious when it comes to the question of the reception of *linguistic* investigations for the sequence, resources, and execution of a methodology concerned with Old Testament exegesis. More thorough discussion is required to utilize apparently chronologically neutral linguistic starting points for describing the distinctive character of very remote historical texts, such as Old Testament texts. Thus, the present manual does not begin its methodologically guided steps with a linguistic analysis or a description of the text's structure. Rather, it allocates this indispensable (!) task to an initial observation phase (see §1) and to a methodological analysis of the linguistic shape of the particular growth elements of a text in the framework of form history (see §7). Still, even in this situation, the significance of linguistic analysis and a structural description is asserted for each (!) of the methodological steps, by means of the constantly required intrinsic examination of the interaction of the individual exegetical procedures.

Among the approaches currently brought into play, "*feminist*" and "*socio-historical*" questions (see §9) in particular are not to be viewed over against the classical stock of methods as competing, alternative methods. Their legitimate concerns, which are not always properly considered in exegetical practice, concerning inquiry into a text's options regarding the position of woman and socially vulnerable persons, can find their place entirely within the frame of the existing methodological perspectives. Additionally, they can also find their place in the procedural steps prior to the explicit execution of the exegetical work (see above §1 II 1), and in the following: the reception history in the time following the Old Testament text, as it is encountered in the disciplines of New Testament and Church History; and a theologically responsible determination of the Old Testament text's meaning for the present (see below, §10 D), as it would be acquired in the disciplines of Systematic and Practical Theology.

The fact that one has agreed upon the goal of Old Testament exegesis is of essential significance for the incorporation of such approaches in the process of exegesis itself. For the exegete, the goal is to act as an attorney for the will of the text. The exegete should reasonably advance that which the text itself originally wanted to witness from God, over against the world and humanity. The goal of exegesis cannot be to subdue the text under a dominating measure of current socio-political wishful thinking or an individual model of experience. Relatedly, the goal is not primarily to determine how the text functioned or how it functions for me. Accordingly, the goal is also not to determine how the text should or should not continue to function. The most decisive thing paving the way for exegesis is not the "I" in the face of the text, but in accordance with the self-understanding of the biblical word, the text in its liberating, critical and reorienting outlook towards humanity and the living world.

Also the concerns of "*structural exegesis*" do not have their place alongside but inside the stock of methods. Structural signals in the formulation provide important insights into the original desire of the statements which form the text, but must be correlated with the contents and formative relationships of the text (see §7).

By contrast, caution and principal objection are offered over against a so-called "*psycho-analytical exegesis*" of Old Testament texts. Especially the writings by E. Drewermann currently come to mind in this arena.[5] Exegetical methodology, in the sense of this workbook, is the methodology for a historically related subject matter in view of its original meaning. It considers the time restriction of the development and formulation of the texts. Correspondingly, it should be said that a so-called "*semiotic exegesis*" should be disregarded, if it abandons the fundamental question of the original meaning of biblical texts in their formulation and inner-biblical transmission; or if it abandons the task of understanding the historical things of the past as such.[6]

Finally, one should object to determining meaning for biblical texts derived from literary studies or New Literary Criticism if one believes one is able to arrive at sound conclusions without the qualification that these texts are historical entities with historical, linguistic, and structural characteristics.[7] The historical origin of biblical texts cannot, under any circumstances, be disregarded in the process of understanding. Recently, R. Knierim has correctly reaccented this when delimiting various false paths of an ahistorical understanding.[8]

The comments in this section hopefully serve students as an initial orientation into current movements in the methodology. Hopefully, they fix the outlook upon the essentials of Old Testament exegesis. Naturally, without already having acquired solid grounding, the brevity in which they are offered here, cannot do justice to the current divergence of exegetical methodology toward new entryways and starting points, which are currently being attempted, probed, and discussed. The workbook cannot, therefore, take up this divergence. It must be satisfied with brief remarks. Above all, these fields of discussion concern the question of the genesis of Old Testament texts as such, as they are treated in the traditional frame of chapters 7–9 of this workbook. Recent methods approach from new starting points: linguistic-structural theory, communication and information theory, and the interpretation of myth and symbol, folklore, anthropology, and sociology. Recent articles by

---

[5] For discussion, compare G. Lohfink and R. Pesch, *Tiefenpsychologie und keine Exegese*, SBS 129, 1987; A Görres and W. Kasper, *Tiefenpsychologische Deutung des Glaubens. Anfragen an Eugen Drewermann*, QD 113, 1988; as well as in condensed form, W. Groß, "Sollen wir ägyptischer werden, um wirklich christlich zu sein?" *ThQ* 166 (1986): 224–226; G. Lohfink, ThQ 167 (1987): 225–227; compare also H. Schweizer, *Biblische Texte verstehen*, 1986, p. 10ff.

[6] Compare, for example, W. Vogels, *Reading and Preaching the Bible: A New Semiotic Approach*, Wilmington, 1986. Culley (See note 9), 175ff, presents significant attempts of semiotic exegesis.

[7] Compare for example, D.A. Robertson, *The Old Testament and the Literary Critic*, Philadelphia, 1977.

[8] R. Knierim, "Criticism of Literary Features, Form, Tradition, and Redaction," in D.A. Knight and G.M. Tucker, *The Hebrew Bible and Its Modern Interpreters*, Philadelphia-Chico, 1985, 123–165, especially p. 123–128.

R. Knierim (see note 8), H.D. Preuß, and R.C. Culley provide an initial over-view of the diverse and divergent endeavors.[9]

In closing, the approaches and the stock of methods of Old Testament exegesis reflect the double aspect of their subject matter. Looking at the origin of the texts, exegesis is a historical discipline. Looking at the intention of the statements of the texts, it is a theological discipline. As such, one single, but decisive fundamental presupposition is imparted in all historical-exegetical work: the admission that the Old Testament means what it says when it speaks of God. God is differentiated from world and humanity, and should not be reinterpreted as an extrapolation of an aspect which stems only from the inner space of the world and humanity.

---

[9] H.D. Preuß, "Linguistik—Literaturwissenschaft—Altes Testament," *VF* 27 (1982): 2–28 (literature); R.C. Culley, "Exploring New Directions," in *The Hebrew Bible* (see note 8), 167–200 (bibliography); compare also more recent works, e.g., P.R. House, *Beyond Form Criticism: Essays in Old Testament Literary Criticism*, Winona Lake, 1992; J.C. Exum and D.J.A. Clines, *The New Literary Criticism and the Hebrew Bible*, JSOT.S 143, Sheffield, 1993. For the "canonical approach," see B.S. Childs §2N and the references in §6DII.

§2 General Bibliography for Exegetical Work

The bibliographic references in this section, as well as the literature sections of §§3–10 must cull a thoughtful selection for the user. Important studies which could not be listed may be easily gathered from the recent publications cited.

A characteristic abbreviation of the title is provided in parentheses for the literature which is more frequently cited in the following.

A. BIBLIOGRAPHIC AIDS

RGG, BHH, TRE, ABD, IDB, commentaries (see section O below), Old Testament Introductions (see section G below)

Biblica. Rome: since 1920, see: Supplement Elenchus bibliographicus Biblicus.

Internationale Zeitschriftenschau für Bibelwissenschaft und Grenzgebiete. Stuttgart, Düsseldorf, since 1951/52.

S. Schwertner. Theologische Realenzyklopädie. Abkürzungsverzeichnis. Berlin—New York, ²1992.

For English Readers:

Religion Index One: Periodicals. Berkeley, since 1949.

Religion Index Two: Multi-Author Works. Berkeley, since 1950.

Old Testament Abstracts. Washington, since 1978.

W.G. Hupper. Index to English Periodical Literature on the Old Testament and Ancient Near Eastern Studies, since 1987.

Additional helps in:

O. Kaiser and W.G. Kümmel. Exegetical Method (look under section H), p. 90–92, footnote 82.

D. Stuart, Old Testament Exegesis. Philadelphia, 1980. p. 93–136.

B.W. Anderson. Understanding the Old Testament. Englewood Cliffs, NJ, ⁴1986, p. 652–676.

P.C. Craigie. The Old Testament: Its Background, Growth, and Content. Nashville, 1986, p. 333–340.

SBL Instructions for Contributors. JBL 107 (1988): 579–596. (standard abbreviations)

B. SOURCES, TEXTS, AND TRANSLATIONS

Biblia Hebraica. R. Kittel, ed. After the 7th edition. Stuttgart, 1951 (BHK).
Biblia Hebraica Stuttgartensia. K. Elliger and W. Rudolph, eds. Stuttgart, 1968 to 1977 (BHS); scaled down edition, 1984.
The Hebrew University Bible. M.H. Goshen-Gottstein, C. Rabin, S. Talmon, eds. Jerusalem, 1975 (begun).
Septuaginta. Vetus Testamentum Graecum auctoritate Academiae Scientiarum Gottingensis editum. Göttingen, 1931 (begun).
Septuaginta. A. Rahlfs, ed. Stuttgart, 1982; scaled down edition, 1979.
The Septuagint with Apocrypha: Greek and English. Grand Rapids, 1993.
Die Apokryphen und Pseudepigraphen des Alten Testaments. E. Kautzsch, ed. 2 vols. Tübingen, 1900 (1921, Darmstadt, 1975).
Altjüdisches Schrifttum außerhalb der Bibel. P. Rießler, trans. and ed., Augsburg, 1928 (Freiburg, [5]1984).
Jüdische Schriften aus hellenistisch-römischer Zeit. W.G. Kümmel, ed. Gütersloh, 1973 (begun).
The Old Testament Pseudepigrapha. J.H.C. Charlesworth, ed. 2 vols. London, 1983, 1985.
E. Lohse. Die Texte aus Qumran. Darmstadt [4]1986.
F.G. Martínez. The Dead Sea Scrolls Translated: The Qumran Texts in English. Leiden, 1994.

C. LEXICA

W. Gesenius. Gesenius' Hebrew and Chaldee Lexicon to the Old Testament Scriptures. Grand Rapids, 1949.
W. Gesenius. Hebräisches und Aramäisches Handwörterbuch über das Alte Testament. Revised by R. Meyer and H. Donner. 18th edition, fascicle I: Berlin—Göttingen—Heidelberg, 1962; fascicle II: 1995.
F. Brown, S.R. Driver, and C.A. Briggs. A Hebrew and English Lexicon of the Old Testament. Oxford: 1907 (reprinted with corrections 1953, 1957, 1972).
L. Koehler and W. Baumgartner. Lexicon in Veteris Testamenti Libros. Leiden, 1953 (1958 with Supplement). (definitions in English and German)
W.L. Holladay. A Concise Hebrew and Aramaic Lexicon of the Old Testament. Grand Rapids, [10]1988.
W. Baumgartner, B. Hartmann, E.Y. Kutscher, and others. The Hebrew and Aramaic Lexicon of the Old Testament. 3 vols. Vol. 1: Leiden, 1994.
D.J.A. Clines. The Dictionary of Classical Hebrew. Vol. I: Sheffield, 1993.

D. GRAMMARS

H. Bauer and P. Leander. Historische Grammatik der hebräischen Sprache des Alten Testamentes. vol. 1: Einleitung, Schriftlehre, Laut- und Formenlehre. Halle 1922 (Hildesheim, 1962, 1965).
E. Jenni. Lehrbuch der hebräischen Sprache des Alten Testaments. Basel, [2]1981.
R. Meyer. Hebräische Grammatik. Berlin, vol. I [3]1966 (1982); vol. II [3]1969; vol. III, [3]1972; vol. IV, 1972; single vol. edition, 1992.

W. Richter. Grundlagen einer althebräischen Grammatik. 3 vols. St. Ottilien, 1978–1980.

W. Schneider. Grammatik des Biblischen Hebräisch. Munich, ⁶1985.

H. Schweizer. Metaphorische Grammatik. St. Ottilien, 1981.

R. Barthelmus. Einführung in das Biblische Hebräisch. Mit einem Anhang: Biblisches Aramäisch. Zurich, 1994.

For English Readers:

E. Ben Zvi, M. Hancock, and R. Beinert. Readings in Biblical Hebrew: An Intermediate Textbook. New Haven, 1993.

J. Blau. A Grammar of Biblical Hebrew. Wiesbaden, 1976.

W. Gesenius and E. Kautzsch. Gesenius' Hebrew Grammar. Oxford, ¹⁷1983.

M. Greenberg. Introduction to Hebrew. Englewood Cliffs, NJ, 1965.

P. Joüon. A Grammar of Biblical Hebrew, trans. and rev. by T. Muraoka. 2 vols. Rome, 1991.

P. Kelley. Biblical Hebrew: An Introductory Grammar. Grand Rapids, 1992.

B. Kittel, V. Hoffer, and R. Wright. Biblical Hebrew: A Text and Workbook. New Haven, 1989.

T.O. Lambdin. Introduction to Biblical Hebrew. New York, 1971.

C.L. Seow. A Grammar for Biblical Hebrew. Nashville, 1987.

J. Weingreen. A Practical Grammar for Classical Hebrew. 2nd ed. Oxford, 1959.

SPECIFICALLY FOR SYNTAX

R. Bartelmus. HYH. Bedeutung und Funktion eines hebräischen »Allerweltswortes«. St. Ottilien, 1982.

C. Brockelmann. Hebräische Syntax. Neukirchen, 1956.

W. Groß. Otto Rössler und die Diskussion um das althebräische Verbalsystem. BN 18 (1982): 28–78.

P. Kustár. Aspekt im Hebräischen. Theologische Dissertationen vol. IX. Basel, 1972.

D. Michel. Grundlegung einer hebräischen Syntax, 1. Neukirchen-Vluyn, 1977.

For English Readers:

F.I. Andersen. The Sentence in Biblical Hebrew. The Hague—Paris, 1974 (1980).

B. Waltke and M. O'Connor. An Introduction to Biblical Hebrew Syntax. Winona Lake, Indiana, 1990.

W.G.E. Watson. Classical Hebrew Poetry. JSOT.S 26. Sheffield, 1984.

R.J. Williams. Hebrew Syntax. Toronto, ²1976 (1982).

E. CONCORDANCES

S. Mandelkern. Veteris Testamenti Concordantiae Hebraicae atque Chaldaicae. Berlin 1937 (Graz 1955; Jerusalem—Tel Aviv, 1971).

G. Lisowsky and L. Rost. Konkordanz zum Hebräischen Alten Testament. Stuttgart, ²1966 (1981).

A. Even-Shoshan. A New Concordance of the Bible. Jerusalem, 1982.

E. Hatch and H.A. Redpath. A Concordance to the Septuagint. 2 vols. Grand Rapids, 1987.

Strong's Exhaustive Concordance. Nashville, 1890 (1986).
Several excellent computerized concordance programs are now available, e.g. Bible
  Windows.

F. BIBLE KNOWLEDGE

M. Augustin and J. Kegler. Bibelkunde des Alten Testaments. Gütersloh 1987.
G. Fohrer. Das Alte Testament. Einführung in Bibelkunde und Literatur des Alten
  Testaments und in Geschichte und Religion Israels. Gütersloh, part 1, ³1980; parts
  2 & 3, ³1980.
H.D. Preuß and K. Berger. Bibelkunde des Alten und Neuen Testaments. vol. 1: Altes
  Testament. Heidelberg, ⁵1993.
O.H. Steck. Arbeitsblätter Altes Testament für Einführungskurse. Zurich, ²1993.
C. Westermann. Abriß der Bibelkunde. Stuttgart, ¹³1991. (English translation of 4th
  edition: Handbook to the Old Testament. Minneapolis, 1967.)

Compare also:
W.H. Schmidt, W. Thiel, and R. Hanhart. Altes Testament. Grundkurs Theologie,
  vol. 1. Stuttgart—Berlin—Köln—Mainz, 1989.

For English Readers:
The German discipline of *Bibelkunde* has no precise parallel in English. Westermann's
  Handbook is one of the few which have been translated. Many of the newer Old
  Testament introductions do, however, provide some overviews of the biblical con-
  tent (cf. section G. below). See also:
R.E. Clements, ed. The World of Ancient Israel. Cambridge, 1989.
A.S. van der Woude. The World of the Old Testament. Bible Handbook, vol. II.
  Grand Rapids, 1989.

G. INTRODUCTORY QUESTIONS

J. Hempel. Die althebräische Literatur aund ihr hellenistisch-jüdisches Nachleben.
  Wildpark-Potsdam, 1930 (Berlin 1968).
O. Kaiser. Grundriß der Einleitung in die kanonischen und deuterokanonischen
  Schriften des Alten Testaments. Vols 1–3. Gütersloh, 1992–1994.
R. Smend. Die Entstehung des Alten Testaments. Theologische Wissenschaft 1.
  Stuttgart—Berlin—Köln—Mainz, ⁴1989.

For English readers:
B.W. Anderson. Understanding the Old Testament. Englewood Cliffs, NJ, ⁴1986.
B. Bandstra. Reading the Old Testament: An Introduction to the Old Testament. Bel-
  mont, CA, 1995.
B.S. Childs. Introduction to the Old Testament as Scripture. Philadelphia, 1979
  (1980).
P.C. Craigie. The Old Testament: Its Background, Growth, and Content. Nashville,
  1986.
R. Coggins. Introducing the Old Testament. Nashville, 1990.
O. Eißfeldt. The Old Testament: An Introduction. Oxford, 1974.

G. Fohrer. Introduction to the Old Testament. Nashville, 1968.
N.K. Gottwald. The Hebrew Bible. A Socio-Literary Introduction. Philadelphia, 1985.
O. Kaiser. Introduction to the Old Testament. Oxford, 1975.
R. Rendtorff. The Old Testament: An Introduction. Philadelphia, 1985.
W.H. Schmidt. Old Testament Introduction. New York, 1990.
J.A. Soggin. Introduction to the Old Testament. Philadelphia, 1976 (^{3}1989).

H. EXEGETICAL METHODOLOGY

H. Barth and T. Schramm. Selbsterfahrung mit der Bibel. Ein Schlüssel zum Lesen
    und Verstehen. Munich—Göttingen, 1977 (^{2}1983, abridged).
G. Fohrer, H.W. Hoffmann, F. Huber, L. Markert, and G. Wanke. Exegese des
    Alten Testaments: Einführung in die Methodik. Uni-Taschenbücher (UTB) 267.
    Heidelberg, ^{6}1993 (Fohrer, Exegese).
H. Gunkel. Ziele und Methoden der Erklärung des Alten Testaments. in: Gunkel,
    Reden und Aufsätze, 11–29. Göttingen, 1913.
W. Richter. Exegese als Literaturwissenschaft: Entwurf einer alttestamentlichen Lit-
    eraturtheorie und Methodologie. (Exegese). Göttingen, 1971.
J. Schreiner, ed. Einführung in die Methoden der biblischen Exegese. Würzburg, 1971
    (Schreiner, Einführung).
H. Schweizer. Biblische Texte verstehen. Arbeitsbuch zu Hermeneutik und Methodik
    der Bibelinterpretation. Stuttgart—Berlin—Köln—Mainz, 1986.
W. Stenger. Biblische Methodenlehre. Düsseldorf, 1987.
B. Willmes. Bibelauslegung—genau genommen. BNB 5. Munich, 1990.

For English Readers:
J. Barton. Reading the Old Testament: Method in Biblical Study. Philadelphia, 1984
    (^{2}1996).
J.H. Hayes, and C.R. Holladay. Biblical Exegesis: A Beginner's Handbook. rev. ed.
    Atlanta, 1987.
O. Kaiser. Old Testament Exegesis. In: O. Kaiser and W.G. Kümmel, Exegetical
    Method, 1–41. New York, 1981.
K. Koch. The Growth of the Biblical Tradition: The Form-Critical Method. New
    York, 1969.
E. Krentz. The Historical-Critical Method. Philadelphia, 1975. (See also the entire
    series by Fortress Press: Guides to Biblical Scholarship).
S.L. McKenzie and S.R. Haynes. To Each Its Own Meaning: An Introduction to Bib-
    lical Criticisms and Their Meaning. Louisville, 1993 (^{2}1999).
R. Morgan and J. Barton. Biblical Interpretations. Oxford, 1988.
D. Stuart. Old Testament Exegesis: A Primer for Students and Pastors. Philadelphia,
    ^{2}1980.

I. INFORMATION ON SPECIFIC TOPICS

Bibel-Lexikon. H. Haag, ed. Einsiedeln—Zurich—Köln, ^{2}1968.
Neues Bibel-Lexikon. M. Görg and B. Lang, eds. Zurich (in fascicles. fascicle 1, 1988).

Dictionnaire de la Bible, Supplément. Begun by L. Pirot et A. Robert. Continued under the direction of H. Cazelles and A. Feuillet. Paris, 1928 (begun).

Evangelisches Kirchenlexikon. E. Fahlbusch, ed. 4 vols. Göttingen, ³1986–1993.

K. Galling, ed. Biblisches Reallexikon. HAT I 1. Tübingen, ²1977.

Biblisch-Historisches Handwörterbuch. B. Reicke and L. Rost, eds. 4 vols. Göttingen, 1962–1979. (BHH)

Theologische Realenzyklopädie. G. Krause und G. Müller, eds. Berlin-New York, 1976 (begun) (TRE).

Reallexikon für Antike und Christentum. Stuttgart, 1950 (begun).

Reclams Bibellexikon. K. Koch, ed. Stuttgart, ⁴1987.

Die Religion in Geschichte und Gegenwart. K. Galling, ed. 6 vols., plus index. Tübingen, ³1957–1965. (RGG)

For English Readers:
The Anchor Bible Dictionary. 6 vols. New York, 1992 (ABD).

Encyclopaedia Judaica, 16 vols. Jerusalem, 1971 (Index vol., 1972).

The Interpreter's Dictionary of the Bible. 4 vols. New York—Nashville, 1962 (Supplement 1976).

Mercer's Dictionary of the Bible. Macon, 1991.

M. Noth. The Old Testament World. London, 1966 (OTW).

J. BIBLICAL ARCHAEOLOGY AND GEOGRAPHY

H. Donner. Einführung in die biblische Landes- und Altertumskunde. Darmstadt, ²1988.

V. Fritz. Art. Bibelwissenschaft I/1. Archäologie (Alter Orient und Palästina). TRE VI (1980), p. 316–345.

M. Noth. Der Beitrag der Archäologie zur Geschichte Israels. VT.S 7 (1960): 262–282 (also in: Noth, Aufsätze zur biblischen Landes- und Altertumskunde. H.W. Wolff, ed. 2 vols. vol. 1, 34–51. Neukirchen-Vluyn 1971.

_____. Das Buch Josua. HAT I 7. o. 142–151: Verzeichnis der Ortsnamen. Tübingen, ³1971.

Orte und Landschaften der Bibel. vol. 1: O. Keel, M. Küchler, and Chr. Uehlinger. Geographisch-geschichtliche Landeskunde. Zurich—Göttingen, 1984; vol. 2: O. Keel and M. Küchler. Der Süden. Zurich—Göttingen, 1982.

H. Weippert. Palästina in vorhellenistischer Zeit. Handbuch der Archäologie II.1. Munich, 1988.

For English Readers:
Y. Aharoni. The Land of the Bible. A Historical Geography. Philadelphia, 1967.

D. Baly. Geographical Companion to the Bible. London, 1963.

Encyclopaedia of Archaeological Excavations in the Holy Land. M. Avi-Yonah, ed. London, vol. I, 1975; vol. II, 1976; vol. III, 1977; vol. IV, 1978. New edition: E. Stern, ed. Jerusalem, 1994.

V. Fritz. An Introduction to Biblical Archaeology. JSOT.S 172. Sheffield, 1994.

Z. Kallai. Historical Geography of the Bible. Leiden, 1986.

K. Kenyon. Archaeology in the Holy Land. Revised edition. New York/London, [4]1985.
A. Mazar. Archaeology of the Land of the Bible, 10,000–586 BCE. New York, 1990.
M. Noth. Old Testament World. London, 1966, p. 2–179.

Also compare the literature in I and L.

BIBLE ATLASES

A. Aharoni, M. Avi-Yonah. The Macmillan Bible Atlas. New York, 1968.
Atlas of Israel. Published by Survey of Israel. Ministry of Labour Israel. Amsterdam, [2]1970.
H. Guthe. Bibelatlas. Leipzig, [2]1926.
The Times Atlas of the Bible. J.B. Pritchard, ed. London, 1987.
Oxford Bible Atlas. H.G. May, ed. London—New York, [2]1974.
J.B. Pritchard, ed. The Harper Concise Atlas of the Bible, 1991.
Palästina. Historisch-archäologische Karte mit Einführung und Register. E. Höhne, ed. Göttingen, 1981 (special printing from BHH, vol. IV).

K. THE HISTORY AND SOCIAL LIFE OF ISRAEL

A. Alt. Grundfragen der Geschichte des Volkes Israel. Eine Auswahl aus den Kleinen Schriften. Munich, 1970.
G. Dalman. Arbeit und Sitte in Palästina. vol. I–VII. Gütersloh, 1928–1942 (Hildesheim 1964).
H. Donner. Geschichte des Volkes Israel und seiner Nachbarn in Grundzügen. 2 vols. Göttingen, 1983, 1986; single volume edition, 1987.
A.H.J. Gunneweg. Geschichte Israels bis Bar Kochba. Theologische Wissenschaft, vol. 2. Stuttgart—Berlin—Köln—Mainz, [5]1984.
E. Kutsch. Art. Israel II. Chronologie der Könige von Israel und Juda. RGG[3] III, col. 942–944; cf. also the time charts in the appendix to the volumes by A. Jepsen, »Kommentar zum Alten Testament (KAT)« and H. Donner, cited above, 229ff.
K. Matthiae and W. Thiel. Biblische Zeittafeln. Neukirchen-Vluyn, 1985.
M. Metzger. Grundriß der Geschichte Israels. Neukirchen-Vlun, [7]1988.
H.P. Müller. Art. Gesellschaft II. Altes Testament. TRE XII (1984), p. 756–764 (bibliography!).
W. Schottroff. Soziologie und Altes Testament. VF 19 (1974): 46–66.
J.A. Soggin. A History of Israel. London, 1984.
W. Thiel. Die soziale Entwicklung Israels in vorstaatlicher Zeit. Neukirchen-Vluyn, [2]1985.

For English Readers:
G.W. Ahlström. The History of Ancient Palestine. Minneapolis, 1993.
R. Albertz. A History of Israelite Religion in the Old Testament Period. 2 vols. Louisville, 1994.
A. Alt. Essays on Old Testament History and Religion. Oxford, 1966.
H.J. Boecker. Law and the Administration of Justice in the Old Testament and Ancient East. Minneapolis, 1980.

J. Bright A History of Israel. 3rd ed. Philadelphia, 1981.
J.H. Hayes and J.M. Miller, eds. Israelite and Judean History. London, 1977.
S. Herrmann. A History of Israel in Old Testament Times. London, ²1981.
J.M. Miller and J.H. Hayes. A History of Ancient Israel and Judah. London, 1986.
M. Noth. The History of Israel. London, ²1960.
J. Pedersen. Israel. Its Life and Culture. London - Copenhagen, vols. I–II, 1926 (last imprint, 1964); vols. III–IV 1940 (1959 with additions, last imprint, 1963).
R. de Vaux. Ancient Israel: Its Life and Institutions. New York, 1961.
_____. The Early History of Israel. London, 1978.
The World History of the Jewish People. B. Mazar, ed. Vols. I–VIII. Jerusalem—London, 1964–1984.

SOURCE MATERIAL

Textbuch zur Geschichte Israels. K. Galling, ed. Tübingen, ³1979.
G.I. Davies. Ancient Hebrew Inscriptions. Cambridge, 1991.
H. Donner and W. Röllig. Kanaanäische und aramäische Inschriften, mit einem Beitrag von O. Rössler. Wiesbaden, vol. I, ³1971; vol. 2, ³1973; vol. 3, ²1969.
K. Jaroš. Hundert Inschriften aus Kanaan und Israel. Fribourg, 1982.
J. Renz and W. Röllig. Handbuch der althebräischen Epigraphik. Vols. I; II/1; III. Darmstadt, 1995.
K.A. Smelik. Writings from Ancient Israel: A Handbook of Historical and Religious Documents. Louisville, 1991.

Compare also the source collections in L.

L. ISRAEL'S ENVIRONMENT

HISTORY

Fischer Weltgeschichte, vols. 2–4: Die Altorientalischen Reiche I–III. E. Cassin, J. Bottéro and J. Vercoutter. Frankfurt/M., 1965–1967.
Fischer Weltgeschichte, vol. 5: Griechen und Perser. Die Mittelmeerwelt im Altertum I. H. Bengtson, ed. Frankfurt/M., 1965.
Fischer Weltgeschichte, vol. 6: Der Hellenismus und der Aufstieg Roms. Die Mittelmeerwelt im Altertum II. P. Grimal, ed. Frankfurt/M., 1965.
Orientalische Geschichte von Kyros bis Mohammed. HO I, 2, 4. Leiden—Köln, fascicle 1A, 1971; fascicle 2, 1966.
W. Helck. Geschichte des Alten Ägypten. HO I,1,3. Leiden, 1968 (1981).
E.A. Knauf. Die Umwelt des Alten Testaments. Stuttgart, 1994.
A. Scharff and A. Moortgat. Ägypten und Vorderasien im Altertum. Munich, 1950 (³1962).
H. Schmökel. Geschichte des Alten Vorderasien. HO I, 2, 3. Leiden, 1957 (1979).

For English Readers:
The Cambridge Ancient History. Cambridge, Vols. I/1-II/2 ³1970–1975; Vol. III, 1925 (1965); Vol. IV, 1926 (1969); Vol. VII/1, ²1984.

The Cambridge History of Iran. Cambridge, Vol. II, 1985.

The Cambridge History of Judaism. Cambridge, vol. I, 1984; vol. II, 1989.

M.A. Dandamaev. A Political History of the Achaemenid Empire. Leiden, 1989.

N. Grimal. A History of Ancient Egypt. Oxford, 1992.

L.L. Grabbe. Judaism from Cyrus to Hadrian. Vol. I. Minneapolis, 1992.

W.W. Hallo and W.K. Simpson. The Ancient Near East. A History. New York—
Chicago—San Francisco—Atlanta, 1971.

H. Sancisi-Weerdenburg, ed. Achaemenid History. Leiden, 1987 (begun).

E.M. Yamauchi. Persia and the Bible. Grand Rapids, 1990.

CULTURAL HISTORY AND THE HISTORY OF RELIGION

J. Assmann. Ägypten. Theologie und Frömmigkeit einer frühen Hochkultur. Urban-
Taschenbücher 366. Stuttgart, 1984.

H. Bonnet. Reallexikon der ägyptischen Religionsgeschichte. Berlin, 1952 (^{2}1971).

H. Brunner. Grundzüge der altägyptischen Religion. Darmstadt, 1983.

H. and H.A. Frankfort, J. A. Wilson, and T. Jacobsen. Frühlicht des Geistes. Wand-
lungen des Weltbildes im Alten Orient. Urban-Bücher 9. Stuttgart, 1954 (English, 1946); revised version, 1981 under the title: Alter Orient—Mythos und
Wirklichkeit.

H. Gese, M. Höfner, and K. Rudolph. Die Religionen Altsyriens, Altarabiens und der
Mandäer. Die Religionen der Menschheit, Vol. 10/2. Stuttgart—Berlin—Köln—
Mainz, 1970.

A. Goetze, Kleinasien, HAW III,1,3,3,1, Munich ^{2}1957.

Handbuch der Religionsgeschichte. J.P. Asmussen und J. Laesøe, eds. Göttingen,
vol. 2, 1972; vol. 3, 1975.

E. Hornung. Einführung in die Ägyptologie. Darmstadt, ^{2}1984.

_____. Grundzüge der ägyptischen Geschichte. Darmstadt, ^{3}1988.

Kulturgeschichte des Alten Orient. H. Schmökel, ed. Stuttgart, 1961 (1981).

Lexikon der Ägyptologie. W. Helck and E. Otto eds. Wiesbaden, vols. I–VIII,
1975–1988.

B. Meissner. Babylonien und Assyrien. Heidelberg, vol. 1, 1920; vol. 2, 1925.

Reallexikon der Assyriologie. Currently 6 vols. Berlin—(Leipzig)—New York,
1932–1983.

Religionsgeschichte des Alten Orient. HO I, 8,1,1. Leiden—Köln, 1964.

G. Widengren. Die Religionen Irans. Die Religionen der Menschheit, vol. 14.
Stuttgart, 1965.

Wörterbuch der Mythologie. Part 1: Die alten Kulturvölker, vol. I: Götter und
Mythen im Vorderen Orient. H.W. Haussig, ed. Stuttgart, 1965.

For English Readers:

British Museum Trustees. An Introduction to Ancient Egypt. New York, 1979.

L.R. Fisher. Ras Shamra Parallels. 2 vols. Rome, 1972, 1975.

J.C.L. Gibson. Canaanite Myths and Legends. Edinburgh, ^{2}1978.

J. Gray. The Legacy of Canaan. The Ras Shamra Texts and their Relevance to the Old
Testament. VT.S 5. Leiden, ^{2}1965.

Historia Religionum. Handbook for the History of Religions. C.J. Bleeker and
G. Widengren, eds. vol. I: Religions of the Past. Leiden, 1969.

J.C. de Moor. An Anthology of Religious Texts from Ugarit. Leiden, 1987.

S. Morenz. Egyptian Religion. London, 1973.

M. Noth. Old Testament World, p. 278–297.

A.L. Oppenheim. Ancient Mesopotamia. Chicago, 1964.

H. Ringgren. Religions of the Ancient Near East. London, 1973.

W. von Soden. Introduction to the Ancient World. The Background of the Ancient Orient. Grand Rapids, 1993.

J.H. Walton. Ancient Israelite Literature in Its Cultural Context: A Survey of Parallels between Biblical and Ancient Near Eastern Texts. Grand Rapids, 1989.

SOURCE MATERIAL

Altorientalische Texte zum Alten Testament. H. Greßmann, ed. Berlin—Leipzig, ²1926 (1970).

Altorientalische Bilder zum Alten Testament. H. Greßmann, ed. Berlin—Leipzig, ²1927 (1970).

Texte aus der Umwelt des Alten Testaments. O. Kaiser. Gütersloh, fascicles since 1981.

For English Readers:

Ancient Egyptian Literature. 3 vols. M. Lichtheim, ed. Berkeley, 1975–1980.

Ancient Near Eastern Texts Relating to the Old Testament. J.B. Pritchard, ed. Princeton, ³1969.

The Ancient Near East in Pictures Relating to the Old Testament. J.B. Pritchard, ed. Princeton, ²1969.

Before the Muses: An Anthology of Akkadian Literature. 2 vols. B.R. Foster, ed. Bethesda, MD, 1993.

Near Eastern Religious Texts Relating to the Old Testament. W. Beyerlin, ed. London, 1978.

Compare the source material mentioned in K.

M. TOPICAL EXEGESIS

ABD, IDB, RGG, BHH, TRE, concordances (see E above), commentaries (see under O), Old Testament theologies (see under N).

J. Barr. The Semantics of Biblical Language. Oxford, 1961.

E. Jenni and C. Westermann, eds. Mark E. Biddle, trans. Theological Lexicon of the Old Testament. 3 vols. Peabody, MA, 1997.

G.J. Botterweck and H. Ringgren, eds. Theological Dictionary of the Old Testament. Grand Rapids, 1971 (begun).

G. Kittel and G. Friedrich, ed. Theological Dictionary of the New Testament. Grand Rapids, 1964 (begun).

N. OLD TESTAMENT THEOLOGY

R. Albertz. A History of Israelite Religion in the Old Testament Period. 2 vols. Louisville, 1994.

B.S. Childs. Old Testament Theology in a Canonical Context. Minneapolis, 1989.
_____. Biblical Theology of the Old and New Testaments. Minneapolis, 1993.
W. Eichrodt. Theology of the Old Testament. 2 vols. Philadelphia, 1961 & 1967.
G. Fohrer. History of Israelite Religion. Nashville, 1972.
_____. Theologische Grundstrukturen des Alten Testaments. Berlin—New York, 1972.
G. Hasel. Old Testament Theology: Basic Issues in the Current Debate. Grand Rapids, [4]1991.
J.H. Hayes and F. Prussner. Old Testament Theology: Its History and Development. Atlanta, 1985.
O. Kaiser. Der Gott des Alten Testaments. Theologie des Alten Testaments. UBT. Göttingen, 1993.
O. Keel and Chr. Uehlinger. Göttinnen, Götter, und Gottessymbole. QD 134. Freiburg, i.B., [2]1993.
M. Oeming. Gesamtbiblische Theologien der Gegenwart. Stuttgart—Berlin—Köln—Mainz, [2]1987.
L.G. Perdue. The Collapse of History: Reconstructing Old Testament Theology. Overtures to Biblical Theology. Minneapolis, 1994.
H.D. Preuß. Old Testament Theology. 2 vols. Louisville, 1995 and 1996.
G. v. Rad. Old Testament Theology. 2 vols. San Francisco, 1962 & 1965.
H. Graf Reventlow. Problems of Biblical Theology in the Twentieth Century. Philadelphia, 1986.
W.H. Schmidt. The Faith of the Old Testament: A History. Philadelphia, 1983.
C. Westermann. Elements of Old Testament Theology. Atlanta, 1982.
W. Zimmerli. Old Testament Theology in Outline. Edinburgh, 1978.

O. IMPORTANT OLD TESTAMENT COMMENTARIES

Das Alte Testament Deutsch (ATD). (V. Herntrich and) A. Weiser, eds. Göttingen, 1949 (begun); O. Kaiser und L. Perlitt, recent editors. (Several volumes in English)
Biblischer Kommentar (BK) Altes Testament. Begun by M. Noth. S. Herrmann, W.H. Schmidt and H.W. Wolff, eds. Neukirchen-Vluyn, 1955 (begun).
Die Botschaft des Alten Testaments. Erläuterungen alttestamentlicher Schriften. Stuttgart.
Commentaire de l'Ancien Testament (CAT). R. Martin-Achard and others, eds. Neuchâtel—Paris, 1963 (begun).
Echter Bibel. Altes Testament. F. Nötscher, ed. 4 vols. and index volume. Würzburg, [2]1955–1960.
Die Neue Echter Bibel (NEB). Kommentar zum Alten Testament mit der Einheitsübersetzung. J.G. Plöger and J. Schreiner, eds. Würzburg.
Handbuch zum Alten Testament (HAT). O. Eißfeldt, ed. Tübingen, 1934 (begun).
Handkommentar zum Alten Testament (HK). W. Nowack, ed. Göttingen, 1892–1938.
Die Heilige Schrift des Alten Testaments. Begun by F. Feldmann and H. Herkenne. F. Nötscher, ed. Bonn, 1924–1960.
Kommentar zum Alten Testament (KAT). E. Sellin, ed. Leipzig 1913–1939; W. Rudolph, K. Elliger, F. Hesse and O. Kaiser, recent eds. Gütersloh, 1962 (begun).

Kurzer Hand-Commentar zum Alten Testament (KHC). K. Marti, ed. Tübingen 1897–1922.

De Prediking van het Oude Testament. Nijkerk.

La Sainte Bible. Begun by L. Pirot, continued by A. Clamer. Paris.

Die Schriften des Alten Testaments (SAT). Göttingen, 1911–1915, ²1920–1925.

Zürcher Bibelkommentare. G. Fohrer, H.H. Schmid and S. Schulz, eds. Zurich (– Stuttgart).

For English Readers:

The Anchor Bible. W. F. Albright and D. N. Freedman, eds. New York, 1964 (begun).

The Cambridge Bible Commentary on the New English Bible. P.R. Ackroyd, A.R.C. Leaney, and J.W. Packer, eds. Cambridge, 1971 (begun).

The Century Bible. New Edition (also: New Series). H.H. Rowley, ed. London.

The Forms of the Old Testament Literature. R. Knierim and G.M. Tucker, eds. Grand Rapids.

Hermeneia. A Critical and Historical Commentary on the Bible. Philadelphia.

The International Critical Commentary (ICC). S. Driver, A. Plummer and C.A. Briggs, eds. Edinburgh, 1895 (begun).

International Theological Commentary (ITC). F.C. Holmgren and G.A.F. Knight, eds. Grand Rapids.

The Interpreter's Bible (IB). Old Testament, 6 vols. New York—Nashville, 1952–1956 (1979).

The Jerome Biblical Commentary. R.E. Brown, J.A. Fitzmyer and R.E. Murphy, eds. London—Dublin—Melbourne, 1970.

New Century Bible. London.

The New International Commentary on the Old Testament. R. Hubbard, ed. Grand Rapids.

Old Testament Library (OTL). London—Louisville.

Peake's Commentary on the Bible. H.H. Rowley, Old Testament Editor. London (etc.), 1962.

Word Biblical Commmentary. J.D.W. Watts, Old Testament Editor. Waco, Texas.

P. TECHNIQUES OF SCIENTIFIC PROCEDURE

G. Adam. Zur wissenschaftlichen Arbeitsweise. Adam, Kaiser, Kümmel. Einführung (see under H), p. 96–128 (p. 127f: bibliography).

A. Raffelt. Proseminar Theologie. Einführung in das wissenschaftliche Arbeiten und in die theologische Buchkunde. Freiburg—Basel—Wien, ⁴1985.

Part Two

The Methods

§3 | Text Criticism

A. THE TASK

From their first recording to the invention of the printing press, Old Testament texts were transmitted and circulated only by transcription, whether in the original language or in translation. Numerous manuscripts and manuscripts fragments in the libraries and museums of the world witness this process which lasted a total of two and one half millennia. The oldest texts found to this date, primarily the manuscripts from the caves of Qumran, date back to the second century B.C. Manuscript transmission is, as a rule, not without error. Deviations between manuscripts[10] and incomprehensible versions ("corruptions")[11] also document this tendency for Old Testament text criticism. Two processes come under primary consideration as the *sources of mistakes:* unintentional oversight during transcription (e.g. confusion of similar letters, haplography, dittography, omission through homoioteleuton), and intentional changes (e.g. improving a supposed mistake in the *Vorlage*, replacing or expanding unusual expressions, and removing objectionable formulations).[12]

---

[10] An example: In Isa 11:1b, the Masoretic text transmission reads, ". . . and a shoot from its roots will bear fruit (*yipreh*)"; the Septuagint, the Vulgate and other ancient translations by contrast offer a verb with the meaning "come forth" (LXX: ἀναβήσεται; Vulg.: *ascendet*).

[11] An example: In the Masoretic text transmission, Isa 11:3 begins with the formulation, *wăhărîhô bĕyir'at yhwh* ("and his—that is the Lord's—smelling is on the fear of YHWH"), a formulation which makes absolutely no sense in this form.

[12] An extensive representation, with commentary, of the mistakes which are typical for the manuscript transmission of the Old Testament is offered with numerous examples in: Delitzsch, *Lese- und Schreibfehler;* Würthwein, *The Text of the Old Testament,* p. 107–112 (there also additional literature); Tov, *Textual Criticism,* p. 6–13, 232–285; McCarter, *Textual Criticism,* p. 26–61.

Correspondingly, text criticism has the *task* of locating mistakes which have crept in during the text history and, if possible, of establishing the "original text of the Old Testament" ("original text," "original wording"), by critically scrutinizing the Hebrew text transmission (or Aramaic in portions of Ezra and Daniel) as well as the ancient translations. The "original text" means, in essence, that wording which existed in the Old Testament at the end of the process of productive, written formation. As a rule, this point is reached at least with the attainment of a text's canonical validity. It does not, however, unequivocally allow itself to be fixed chronologically. Moreover, the endpoint of productive formation differs among the various groups of Old Testament writings and even in the individual writings. An approximate arrangement leads into the time period between the 4th century B.C. and the 1st century A.D.

B. COMMENTARY ON THE APPROACH AND THE METHOD

I. Relationship to Literary Criticism

Prior to the endpoint of productive text formation, *intentional* changes within the arena of the written transmission of a text block mentioned in section A (such as additions, and corrections of formulation), fall within the arena of literary criticism. *All* changes in the text occurring *after* the above mentioned break constitute text critical problems (such as transcription mistakes, transcriber glosses, dogmatic changes).

Obviously, transcription *oversights* can intrude into the text transmission, even *before* this break. Their explanation devolves principally to text criticism. Nevertheless, it is difficult to determine in a given instance when the transcription oversight has entered. In certain situations, a text critical diagnosis can also refer to the processes prior to the end of productive Old Testament formulation of transmission. Correspondingly, this diagnosis must then be treated within the framework of literary criticism or transmission history. Hence, deviations of the Septuagint from the Masoretic text in a number of Old Testament books raises the question whether or not we are dealing with two separate ancient transmission lines, i.e. two (or more mixed) "original texts" at the end of the formation process.[13]

---

13 Compare Old Testament introductions for the arrangement and size of Jeremiah, or the thesis of H.J. Stoebe for 1 Sam 17:1–18:5 (*VT* 6 [1956]: 397–413, especially 411f).

II. The Procedural Steps[14]

1. Establishing and Critically Scrutinizing the Transmitted Text

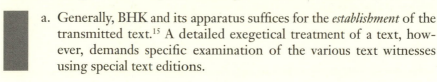

a. Generally, BHK and its apparatus suffices for the *establishment* of the transmitted text.[15] A detailed exegetical treatment of a text, however, demands specific examination of the various text witnesses using special text editions.

In the first place, the text transmission of the original Hebrew (or Aramaic) should be taken into account, followed in the second place by the text transmission of ancient translations. These text transmissions allow deductions concerning their Hebrew (or Aramaic) *Vorlage*. For orientation concerning the paths of transmission for Old Testament texts, compare the graphics in Fohrer (*Introduction*, 515 and *Exegese*, 40).

Under the limitation of those languages normally learned, the following should be consulted:

1. Text witnesses from the recent Palestinian manuscript discoveries (particularly Qumran)[16]
2. Samaritanus[17]
3. LXX[18]
   — Brooke—McLean—Thackeray—Manson (begun 1906)
   — Göttingen edition (begun 1931)
   — Rahlfs
4. Vetus Latina[19]
   — Sabatier
   — Edition of Erzabtei Beuron (begun 1949)
5. Vulgate[20]
   — Edition of the Benedictine order (begun 1926)
   — Edition of the Württ. Bibelanstalt (ed. R. Weber)

---

14 Here we follow Würthwein, *Text*, p. 113–120; see also McCarter, *Textual Criticism*, p. 62–75.

15 The BHS evidence is greatly reduced, and the apparatus also contains literary critical propositions. The Hebrew University Bible (HUB) project stands out at the forefront. For deciphering the language of the apparatus, compare H.P. Rüger, *An English Key to the Latin Words and Abbreviations and the Symbols of Biblica Hebraica Stuttgartensia* (Stuttgart, 1981); and R. Wonneberger, *Understanding BHS*, p. 40ff.

16 For references to the text distribution, see Würthwein, *Text*, p. 30–32, especially footnotes 60,61; and Tov, *Textual Criticism*, p. 21–79, 100–121.

17 For references to the text distribution, see Würthwein, *Text*, p. 45; Tov, *Textual Criticism*, p. 80–100.

18 Würthwein, *Text*, p. 76ff; Tov, *Textual Criticism*, p. 134–148.

19 Würthwein, *Text*, p. 92ff; Tov, *Textual Criticism*, p. 134.

20 Würthwein, *Text*, p. 99; Tov, *Textual Criticism*, p. 153.

b. *Critical scrutiny* means grouping the text witnesses according to their weight (see III 1); eliminating easily recognizable textual corruptions and changes; and correlating text witnesses dependent upon one another.

2. Linguistic and Material Examination of the Various Text Transmissions

  a. *Linguistic* examination aims specifically at the lexical, metrical-stylistic, and grammatical analysis of the text:
  1. Lexical inspection: Does the formulation under investigation provide meaning in the context? In addition to the familiar dictionaries, the concordance can be consulted for illuminating a word's range of meaning.
  2. Metrical-stylistic inspection: Is this particular (portion of the) verse possible metrically-stylistically? With poetic texts, one should consider the *parallelismus membrorum*. In light of the problems concerning Hebrew meter, caution is advised regarding changes based on metrical observations.
  3. Grammatical inspection: Is this particular (portion of the) verse possible grammatically? In text criticism, the grammatical analysis finds its expression primarily in the elucidation of unusual forms, peculiar constructions, as well as rare syntactical figures.
  b. *Material* examination asks: Is this word or this verse possible in this location for reasons of content, history, or the history of theology? This question comes closely into contact with other exegetical approaches. Often, it can only be answered when the results of further exegetical procedures are taken into consideration. Here it is shown that text criticism stands in comprehensive correlation with the remaining methods.

3. Reasoned Decision

  See the following for the methodological principles which enable a decision regarding which text form is considered as the "original text."

III. Principles for the Text Critical Decision

1. Importance of the Text Witnesses
  The old text-critical rule *manuscripta ponderantur non numerantur* ("manuscripts evaluated, not counted") means that the decision for a particular read-

ing cannot be grounded in the sheer numerical majority which the text witnesses afford. Rather, a decision can only be grounded in the importance of the witnesses. The importance of the individual text witnesses ensues from the text history with its changing relationships and dependencies.

a. As a rule, MT takes preference over every other transmission, as long as it is not defective linguistically and materially. The reason for this precedence is that it is the transmission of the original language and rests upon a calculated process of transmission of the text through careful studies. Within MT, the consonantal stability has a higher status than the vocalization. When MT offers a faultless and understandable text, a decision against MT is conceivable, and even probable in several places, but it must be careful grounded.

b. According to their significance for text criticism, the *further sequence of text witnesses* is: text witnesses from recent Palestinian manuscript finds (particularly Qumran), and Samaritanus; further, witnesses (retroverted into Hebrew) from LXX, Aquila, Symmachus, Theodotion, Peshitta, Targum, Vulgate, Vetus Latina, the coptic translations, and the Ethiopic, Arabic and Armenian translations.[21]

As findings which are to be taken seriously alongside MT, such text witnesses only come into question, if it is demonstrable that they are not already dependent upon MT, and do not owe their deviations to tendencies of their own transmission or translation.

2. Decision between Equally Important Text Witnesses

If a decision between two equally important text witnesses becomes necessary, then the following holds force:

a. *Lectio difficilior lectio probabilior* ("the more difficult the reading, the more probable a reading"—to the extent that the *lectio difficilior* is not meaningless, and is more readily explained as a transcription oversight). This rule, however, is only a result of the more general principle:

b. That reading is secondary whose origin from the other can be conceived with the least constraint.

3. Explanation of the Discarded Reading

After deciding for a particular reading, one must explain how the deviating reading of the text transmission came to be (at least for MT).

4. Conjectures

Free textual reconstructions, that is suppositions about the original wording, which are not supported through any available text witnesses, are to be used with the greatest frugality. As a rule, they are only acceptable if no

---

21 Würthwein, *Text*, p. 114.

available text transmission provides a meaningful text. However, it should be noted that the text witnesses themselves may already contain conjectures over against an incomprehensible text. If a conjecture is unavoidable, then it should be appended as closely as possible to the imagery of the letters of MT.

IV. Summary of the Text Critical Procedure

1. Establishing and critically scrutinizing the transmitted text
   a. What does MT offer?
   b. What does the critical apparatus of BHS, as well as BHK³ (!), offer? It is recommended that one consulting the witnesses mentioned in B II 1a based on special text editions.
   c. What do the commentaries offer?

   If the need arises, deviations from MT in the text witnesses are to be contemplated in their own textual context, and customarily translated into English.

   d. How do the texts allow themselves to be grouped, critically evaluated, and sorted, according to B II 1b and III 1?

2. Examining the various text witnesses
   a. linguistically (lexically, grammatically, stylistically)
   b. materially
   Aids: concordance, dictionary, grammar, commentaries

3. Decision according to the following criteria:
   a. MT takes preference as a rule! (*manuscripta ponderantur non numerantur*).
   b. With equally important readings: *lectio difficilior lectio probabilior*.
   c. Corroboration: Secondary readings should be explainable from the preferred.
   d. If no reading lays claim to the original wording (crux): conjecture.

Note: Further methodological treatment of the text can, if need be, necessitate revision of one's text critical judgment.

C. RESULTS

Text criticism is the fundamental endeavor concerning the wording of the text. It seeks to restore the "original" wording of the text by critically assessing the text transmission. Determining the textual base provides the indispensable preliminary work for subsequent exegetical procedures. Once the wording is established, then these procedures can and must be applied.

D. LITERATURE

I. INTRODUCTION, FOUNDATION, AND OVERVIEW

O. Eißfeldt. The Old Testament: An Introduction, §§ 113–125: p. 669–721 (additional references throughout and p. 778–785; for the execution of text criticism, see especially p. 718–720, 785).

F.E. Deist. Witnesses to the Old Testament: Introducing Textual Criticism. The Literature of the Old Testament 5. Pretoria, 1988.

G. Fohrer. Introduction, §§ 78–80: p. 489–515 (additional references throughout and p. 529–530).

_____. Exegese, § 4 (L. Markert).

O. Kaiser & W.G. Kümmel. Exegetical Method, p. 5–11.

P.K. McCarter. Textual Criticism: Recovering the Text of the Hebrew Bible. Philadelphia, 1986.

M. Noth. OTW, §§ 40–47: p. 301–363.

R. Smend. Einleitung des AT, §§ 3–5.

E. Tov. Textual Criticism of the Hebrew Bible. Minneapolis, 1992.

_____. "Textual Criticism." ABD, Vol. 6, 393–412.

R. Wonneberger. Understanding BHS: A Manual for the Users of Biblia Hebraica Stuttgartensia. Rome, 1990.

E. Würthwein. The Text of the Old Testament: An Introduction to the Biblia Hebraica. Grand Rapids, ²1995.

Regarding Hebrew *Poetry:*

Alter, R. The Art of Biblical Poetry. New York, 1985.

O. Eißfeldt. The Old Testament: An Introduction, § 6: p. 57–64 (additional references also p. 988f).

G. Fohrer. Introduction, § 5, p. 43–49 (additional references also p. 517–518).

O. Kaiser. Introduction, § 27, p. 326–337.

K. Koch. The Growth of Biblical Tradition, p. 91–100.

J.C. Kugel. The Idea of Biblical Poetry: Parallelism and Its History. New Haven, 1981.

M. O'Connor. Hebrew Verse Structure. Winona Lake, Indiana, 1980.

D.L. Petersen and K.H. Richards. Interpreting Hebrew Poetry. Minneapolis, 1992.

W.G.E. Watson. Classical Hebrew Poetry. JSOT.S 26. Sheffield, 1984.

For *lexicons, grammars* and Literature on *syntax*, see § 2 C.D.

II. FURTHER STUDY AND CRITICAL ALTERNATIVES

A. Aejmelaeus, ed. On the Trail of the Septuagint Translators: Collected Essays. Kampen, 1993.

P.S. Brock. "A Classified Bibliography of the Septuagint." In: Arbeiten zur Literatur und Geschichte des Hellenistischen Judentums VI. Leiden, 1973.

F. Delitzsch. Die Lese-und Schreibfehler im Alten Testament. Berlin—Leipzig, 1920.

J.A. Fitzmyer. The Dead Sea Scrolls. Major Publications and Tools for Study. p. 205–237. Atlanta, [2]1990.

R.W. Klein. Textual Criticism of the Old Testament: The Septuagint after Qumran. Philadelphia, [3]1981.

S. Olofsson. The LXX Version: A Guide to the Translation Technique of the Septuagint. Coniectanea Biblica. Old Testament Series 30. Stockholm, 1990.

M.H.K. Peters. "Septuagint." ABD, Vol. 5, 1093–1104.

Qumran and the History of the Biblical Text. F.M. Cross and S. Talmon, eds. Cambridge, MA—London, 1975.

De Septuaginta. Festschrift for J.W. Wevers. A. Pietersma and C. Cox, eds. Mississauga, Ontario, 1984.

H.-J. Stipp. Textkritik-Literarkritik-Entwicklung. EThL 66 (1990): 143–159.

Studies in the Septuagint: Origins, Recensions, and Interpretations. Selected Essays with a Prolegomenon by S. Jellicoe. New York, 1974.

Additional Bibliography in E. Würthwein. The Text of the Old Testament, p. 242–276, as well as in the notes and work of R. Wonneberger. Understanding BHS, p. 77–85.

III. ILLUSTRATIVE EXECUTION

D. Barthélemy. Critique textuelle de l'Ancien Testament. vol. 1: Josué, Juges, Ruth, Samuel, Rois, Chroniques, Esdras, Néhémie, Ester. OBO 50/1. Fribourg, 1982; vol. 2: Isaïe, Jérémie, Lamentations. OBO 50/2. Fribourg, 1986; Vol. 3: Ezéchiel, Daniel, et les 12 Prophètes. OBO 50/3. Fribourg, 1992.

R.W. Klein. "Doing Textual Criticism." In Textual Criticism of the Old Testament: The Septuagint after Qumran. p. 62–84. Philadelphia, [3]1981.

R. Wonneberger. Understanding BHS (in entirety).

Additional examples of text critical work may be found in the volumes and fascicles of the Biblischer Kommentar series (or Hermeneia and Word in English), where the results of the text critical procedure are summarized extensively in connection with the translation.

§4 Literary Criticism

A. THE TASK

I. The Overarching Question of the Development of an Old Testament Text

In practice, the subject of exegetical work is an Old Testament text several verses in length, once it has been text critically clarified. During the historical observation phase of this work (see above §1 B II 2), this text's train of thought may appear *consistent*. Not infrequently, however, it may also appear to be without inner coherence. The text may be confusing because it exhibits repetitions, multiple climaxes, or multiple statements of intention. The text can exhibit gaps or breaks where a transition is missing. It can even manifest contradictions whichin fact should be mutually exclusive. Both impressions— consistency or *inconsistency*—can prove either true or false in the subsequent methodological treatment of the text. For example, supposed inconsistency can be disproved when consistency arises from the inclusion of the context, by noting conventions of form (see §7), by noting content associations bound to the formulation at that time (see §8) or by noting historical realities (see §9). The apparent deficiency of the text's material coherency which causes the impression of inconsistency is then, in reality, our deficiency of knowledge. However, this impression of inconsistency can be true if these inconsistencies remain, or if new ones become visible, even after dismantling our lack of knowledge by the methodological treatment of the text. As far as we can see, with all exegetical responsibility, the Old Testament is full of such cases of enduring inconsistencies or of supposed consistencies. How does one explain that?

In the *Biblia Hebraica*, we encounter individual Old Testament texts in the framework of Old Testament books. However, these *books* are a *particular type* which is unfamiliar to us as contemporary users of the book. From the outset, these books could be completely independent works of literature—for example, Isaiah, Jeremiah, the Book of the Twelve, or the book of Psalms. However, Old Testament books can also have originally been only parts of larger works of literature. For example, the books of Leviticus and 1 Kings were never formulated as isolated works. For understanding a particular text, both cases are significant because we cannot adequately understand a text without the *contexts* to which it belongs. As a rule, the literary works to which the text belongs have not been written down in a single sitting, regardless of whether they cover the entire biblical book at hand. What we have before us in such a work, in many cases, is nothing more than the *final literary state* which has developed into a writing over time. The most significant thing about the process is that the more recent editions of a literary work do not replace the formulated material of the older version. Rather, they maintain it, but they expand, enlarge, and reorder it. Indeed, newer editions incorporate other transmissions, or even other writings, into the text; or they transport the received text into other literary works. This process is not just presented as the faithful transcription of that which was given, as seen later in the conscientiousness of the Masoretic transmission. It also represents a productive continuation which enlarges the text. The process is motivated by the effort to add interpretation, appropriation, and actualization for a new time to the older edition. It also structures the corresponding enlarged edition. Old Testament exegesis operates within the framework of this history of productive growth. In order to secure the original context's contribution to understanding a text in a writing, exegesis must therefore necessarily ask: During which phase of the literary growth were the text's component parts originally formulated? And how did that writing look during this phase? Exegesis must pay attention to the larger path of meaning which a particular text takes when the writing in which it stands is expanded.

The manifestation of undeniable inconsistencies is connected with this expanded character of the origin of Old Testament writings, even in the narrow confines of a single text. The great faithfulness with which older formulations remained protected during a writing's continuing productive development brings with it another situation. Many Old Testament literary works demonstrate inconsistencies between the actualizations and expansions which are older and those which are more recent. The inconsistencies are noticeable in the current shape of the entire work, but occasionally they may even be noticed in a single passage where formulations from different phases of the work's development stand side by side. Exegetically confirmed inconsistencies are therefore signs of the writing's development, its *productive evolution*, or even the development of an individual text within that writing.

How do enduring inconsistencies reveal themselves? And why do they necessitate that one not view individual Old Testament texts (such as a narrative or a prophetic speech) or especially larger text complexes (such as the Pentateuch or an entire prophetic book) as the result of one original formulative act? In other words, why not view the inconsistencies as texts which have been formulated in one setting by one author? In scholarly circles a whole series of *indicators* has long confirmed the impression that the texts have grown to the current form by means of an anonymous process.[22] Above all, material differences and tensions within a text, or a text-complex, stand in the way of their derivation from a single author. Instead, these differences imply that one must reckon with several layers of growth, different sources, or relatedly the act of collection.[23] The fact that the text has attained its current wording through several formulative acts over an extended period is also frequently proven by divergences in the language and formation of the text[24]—or its historical background (including cultic and historical-theological realities).[25] Additionally, it is proven by confirming that the same text appears more than once, occasionally in different versions.[26]

If one thinks of the origin and character of today's texts, then it will surely seem strange to learn that many Old Testament texts have been processed over the course of centuries by reformulation, broadening, expansion, and even by insertion into larger contexts. One must, however, take into account the realities of antiquity in general and of Ancient Israel in particular. At that point, the intellectual creation of a single person, and the specific form of the linguistic utterance do not yet represent an independent asset. In the present time, the dynamic narration of sagas and fairy tales provides a certain analogy. The essential stimulus for the productively developing transmission within the Old Testament lies in *changes in experiential perspective*. Even these changes require

---

[22] The perspectives are only mentioned here. For specification and expansion, see below B II 1 (p. 53f) and §5 B III (p. 65).

[23] For example: The two versions of the miracle of the sea in Exod 14:21f can hardly have stood side by side in the same narrative from the beginning: 1) Moses divides the sea into two dams of water on the right and left; 2) an east wind blowing through the night causes the water to recede.

[24] For example, in the main portion of the book of Judges (2:6–16:31), it is possible to isolate different independent transmissions (e.g. the Deborah-Barak narrative, in chapter 4, and the song of Deborah, 5:2–31a) and a bracketing, schematizing frame (4:*1–3; 5:31b) based on linguistic and formal criteria. This determination indicates redactional reworking of older narrative material.

[25] For example, in Isaiah, the historical background of chapters 1–39 is fundamentally different from chapters 40ff. After chapter 40, there is no reference to the historical situation of the latter eighth century, in which the prophet Isaiah appeared (1:1; 6:1; 7:13, etc.). Instead, the speeches are spoken in the time of the exile (45:1: Cyrus; 47; 52:7–12, etc.). Chapters 40ff were therefore attributed to an unknown prophet of this period (»Deutero-Isaiah«). Also, the historical background of chapters 1–39 is not unified (cf. 11:11–16 or 21:1–10). This variety leads to the differentiation of later, post-Isaianic pieces.

[26] Examples include: the parallels Gen 12:10–20; 20:1–18; and 26:1–13; 1 Sam 23:19–24: 23 parallels 26:1–25; 1 Kgs 17:17–24 parallels 2 Kgs 4:8–37; and Ps 14 = Ps 53.

interpretive and actualizing revisions of the texts in light of the authority of existing transmissions. These revisions reveal that one's own time is interpreted and mastered with the received texts and by the received texts.

In order to see the range of possibilities, one can become oriented with the following *portrayal of the chronological sequence of the phases of development for an Old Testament literary work*. The following picture is suggested in many cases:

1. Initially, *individual units* are formulated and transmitted *orally*. For example: a prophetic speech, a wisdom saying, a legal saying, a cultic psalm, or an ancestral narrative.
2. While still *orally* transmitted, individual texts can be strung together or *collected*. Beyond the setting for the *speech* in stage (1), now *the context of the collection* also influences the meaning of the single unit.
3. An important station on the path of transmission is the *initial written record* of these units or collections and their attachment to a writing. Now a literary entity arises. In order to fashion this literary entity, new text components can be attached which are specifically formulated to unite and to structure the whole. From the outset, these text components serve the redaction of the transmitted material within the framework of this writing. Additionally, however, individual interpretive additions can occasionally appear in this stage which do not have the entire writing in their horizon. Apparently, this stage quite decisively affected the transmission of prophetic speeches. The prophetic pronouncements, for example, stripped of their original communicative setting, were now compressed into a condensed formulation for written transmission in a future time.
4. With this initial recording phase, the end of an Old Testament *writing's* productive path of transmission is, as a rule, a long way from complete. The writing which originated in this manner *develops further*. How? Different possibilities come into view which are also partially related to one another: (a) The writing grows in size and becomes a corpus when it incorporates similarly developed writings; or it grows when it enters another writing. With such processes, newly formulated text material arises to unite and to structure the new totality. Quite obviously, the entire construction is organized anew during this stage. (b) The writing is not intertwined with other writings to become a new corpus, but it grows from within (e.g. the book of Ezekiel). In this case, one must also reckon with the following for each growth stage: isolated additions, additions structuring the whole, and new accents based on arrangement. (c) Some of the latest text components of an Old Testament writing can even have the intention of literarily anchoring this writing to large "canonical" corpora: Ps 1, with its accentuation of the Torah and its use of Josh 1, anchors the psalter to the Torah and the *Nebiim*. Mal 3:22–24 also anchors the Book of the Twelve to the prophetic canon.

This process reveals the following: The *accents of meaning* from an individual text are *changed* over the course of the productive transmission of Old Testament writings. Exegetical work seeks these accents of meaning in order to discern the fullness of the witness within the Old Testament itself. Exegetical work must illuminate the changes by differentiating and coordinating the text components according to developmental phases. Inconsistencies in a particular text are neither reasons to destroy biblical entities by arrogant attack nor to overemphasize the individual parts. Rather, inconsistencies aid in questioning and observing the *multiplicity of perceptions of God* which a text can already accrue in the process of its transmission within the Old Testament. §§4–6 serve as the methodological investigation of this state of affairs.

With §4 we enter a field of closely related methods, which all concentrate upon the text's development during the time in which the text is productively fashioned within the Old Testament. The procedures of literary criticism (§4), transmission history (§5), and redaction history (§6), which will be more extensively presented in the following, each concentrate on a particular aspect of this phenomenon, the development of an Old Testament text. By contrast, changes to the text which have taken place on the other side of the boundary of productive, developing transmission do not belong in the methodological field which we now enter. Rather, as we stated in §3, they belong in the area of text criticism.

If one looks at the concrete transmission processes in the Old Testament, then one distinction is certainly important in principal: Are the *processes oral or written in nature?* A number of Old Testament texts have existed only in written form (such as annals, lists, and probably also the Succession History of 2 Sam 9–20 + 1 Kgs 1–2). For a majority of texts, however, one should accept an oral *and* written transmission phase. Accordingly, the processes of productive transmission look different. They are recorded in the texts differently, and methodologically, they must be approached differently. They must be approached on the written level with literary criticism and redaction history, and they must be approached on the oral level with transmission history.

II. Determining the Task of Literary Criticism

Literary criticism is associated with the realm of written transmission, and it therefore investigates the text at the stage of its *fixed, written* formulation. This formulation could have been fixed in a single setting and within the frame of a larger literary context which still exists within the Old Testament without modifications.[27] If so, the literary critical inquiry provides no results. In the vast majority of cases, however, a given formulation, and its current context within the Old Testament, materialize during a literary history which may be rather brief or lengthy. A particular formulation can later be incorporated into a larger literary complex without notable changes.[28] However, it

---

[27] Examples include the book of Ruth and perhaps Lamentations.

[28] Examples include the Holiness Code (Lev 17–26) which was inserted into the Priestly writing and the Succession story (2 Sam 9–20+1 Kgs 1–2), which was incorporated into the Deuteronomistic history.

can also have grown in several phases. For example, during the composition of new literary entities, it can be compiled from several previously independent formulations.[29] Additionally, it may or may not have experienced expansions and additions.[30]

Accordingly, literary criticism asks:[31]

1. Is the text under investigation formulated in one setting or at different times and as a rule by different authors? This is the question of the *text's literary integrity*, or in other words, the question of its original coherence and consistency.

2. In the case of unity, for which wider literary context was the text first formulated? Or, in the case of disunity, for which wider literary contexts was the text transmitted and formulated during its various developmental stages? Or, in which expanding wider literary contexts has a unified text developed over time?[32] This is the question of the *larger literary contexts*,

---

[29] Examples include the flood story (Gen 6:5–8:22) and the miracle-story of the crossing of the sea (Exod 13:17–14:31). Relatedly, one may also include the Pentateuch itself to the extent that one views it as a combination of written sources.

[30] Examples include Deut 28 (Verses 45–68 are a later expansion; see the commentaries.); Isa 11 (Verses 6–9,10,11–16 are later additions, compare the discussion in the commentaries); the book of Job (Chapters 32–37 are clearly recognizable as an addendum. See further the Old Testament introductions).

[31] Kaiser (*Exegetical Method*, p. 12–14; for delimitation see also Huber in Fohrer, *Exegese*, p. 45,48f) considers the delimitation of the texts and the analysis of their structure part of the task of literary criticism. According to his presentation, they cannot be performed without the instruments of form-criticism. These tasks will therefore be assigned to the form critical process (See below, §7B II, III.1. [p. 102–108] and C I [p. 115]), where the scope of a passage can be clarified out of its larger literary context. Conversely, by investigating the text in light of its immediate context, literary criticism can occasionally provide the impression that the given text, with its scope, presents no independent pericope, because apparent pronouncements from the immediate context must be included (for example, if Isa 6:4–6 were the subject of the exegesis).

[32] For Richter (*Exegese*, p. 49f,63–65,69), literary criticism cannot overstep the inner realm of the text, or text-complex, under analysis. For him, the larger literary contexts in which the text/text complex belong (and relatedly the smaller units contained therein), are not yet determinable in this methodological step (cf also Huber, p. 48,57f). However, one should ask whether Richter's literary critical starting point is achievable according to the character of the act of historical recognition and in executing historical work. He seeks to exclude prejudices by preconceptions that are conditioned by the history of research, and therefore limits himself solely to the observation and the evaluation of formalized linguistic indicators. In order to avoid erroneous conclusions, the literary critical process should begin more broadly, in the sense of a comprehensive historical approach. A text, in its literary "unity or composition," is not just a linguistic phenomenon, it is also a historical phenomenon. This *historical aspect* and the process of analysis must continually correct one another interactively. Therefore, the analytical result requires cross-checking with those things which are historically conceivable (see below, p. 56). Also, the analytical procedure must observe, from the beginning, that the origin and development of the text may not be seen without the historical events associated with it. In the practice of exegetical work, this cross-checking happens intentionally, repeatedly, by taking up insights already acquired from the

to which also belongs the question of the structure of these contexts and the position of the text under investigation within those contexts.

Both questions are therefore *analytical* approaches of literary criticism. The first analyzes the *individual text* while the second analyzes the *literary contexts* of the layers of the individual text. The synthetic flip side of this approach is the task of the redaction critical investigation (see §6). It deals with the manner in which these layers grow together, their relationships and their changes, and the manner in which they come to be situated in their current literary context.

III. Terminology

The component "literary" in the term literary criticism should connote the delimitation of literary criticism to the period in which the development a text proceeds to the level of its *fixed, written formulation*. The definition and aims of "literary" by the discipline of literary studies or (modern or new) literary criticism are not intended here (see the discussion of New Literary Criticism above, §1 C V).

B. COMMENTARY ON THE APPROACH AND METHOD

I. The Question of a Text's Literary Integrity

This approach traditionally dominates literary critical research. It finds its primary utilization in the narrative writings of the Old Testament as well as in the prophetic writings. Recently, however, through the work of W. Beyerlin and K. Seybold, and others, it has also become important for the Psalter. It examines whether a text has been fixed in written form by *one* author, or a group of authors, in the course of a *single* formulative act. If not, and literary disunity is determined, then the additional task results, namely separating the

---

sub-disciplines of "Introduction to the Old Testament" and the "History of Israel" (see 1f and 1g below, p. 54, and footnote 41). Without doubt, caution is also recommended over against an uncritical, uncontrolled acceptance of scholarly opinions. Still, in this regard, the interdependency between the literary critical result and the insights of other exegetical techniques operates as the crucial stage. This interdependency already makes it necessary, within the literary critical analysis, to consider those processes of a text's development to which the other methodological aspects of exegesis are related (especially transmission history, below, p. 55, and further pp. 63ff). At the same time, however, it requires that one hold open the literary critical result. This broader starting point of literary critical work is also consistent with the fact that, if need be, the larger literary contexts of a text can be determined within its scope. Limiting the literary critical question only to the text under investigation will not be the procedure of this textbook, since text elements, several verses in length, have never experienced a literarily independent existence (cf also Knierim, [see above footnote 8] p. 131f).

fixed, written formulations analytically.[33] As a rule, those possibilities already mentioned (A.I. and A.2.) will come into play.

II. Methodological Principles for the Question of a Text's Literary Integrity

1. Indication of Literary Disunity

When investigating the literary integrity of texts, literary criticism must be methodologically careful to ask only those questions which are strictly related to the transmission stage of the written fixation, that is, to the layer of the given formulation.

> The following matters are thus important:
>
> a. Doublets: The same line of content is formulated twice within the same paragraph.
> b. Double or multiple transmissions: The same piece appears more than once within larger text complexes (in a different version).
> c. Secondary brackets: The formulations of various text components are clearly recognizable as balanced and are related to one another.
> d. Tensions in vocabulary (lexical, grammatical, syntactical, terminological), especially contradictions and breaks in the text's progression.
> e. Differences in the manner of speech and style (form, linguistic usage; poetry and prose in the same text).
> f. Differences of historical background (different historical realities which are chronological, cultic, legal, and theological).
> g. For certain literary layers, or sources, significant theological assertions, phrases, and linguistic peculiarities.
> h. Tensions and unevenness of content as well as elements typical for a genre. For the examination of the context, see footnote 31, and III below.

It is self-evident that interdependency also exists with the procedures of §7–9 at this point. Moreover, carefully processed impressions from the observation phase (see above, §1 II 1, and especially II 2) can be applied to the text here with profit. They are now processed methodically and explained while excluding possible alternatives.

> In the case of literary disunity, the various text components should be *ordered chronologically, relative to one another* (What is older/younger? What is dependent/independent?), if the literary critical analysis has produced criteria for doing so (cf further §6A)

---

[33] Huber, p. 54–57, attempts to classify the resulting possibilities.

2. Limitations

The validity and effectiveness of the questions about the text produced by 1a–h are subject to limitations in certain cases:

a. Observations from *1a and b* remain ambiguous without additional support by 1d,e,f, and/or g. For today's exegete, a danger exists with 1a which is obvious. One presupposes a strictly logical, consistent train of thought, in our sense, as the ideal (the exorbitant demand of modern logic upon an ancient text). However, precisely for that reason one is able to scrutinize that danger. This presupposition of a strictly logical text, however, would misconstrue the *historical character of the texts* as much as if the question of a text's particular stylistic devices were neglected (e.g. repetition, and the complex use of images and metaphors). Under certain circumstances, 1b, taken by itself, can too quickly give way to a modern perception about a text's multiple appearance.[34]

b. Moreover, the strength of the facts mentioned in *1b* also depends upon the *character* of the work under investigation (intention, structure, acquaintance with the transmission). Double and multiple transmissions weigh heavier in a closed work that is fashioned by a unified concept (such as if the Succession History of David contained such a concept) than in a work which is dependent upon pre-existing text material, and which collects, composes, and reworks transmissions which have been passed down (such as the History of David's Ascendency in 1 Sam 16–2 Sam 5).

c. The criteria of *1d–h* likewise do not operate without limitations.

(1) At any rate, with early Old Testament texts one may frequently observe that the *authors of larger literary works* incorporate various types of oral transmissions which come to them, virtually unchanged. They even protect the ancient, transmitted wording. Thus, within the same literary work, tensions in vocabulary, manner of speech, style, and content can be due to this collecting and codifying (by contrast, the Priestly writing and the Books of Chronicles are different). Thus, these tensions do not derive from literary disunity.[35]

(2) The facts mentioned in (1) apply not only in view of the collective character of the larger work as a whole, but even more for the *individual sections* of such works. Here, one may demonstrate that a list of criteria used by literary criticism at the turn of the century, which continue to be partially operative today, cannot be utilized unconditionally in literary critical analysis. Certain features can already derive from processes in the oral pre-history of a text and thus find a transmission historical solution.[36] These features include differences in language (words, style), in historical and chronological details, in the presuppositions of legal, social, and religious (cult and piety) conditions, in ethical and theological understanding, and in material contradictions.[37] Likewise, the impression of literary disunity can be misleading in redactionally formulated texts because the complexity of the statements, or the order of the statements, stems from their relatedness to the entire writing (see below, §6).

Observing tensions of the type mentioned in 1d-h therefore demands, for methodological reasons, that one suspend judgment during a text's literary critical treatment

---

34 Compare Gen 12:10ff and 26:1ff within the Yahwist's narrative and the consequences of the undifferentiated appraisal by exegetes who ascribe Gen 12 and 26 to two sources.

35 Compare again Gen 12 and 26.

36 Cf Noth, *Pentateuchal Traditions*, p. 20f.

37 F. Baumgärtel, "Bibelkritik I. AT." in RGG³, vol 1, column 1186 (literary criticism).

until one concludes the *transmission historical* and the *redaction historical* investigation. As a result of the interdependence of the methods, even the procedures in §§7–9 can once again provide viewpoints for the question of the literary integrity. The intention of this observation is not to dwell on our impressions of the text's inconsistency (or consistency). Rather, the intention is to push forward to the emergence of the text itself. Stated simply: Literary criticism is not persuasive just because one can use it, rather it is persuasive where the text forces one to use it. Only when the tensions cannot be explained in favor of literary unity must the literary critical consideration be applied anew. Then the criteria cited in section I can be evaluated for the formative layer without impediment.

d. The convincing proof that a literarily fixed *Vorlage* (e.g. source text) has been used, can only be presented if the copy's original formulation can be extricated as an adequately closed entity, free of influence from the borrowing author. Acceptance of several factors will necessarily weaken such proof, although it must not eliminate it. These factors include: accepting that the author has only taken up the copy incompletely, accepting that numerous places adapt their formulation to the new context, or accepting that transpositions of the original text occurred with the borrowing.

e. In order to counteract the danger of analytical oversensitivity, one should, by contrast, attempt to understand and to interpret a given text synthetically, as a *substantive totality*, in the sense of synchronic reflection. In the course of such a process, individual threads, which appear to be full of tension, can also be seen diachronically and developmentally as complimentary aspects added to a complete and thoughtfully constructed totality.[38] Here, one must also observe the interdependence of the various methodological approaches. The Old Testament author's genre, opinion, and the type of presentation play an important role as the subject of cross-checking questions. They can delimit the literary critical endeavor because literary analysis cannot depend upon that which appears inconsistent to the modern reader's logical, stylistic, and material demands upon a text. Rather, the historical approach of literary analysis has to infer what was literarily possible at the time of the text's literary formulation, and what was not.

f. One critically corrective function of the literary critical analysis, similar to the approach in section e), finally requires a procedure by which one must test whether the achieved result is even *historically conceivable* for the development of an Old Testament text. In so doing, one must consider the diverse character of Old Testament transmissions.[39]

Generally in those places where *longer transmission historical growth* of material becomes apparent on a broad basis (as for example in Genesis), comprehension has to make room for the thoughtful transmission historical perspective. In light of the independent narrative units it is difficult to conceive historically that the texts are combined from literary sources even to the level of half-verses. By contrast, the literary critical view has proven itself in the Pentateuch in those places where entire narrative units have been literarily distinguished.[40] If texts provide *little in the way of reference points for a transmission historical development*, then, on the basis of observations which indicate disunity, one may

---

[38] Compare O.H. Steck, *Wahrnehmungen*, p. 16–35 (especially 26ff), for Gen 2:46–3:24. Also, Steck, *Der Schöpfungsbericht der Priesterschrift*, ²1981 (especially p. 26–30, 244–255); also H. Barth, *Die Jesaja-Worte in der Josiazeit*, 1977, p. 10f, 86–88, 187–189, for Isa 28:7b–22; 29:1–7; and 31:1–4+8a.

[39] Compare also §5 B II 1 (p. 66f).

[40] Compare, Noth, Pentateuchal Traditions, p. 24f.

reckon historically with the literary adaptation of a fixed, written text. These observations allow one to confirm short explanatory additions and glosses. They also confirm expansions, revision into collections, and supplemental redactions. Those places where one must account for fixed statements *already in oral tradition* (prophetic speeches, partial psalms, legal sayings, wisdom speeches, and apparently even in prophetic narratives) create a particularly difficult problem for literary criticism and transmission history. In these cases it is scarcely possible to decide from the text itself whether the processes represent written or oral expansion. Overlapping viewpoints must be taken into account regarding the place of origin, the tradent, and purpose in order to reach a decision. If material arguments dictate an oral development of the text, then the analysis must insure critically that the results correspond to the growth process as it would be possible in oral tradition.

III. The Question of Larger Literary Contexts

If the text under investigation is itself not already the larger literary context (as for example, if an entire prophetic book will be analyzed), then the text's relationship to the preceding and the following context should be examined literary critically. This procedural step begins by *taking stock* of the given immediate and broader context. This step is pursued by the *literary critical inquiry* into the context. It takes into account this context's contents, its arrangement (in the sense of structure and composition—see footnote 80), and its thought progression. It does so in order to distinguish that which originally belonged together literarily from more recent contexts if necessary. This process leads to the *determination* of the original literary layer as well as, if necessary, determination of more recent layers to which the entire text under investigation belongs.[41]

Thus, the task of classifying a text into the respective literary context to which it belongs must even be performed if the text under consideration is literarily homogenous.

In the beginner's practice, literary critical results will be applied from the present state of the discipline of introduction. This discipline will provide information for the historical identification of the literary layers[42] as well as results regarding linguistic contour and form (§7).

---

41 Examples: The larger literary context of Amos 8:1–2 (the harvest basket vision of Amos) was originally the vision cycle of Amos 7:1–8; 8:1–2; 9:1–4. This cycle was later expanded and has been combined with other transmission complexes to make the current book of Amos (cf Kaiser, *Old Testament Introduction*, p. 217f). The larger literary context of 1 Sam 26 is first the history of the ascendancy of David. Later, the context becomes a narrative work which combines the history of the ascendancy with the Succession History to the throne. Later still the context becomes the Deuteronomistic history. The larger literary context of Gen 9:1–6 is first the Priestly writing, then developmental stages in which the priestly writing has been worked into larger literary works.

42 Naming the layer, author, date and place of composition, material profile, etc.

The reconstruction of larger literary contexts essentially occurs within the frame of literary criticism. However, these results require expansion, differentiation, and verification by the remaining methodological procedures. These procedures will evaluate the result of the text—immanent literary analysis for its historical plausibility. It is important to pay attention to the following: the unified profile of statements of a larger literary context; the transmission *process* standing behind that context including the redaction historical perspective; the form and the historical setting of that context.

IV. Summary of the Literary Critical Procedure

1. The question of the text's literary *integrity*:
   a. Is the text understandable by itself, or does it represent only a segment which requires the context?
      Examination of the edges of the text, examination of the corpus with regard to linguistic reference signals which relate the text to the context (e.g. suffixes, unintroduced persons, presuppositions of the action).
   b. Is the formulation of the corpus literarily homogeneous or not?
      Use of the guiding question and the controlling question above in B II.
   c. In the case of literary disunity:
      — precise delineation and division of the text formulations into different literary layers.
      — content relationship of the layers to one another: For example, two originally independent formulations are combined secondarily with or without redactional formulations connecting and compensating them. Also, an existing literary formulation receives a gloss, is expanded, or enlarged (in conjunction to what?).
      — relative chronological relationship of the layers to one another, if the literary critical analysis offers indices for this task.

Observe: Possible alternatives must be expressly eliminated with rationale, and a revision on the basis of the procedures of §§5–9 must be held open during the process.

2. The question of the larger literary *contexts* of the unified text or, relatedly, of the different literary layers:
   a. Reconsideration of question 1a: Which passage of the immediate context (previous or subsequent) does the text (or the particular literary text layer) specifically presuppose?
   b. For which Old Testament literary work was the text (or the individual literary layer) first formulated?
      How is this literary work arranged, and where does the text (or text layer) stand within that arrangement? (preparation for the

redaction historical question regarding the intended position of the text (or text unit) in the literary work, cf §6 B II 2).

Do the more recent layers of the text have parallels in other places of this literary work? (preparation for the redaction historical question: Do these internal stages relate to one another as individual expansions or redactional processes? Cf § 6 B II 2.)

Corroborating question: To what extent do the literary critical findings in the text under investigation correspond to the linguistic and material character of the larger literary framework?

c. In what broader literary contexts was the text under investigation transferred with its literary layering, even if this transferring did not affect the formulation of this particular text? (Correlation with §6)

The component questions b and c strive toward the larger context in which a statement has been formulated or the context in which it entered the Old Testament. They prepare the redaction historical investigation (§6) and the determination of an individual statement's meaning within the frame of its entire context (§10). Practically, one must rely upon secondary literature (Old Testament introductions, commentaries and their introductions, monographs) for clarification of b and c. Even for the beginner, this reliance in no way excludes the possibility of limited contributions on the basis of the text under investigation.

C. RESULTS

The results of literary criticism can be seen in the fact that it performs the necessary *groundwork* for other exegetical stages. *Transmission history* can begin its analysis with the oldest literarily homogenous version of the passage under consideration (or relatedly its [source] components) which was obtained by literary criticism. *Redaction history* employs the results achieved by literary critical analysis when it coherently presents the history of the encountered text in the realm of written transmission and when it coherently presents the operative working procedures and motifs. At the point in which the larger literary context of a text is demonstrated, and at the point in which the text's place in the context is determined, literary criticism makes it possible *to inquire into* the *author, place, and time* for the literary version. Simultaneously, this demonstration provides the respective literary context in whose framework the text can be materially interpreted in the concluding section of *determining the historical meaning.*[43]

---

[43] Examples: Amos 8:1–2 should first be interpreted in the context of the vision cycle. Correspondingly, the components of the Yahwistic primal history should be interpreted first and foremost in the frame of the Yahwistic work, etc.

D. LITERATURE

I. INTRODUCTION, FOUNDATION, AND OVERVIEW

J. Barton. "Source Criticism." ABD, vol. 6, 162–165.
G. Fohrer. Exegese, § 5 (F. Huber), § 9B (G. Fohrer).
N. Habel. Literary Criticism of the Old Testament. Guides to Biblical Scholarship. Old Testament Series. J.C. Rylaarsdam, ed. Philadelphia, 1971.
O Kaiser. Exegetical Method, p. 11–16.
K. Koch. The Growth of the Biblical Tradition, p. 68–78.
M. Noth. A History of Pentateuchal Traditions. p. 5–41 (esp. p. 20–25). Atlanta, 1981 (reprint, 1972 translation).

II. EXPANSION AND CRITICAL ALTERNATIVES

I. Engnell. Methodological Aspects of Old Testament Study. VT.S 7 (1960): 13–30 (esp. 21ff).
R. Rendtorff. "Literarkritik und Traditionsgeschichte." EvTh 27 (1967): 138–153.
_____. The Problem of the Process of Transmission in the Pentateuch JSOT.S 89. Sheffield, 1990.
W. Richter. Exegese, p. 49–72.
H. Ringgren. "Literarkritik, Formgeschichte, Überlieferungsgeschichte. Erwägungen zur Methodenfrage der alttestamentlichen Exegese." ThLZ 91 (1966): col. 641–650.
S. Segert. "Zur Methode der alttestamentlichen Literarkritik." ArOr 24 (1956): 610–621.
H.J. Stoebe. "Grenzen der Literarkritik im Alten Testament." ThZ 18 (1962): 385–400.
J.H. Tigay, ed. Empirical Models for Biblical Criticism. Philadelphia, 1985.

III. EXEMPLARY EXECUTION

H. Gunkel. Genesis. HK I/1. p. 137–140. (Literary criticism on Gen 6:5–9,17,28f.) Göttingen, ³1910 (=⁹1977).
H.-J. Hermisson. Deuterojesaja. BK XI. Fascicle 7. p. 1–80. Neukirchen-Vluyn, 1987.
W. Richter. Die Bearbeitungen des »Retterbuches« in der deuteronomischen Epoche. BBB 21. p. 1–62 (Literary criticism on Judg 2–12). Bonn, 1964.
C.R. Seitz. "The Crisis of Interpretation over the Meaning and Purpose of the Exile." VT 35 (1985): 78–97 (Literary Criticism on Jer 21,24,27,37–43).
K. Seybold. Bilder zum Tempelbau. Die Visionen des Propheten Sacharja. SBS 70. p. 11–23. (Literary criticism on Zech 1–8). Stuttgart, 1974.

IV. HISTORY OF RESEARCH

R.E. Clements. A Century of Old Testament Study. Rev. ed. Guildford, 1983.
O. Eißfeldt. "Literarkritische Schule." RGG³, vol. 4, col. 388–390.
H. Greßmann. "Die Aufgaben der alttestamentlichen Forschung." ZAW 42 (1924): 1–33 (esp. 2–8).

N.C. Habel. Literary Criticism of the Old Testament. Minneapolis, 1971.

H.F. Hahn. "The Critical Approach to the Old Testament." Old Testament in Modern Research. p. 1–43. Philadelphia, 1954.

R. Knierim. "Criticism of Literary Features, Form, Tradition, and Redaction." In D.A. Knight and G.M. Tucker, The Hebrew Bible and Its Modern Interpreters. Philadelphia-Chico, 1985, p. 128–136.

D.A. Knight, ed. Julius Wellhausen and His *Prolegomena to the History of Israel.* Semeia 25 (1983).

K. Koch. The Growth of the Biblical Tradition. p. 68–76.

H.-J. Kraus. Geschichte der historisch-kritischen Erforschung des Alten Testaments. (see the subject index under "Literarkritik."). Neukirchen-Vluyn, [3]1982.

§5 The Transmission Historical Approach

A. THE TASK

I. Determination

If an Old Testament text or text complex developed in the realm of *oral* speech before its transcription, then one utilizes the transmission historical approach.

Above all, the following state of affairs offers the *reason for inquiry* behind a text's oldest ascertainable written phase into the realm of its previous oral transmission. The content of a text, or even parts of a text, appears to be independent of its immediate context (including aspects of both form and genre, in anticipation of §7). Thus, in the time of its first utterance, the text was originally understandable without additional text material. One thus appears to encounter the phenomenon of a *"small unit."* On the one hand, literary entities so small in size were not transmitted in written form separately, and their combination with other "small units" into a collection is a secondary process. One the other hand, such phenomena arise in conjunction with spoken actions (cult, school wisdom, legal oration, prophetic pronouncement, narrative activity). For these two reasons, the assumption is offered that here one encounters the recording of small, originally *oral* speech units. Indeed, in special cases it even appears that these small units experienced changes during oral their transmission which is still detectable, as text observations can suggest (along with investigation on the basis of §§ 7 and 9).

The *transmission historical approach* concerns itself with such justifiable deductions from the oldest written form of the text back into the arena of the oral development and transmission. Accordingly, the precision of these transmission historical deductions manifests itself differently depending upon the extent of the first written recording upon the formulation of the text. Often in the area of cult, wisdom, and law, one can situate the given formulation in the oral phase for reasons of usage. With prophetic logia, it is frequently not possible to reconstruct the complete, originally oral formulation behind the condensed, written form. The written form can even take account of the effect of the prophetic word. With individual narratives, the possibility that one can trace the formulation's oral phase is generally even smaller, as will be shown below.

At the same time, the transmission historical approach is of essential significance. It provides insight into the development and origin of the text, into the text's purpose and use in concrete situations, and into the institutions of Israel. Further, the transmission historical approach illuminates the appearance, independence, and contour of "smaller units" within the written transmission of the Old Testament.

The *task* of transmission history is therefore to determine the form and development of the text in this oral transmission phase, in as much as that is possible, and to extract any other supportable conclusions from this area.[44]

Transmission history first proceeds *analytically*. It begins with the oldest literarily homogenous version of a text, or relatedly its component (source) parts, as established in the literary critical stage. It then inquires further, back into the realm in which the text has been orally transmitted and in which it was originally formulated. Transmission history thereby aims at a phenomenon frequently encountered in Ancient Israel: a majority of texts have their origin in the realm of living speech (such as individual narratives, legal stipulations, prophetic speeches, and cultic songs). They are first conveyed in oral transmission. During this oral transmission, changes can also enter the transmitted material.

A *synthetic stage* begins with the analytical results, but reverses the direction of inquiry. To the extent that it is possible and that it is suggested by evidence, this stage attempts to portray the development of the transmitted text, in its historical derivation and context, from its first recognizable oral form to the oldest written formulation. It highlights the effective changes and historical factors.

II. Terminology

Elsewhere in exegetical literature, one also finds the term "transmission history" limited to the history of a transmission unit, or the merger of individual pieces, during the stage of *oral* transmission.[45] It must also be noted,

---

44 The task is thus a constituent question within the framework of the overarching question about the development of an Old Testament text (see above, §4 A I [p. 47ff]).

45 Compare Fohrer, *Introduction*, p. 29f,31 (chart). Recently Fohrer (*Exegese*, p. 119ff) has modified his definition in so far as he also attributes "*possible* earlier, and therefore "precursory", stages of codification" (p. 120, emphasis ours) to transmission history. However, for Fohrer, this

however, that "transmission history" will often be perceived in another sense which includes redaction history[46] or which is related to the analysis of a specific text's written or oral prehistory.[47] Many use the term "tradition history" as a synonym for "transmission history" in the narrower sense, as used by us.[48] Likewise, many use the term "transmission history" in a broader sense which includes written transmission.[49] Finally, in order to differentiate between the methodological process and the subject which it investigates, the designation for the method contains the component of "criticism", which many researchers use in the sense of forming scientific judgment (transmission criticism, tradition criticism). The same goes for the methods of redaction history, form history, and tradition history.[50]

B. COMMENTARY ON THE APPROACH AND THE METHOD

I. Relationship to Literary Criticism[51]

1. Expansion
Methodologically reflective literary criticism and transmission history complement one another meaningfully. Analytically determining a text's development during the written transmission stage is conducted by literary criticism, while determining the oral transmission stage is conducted by the transmission historical approach.

2. Delimitation
When critically distinguished from literary criticism, the transmission historical approach should bring the following to bear:

a. The origin and formation of numerous Old Testament texts derive from the arena of oral transmission.
b. The principles of oral transmission can be considerably differentiated from those of written transmission.[52]

---

expansion has a purely theoretical character, since the "precursory" codification stage is no longer something which is "immediately available."

46 Classic examples: Noth's *The Deuteronomistic History* and *The Chronicler's History* (see below, §6 D III [p. 93]) and *Pentateuchal Traditions* (see above, p. 60).

47 So Koch, *Growth of Biblical Tradition*, p. 38,51,53f,57.

48 So, for example, F. Baumgärtel, RGG³, vol. 1, col. 1187.

49 So, for example, von Rad, *Old Testament Theology*, vol. 1, p. 11f,187,306f, etc.; A.H.J. Gunneweg, BHH, vol. 3, col. 2018–2020.

50 Compare, for example, Fohrer, *Exegese*, p. 7,121f.

51 Cf also §4 B II 2f (p. 55).

52 Cf. §4 A II (beginning on p. 51) with §4 B II 2f (p. 55). See also Koch, *Growth of Biblical Tradition*, §7 (especially, p. 89–91.)

One should thus certainly note the following: Frequently, the outline, contour, and essential traits are determined in the realm of oral transmission, especially in narrative texts. However, not every specific formulation is determined therein.[53]

II. Transmission Historical Processes[54]

Transmission history can be applied with a prospect for concrete results[55] to those texts which arose in the realm of oral transmission and to those which were also occasionally subjected to certain changes and formative influences during oral transmission.

1. Type and Manner of Changes

In order to understand the type and manner in which the transmission segments (small units) were changed during oral transmission one must consider that Old Testament texts derive from extremely diverse formative relationships. The means of influence upon individual segments are very different depending upon the *formative circumstances.*

In those places where traditions had been *popular narrative material* before they were recorded in written form, one should consider that only the contents were initially fixed during the oral phase.[56] Thus, these transmissions were still relatively open for reformulation, broader development, correlation, and intertwining with other narratives and with portions of other narratives. The composition of different elements necessarily produces certain tensions. By contrast, it is less apparent that the original wording was constantly changed during oral transmission when institutional frameworks (or relatedly *reflective procedure*) lead to fixed formulations which could then be orally transmitted.[57] In those cases, the effect of the transmission tradent

---

53 The following is valid in these cases: If verse numbers are assigned during the course of a transmission historical analysis, then, in contrast to literary criticism, the isolation of verses or verse parts does not generally intend a fixed vocabulary. Rather the assignation indicates the extent of transmission components they contain.

54 Hermisson, *Jakobs Kampf am Jabbok*, 251–257, offers important, extensive reflections upon the presuppositions for the origin and transmission of orally transmitted products in light of narratives.

55 Cf. section V below, p. 69.

56 Sociologically: in the main, the period of the tribal system of Israel before 1000 BCE, but still in the Northern Kingdom; tradents: perhaps travelling story tellers. Texts in the Old Testament: especially in Genesis to Samuel; Example: Gen 32:23–33 (cf. Elliger, *Der Jakobskampf am Jabbok*, and Hermisson, cited above). J.P. Floß, *Wer schlägt wen?*, demonstrates that one may track a preliterary phase of this text by linguistic investigation, in contrast to E. Blum, *Komposition* (p. 140ff, 175ff).

57 Sociologically: in the monarchial period of Israel and under the influence of courtly culture these institutional frameworks are expanded; tradents: schools and school-like groups. Texts in the Old Testament: especially cult songs, legal sayings, and, in part, prophetic logia, wisdom sayings, but also theologically contemplative narratives about prophets.

more likely manifests itself in the ordering of the collection, in interpretive and actualizing introductions, expansions, appendixes, or connective pieces (as long as these are not better attributed to the written transmission phase).

2. Material Character of the Changes

To understand the substantive material character of the changes whose transmissions can be attributed to the course of the transmission history, one must consider a broad array of possibilities:

a. new material accents[58] (especially narrative);
b. substantive theological transformations (for example, the incorporation of pre-Israelite material into the sphere of Israelite religion)[59];
c. changes on the basis of displacement (regarding populations, territory, setting, leading figures) or particular (historical) events in the realm of transmission[60];
d. changes on the basis of institutional or theological alterations in the tradent circle[61];
e. changes associated with uniting individual pieces into a collection (assimilations, harmonizations, tetherings, entire connective pieces).[62]

58 Example: In the Penuel saga of Gen 32:23–33, the naming scene (32:28–30a) is a secondarily added narrative motif because it interrupts the demand and the bestowal of blessing (32:27b,30b) and forms a second climax to the narrative beside the naming of the place (32:31).

59 Example: In the pre-Israelite/Canaanite form of the Penuel saga, the man had really threatened his divine counterpart (as 32:26f demonstrates). However, the Israelite version, through its additions of 32:29,31bß (even clearer in the version of Hos 12:4f), expresses that Jacob was fundamentally the loser in this battle. He had only endured (*ykl* in 32:29), and thus is his life spared (32:31). The formulations of 32:26f have been implicitly transformed without change to the wording (these are also transmission historical changes).

60 Example: The original Carmel story in 1 Kings 18 wants to show how a people vacillating between YHWH and Baal were led to a significant YHWH confession in the time of Ahab (correspondence between 18:31 and 18:39!). By contrast, 18:19b,20,40 highlight the events of the killing of the Baal prophets. This displacement of accent signifies a reworking which actualizes the older Carmel transmission under the impression of the reign of Jehu and his eradication of the Baal worshippers (2 Kgs 10:18–27).

61 Example: The expansion of the Penuel saga in 32:33, which etiologically connects a certain table custom with Jacob's limp, happens first when the saga leaves its pre-Israelite and its proto-Israelite transmission circle, which was still limited to the people of Jacob, and was passed on by transmission tradents oriented toward all Israel.

62 Example: 1 Kings 18:18b,19a are components of a collector's transition (because of later reworkings, only incompletely received) from the drought narrative (17:1–6; 18:1–2a [2b–16?], 17–18a) to the Carmel story (18:21–39). For examples from the Pentateuch, see Noth, *Pentateuchal Traditions*, especially p. 198–227.

Fohrer's (*Exegese*, p. 120f,128f,139f,141f) differentiation within the realm of oral transmission represents an unnecessary complication, which is also impractical in light of the text material. He distinguishes between "collector's ordering," which he assigns to transmission criticism, and "composition," which should be investigated in composition criticism and redaction criticism. By contrast, we assign *all* proceedings taking place in the realm of oral transmission to transmission

III. Methodological Questions for the Analytical Process[63]

1. Is the text under investigation transmitted elsewhere in the Old Testament or in Israel's environment in a manner which does not indicate literary dependence (*double and multiple transmission*)?[64] What does comparison provide?

2. How does this text appear under *form critical inspection*?[65] Does this inspection indicate an entity which is complete, free-standing, and independent of the context?

   In a narrative text, what do the scenic structure and, above all, the lines of tension produce for the question of the coherence and consistency of a small unit?

   Can one determine lines in the profile of the genre (climax, lines of tension, introduction, conclusion; expanded genre, mixed genre) or by comparing genre historical results which allow conclusions concerning the transmission historical processes and which allow a reconstruction of the preliterary form(s)?[66]

3. Where do *material tensions and curiosities* exist which, however, no longer allow literary division? Which lines are not conceivable, or are even improper, at the time of the text's literary composition and thus point to a prior arena of transmission history?[67]

4. Which lines allow themselves to be classified to a *specific transmission stage* for theological, historical, linguistic, or history of religions reasons?[68]

---

history, and all proceedings taking place in the written transmission realm we assign to literary criticism and redaction history.

63 Richter rejects argumentation solely on the basis of content criteria for transmission historical analysis (*Exegese*, 44,152–163; there under the term "tradition criticism," cf. discussion above, p. 65). Such caution is warranted. However, one should also doubt whether deductions concerning preliterary stages of a text are possible exclusively on the basis of linguistic-structural indices. It is not conceivable why material tensions, history of religions phenomena, or cultural history phenomena (that is to say phenomena related to the content of the text) may not be evaluated as signs of an oral prehistory of the text unit as such, especially since linguistic-structural tensions can be missing from a text with a preliterary prehistory. Reaching beyond the transmission historical process to other exegetical processes is therefore again essential.

64 For examples, see footnote 26.

65 Again, the interdependence of the methods is revealed!

66 Example: the multiple climax of Gen 32:23–33 (see above, footnotes 58 and 61).

67 Example: the presentation of YHWH's wrestling with Jacob in Gen 32:26f (see above, footnote 59).

68 Example: the killing of the Baal priests in 1 Kgs 18:40 in distinction to the historical setting of the Carmel scene as a whole (see above, footnote 60).

5. Does the homogenous genre property (§7) necessitate the acceptance of the oral origin of a small unit for a text whose formulation
is fixed because of the *arena in which it is utilized* (cult, wisdom, law)?
6. Does a corresponding finding simultaneously necessitate further inquiry into an oral transmission form *despite redactional reworking* of
the formulation (prophetic logia)?

IV. The Synthetic Process

By mobilizing historical (§9) and form critical (§7) considerations, the
synthetic presentation of a transmission unit's path in oral tradition should
illuminate the reasons for the origin of that transmission unit.

The synthetic presentation should endeavor to explain the historical
necessities and the intentions which have determined the transmission
unit's development and the changes within the frame of oral transmission.[69]

The same is true for the process of the connection of several such transmission units in the realm of oral transmission into a larger transmission complex
(collections, narrative cycles). With the question of the intentions of transmission, the synthetic process of the transmission historical approach already
furnishes elements for determining historical meaning (§10).

V. Applications for the Transmission Historical Approach

Individual texts as well as large text complexes (for example, pentateuchal
sources) allow themselves to be treated transmission historically regarding
the transmission components assimilated in them and their shape in oral tradition. Among the Old Testament writings, the historical books generally
prove productive for a transmission historical investigation. In addition to the
narrative transmission, it is especially important to consider the legislative
material as well.[70] By contrast, changes scarcely appear in older wisdom and
cult texts in the phase of oral transmission.[71] With prophetic logia, the trans-

[69] A close correlation thus exists between the transmission historical approach and the determination of the historical setting of transmission layers!

[70] For example, one has to consider the problems which the Book of the Covenant creates in
this regard. See the recent work of E. Otto, *Wandel der Rechtsbegründungen in der Gesellschaftsge-
schichte des antiken Israel. Eine Rechtsgeschichte des »Bundesbuches« Ex XX 22–XXIII 13*, Leiden, 1988.

[71] In the Psalter, however, transmission historical and literary critical problems are nevertheless settled in the arena of the formulations of individual psalms. This fact is demonstrated, for
example, in the investigations of W. Beyerlin and K. Seybold. Cf. K. Seybold, *Introducing the
Psalms*, Edinburgh, 1990, p. 255ff (more extensive bibliography in the German edition, *Die
Psalmen. Eine Einführung*, 1986, p. 208ff).

mission historical inquiry is in principal necessary, but progress toward the preliterary formulations is frequently blocked.

VI. Summary of the Procedure of Transmission History

1. Analytical Questions
   a. Does the literarily homogenous text, or one of its literarily inde-pendent layers, suggest *material reasons* indicating an orally trans-mitted piece existed previously? And can one exclude a purely literary (!) imitation of the character of small units (perhaps in re-lation to the genre)?
   b. Does B III 1–6 provide *analytical text indicators* which strengthen this supposition?
   c. What *shape* did the *oral* transmission take?
      — Possibly, the formulation is received completely intact (for example, in cult songs, sacral and profane legal stipulations, wisdom sayings, even, with qualification, the incorporation of prophetic logia).
      From the other side, can one isolate elements of the formulation which more likely belong to the written recording?
      — Less of the formulation is received intact (for example, with prophetic logia).
      What can one isolate as a linguistic or material presupposition of the literarily-compressed prophetic logia which comes closer to their oral linguistic shape?
      — The formulation is probably not received intact, but possibly the outline, perspective, or emphases are received (for ex-ample with individual narratives).

2. Synthetic Questions
   a. What are the *reasons for the origin and transmission* of the text's reconstructed oral phase, and what are the conditions of its insti-tutional framework (§9)?
   b. Are there indeed indicators of a *change* (transmission history) within the oral tradition, and what are the reasons and the ma-terial signals of this change (see B II 2)?
   c. Are there compositional indicators in the context that the text, or text layer, was incorporated into *orally* transmitted *collections* of correspondingly small units?
      If so, what material change does this process produce?

Note: Transmission historical investigations are necessary, but they are to a large degree reconstructions. For this reason, they require support from similar findings according to §7 and §9.

C. RESULTS

I. Insight into the Origin and Changes of a Transmission Unit within Oral Tradition

If one is able to trace a text's origin and, if necessary, its formative changes back into the realm of oral tradition, then transmission history prepares indispensable insights for understanding this text. One can detect locality, time, rationale, and the arena of usage concerning the origin and the changes. Together with the transmission form's characteristic components, these insights leave traces in oral tradition up to the oldest literary version of the text. Also, on the basis of this prehistory, these insights make the text understandable.

II. Transmission History as Actualizing Procedure

Transmission historical research makes the transmission procedure understandable as a process of continual realization and actualization beginning with the realm of oral tradition.[72] It does so even when this process primarily shaped the present text in the subsequent written phase (see §6). This procedure may be classified in three aspects:

1. The revision of older transmission pieces and, at times, their new realization is a conspicuously frequent feature in the Old Testament. Those responsible for such transmission apparently operated from the conviction that both texts and speeches are not simply "finished" if their concrete chronological reference has faded. Now, as before, these texts conceal an inner *actuality* "which could always have fresh meaning extracted from them" in a changed situation.[73]
2. The old transmission piece gains its actuality in the changed situation, but only through reappropriation and *interpretation*. Simple repetition does not suffice.
3. The structure of the transmission process inside the Old Testament, in a certain respect, can stimulate and orient the task of reappropriating and actualizing Old Testament texts in the *present*.

III. Transmission History as the History of the Religion and Faith of Israel

The analytical portion of the transmission historical investigation of texts can provide access to historical data.[74] The synthetic aspect of the transmis-

---

72 Compare especially von Rad, *Old Testament Theology*, vol. 1, p. 3–5,129f, and Vol. 2, p. 42–44, 45–49, and context.

73 V. Rad, loc. cit., Vol. 2, p. 46.

74 Cf. IV below.

sion historical investigation creates the condition that one may furthermore observe a very particular kind of history.[75] Under transmission historical observation, even a small text unit like Gen 32:23–33 presents itself as a series of developmental stages which conceal a kind of religio-historical compendium. Furthermore, one may recognize the history of Israel's faith from the transmission history of larger text complexes. One recognizes this history as a response to specific historical experiences understood as coming from YHWH, and as the integration of newly encountered intellectual conceptions. Transmission history thereby opens the possibility of retracing the path of Israel's faith and its inclinations, especially in the realm of Israel's beginnings.

IV. Access to Historical and Religio-Historical Data

In their final form which now lies at hand, statements from Old Testament texts frequently stand in tension with the image which the historian must depict for the history of Israel. This fact at first appears to diminish greatly the value of the Old Testament as a source of research for the history of Israel.[76] Transmission history, however, has changed this situation. One must differentiate the question of the text's historical content, to the degree that tradition history allows one to perceive the text in various developmental stages. Now each of the developmental stages allows itself to be investigated separately for its historical content. On the one hand, the historical content can relate directly to details offered in the text. On the other hand, however, it is given indirectly in the relationships and the processes by which those responsible for transmission were determined in their own time period. Only then do cross references between archaeology, or the history of religion, and reports of the Old Testament texts often become clear.[77]

D. LITERATURE

I. INTRODUCTION, FOUNDATION AND OVERVIEW

G. Fohrer. Exegese, § 9A+B
D.A. Knight. "Tradition History." ABD, Vol. 6, p. 633–638.
K. Koch. The Growth of Biblical Tradition, p. 38–57.
W.E. Rast. Tradition History and the Old Testament. Guides to Biblical Scholarship. Old Testament Series. J. C. Rylaarsdam, ed. Philadelphia, 1972.

---

75 Compare Rendtorff, *Geschichte und Überlieferung*, especially p. 83,85,88ff.

76 This fact should not be evaluated as negative too quickly. For the problem, cf. von Rad, *Old Testament Theolgy*, vol. 1, p. 3–5,105–111.

77 For discussion of the whole question, see especially Koch, *Growth of Biblical Tradition*, p. 54–56.

II. EXPANSION AND CRITICAL ALTERNATIVES

H. Birkeland. Zum hebräischen Traditionswesen. Die Komposition der prophetischen Bücher des Alten Testaments. ANVAO II. Hist.-Filos. Klasse. 1938 No. 1, Oslo, 1938.

E. Blum. Die Komposition der Vätergeschichte. WMANT 57. Neukirchen-Vluyn, 1984.

K. Jeppesen and B. Otzen, eds. The Productions of Time. Tradition History in Old Testament Scholarship. Sheffield, 1984.

D.A. Knight, ed. Tradition and Theology in the Old Testament. Philadelphia, 1977.

S. Mowinckel. Prophecy and Tradition. ANVAO II. Hist.-Filos. Klasse. 1946 No. 3. Oslo, 1946.

G. v. Rad. Old Testament Theology, Vol. 1, esp. p. 8–10,12–14,121–135; Vol. 2, everywhere.

R. Rendtorff. Geschichte und Überlieferung. In: Studien zur Theologie der alttestamentlichen Überlieferungen (Festschrift. G. von Rad). p. 81–94. Neukirchen, 1961.

_____. Literarkritik und Traditionsgeschichte. EvTh 27 (1967): 138–153.

W. Richter. Exegese, 152–165.

H. Ringgren. Literarkritik, Formgeschichte, Überlieferungsgeschichte. ThLZ 91 (1966): 641–650.

Works Dedicated to the Discussion of *Oral Tradition:*

R.C. Culley. "Exploring New Directions." In D.A. Knight and G.A. Tucker, The Hebrew Bible and Its Modern Interpreters. Philadelphia, 1985. p. 167–200.

_____, ed. Oral Tradition and Old Testament Studies. Semeia 5 (1976).

G. Fohrer. Introduction to the Old Testament, § 3: p. 36–41 (see also additional literature on 568f).

R. Knierim. "Criticism of Literary Features, Form, Tradition, and Redaction." In: D.A. Knight and G.A. Tucker, The Hebrew Bible and Its Modern Interpreters. Philadelphia, 1985. p. 123–165.

K. Koch. The Growth of Biblical Tradition, 78–91 (note especially the most important literature on p. 78f).

A.B. Lord. The Singer of Tales. Cambridge, MA, 1960.

B.A. Stolz and R.S. Shannon, eds. Oral Literature and the Formula. Ann Arbor, 1976.

III. EXEMPLARY EXECUTION

G.W. Coats. Genesis. FOTL 1. Grand Rapids, 1983.

K. Elliger. Der Jakobskampf am Jabbok. Gen 32,23ff als hermeneutisches Problem. ZThK 48 (1951): 1–31 (also in: Elliger, Kleine Schriften zum Alten Testament. ThB 32. p. 141–173. Munich, 1966).

J. P. Floß. Wer schlägt wen? Textanalytische Interpretation von Gen 32,23–33. BN 20 (1983): 92–132; BN 21 (1983): 66–100.

H.-J. Hermisson. Jakobs Kampf am Jabbok (Gen. 32,23–33). ZThK 71 (1974): 239–261.

J. Jeremias (s. § 6 D III).

M. Noth. A History of Pentateuchal Traditions. Atlanta, 1981.

O.H. Steck. Überlieferung und Zeitgeschichte in den Elia-Erzählungen. WMANT 26. Neukirchen-Vluyn, 1968.

IV. HISTORY OF RESEARCH

H.-J. Kraus. Zur Geschichte des Überlieferungsbegriffs in der alttestamentlichen Wissenschaft. EvTh 16 (1956): 371–387.

___. Geschichte der historisch-kritischen Erforschung des Alten Testaments. Neukirchen-Vluyn, [3]1982 (See the subject index under "Überlieferung", "Überlieferungsgeschichte").

§6 | Redaction Historical Approach

The introduction to §§4–6 above (§4 A I) offered an ideal model concerning the origin of an Old Testament writing. In most cases, this origin does not occur in a single act which conceives and composes a writing in the final form which comes to us. Rather, this origin occurs in a multi-stage process over an extended period during which an older portion is occasionally expanded and newly accented. As a rule, *the origin of an Old Testament literary work* therefore means the *history of origin!* This history of origin of an Old Testament writing can even stand out sharply in a specific text. This contrast is particularly true if transmission historical and literary critical analysis establish that the text contains transmission elements, and especially formulations, from different times. The more recent material is thereby attached to older, pre-existing material and enriches the older material with new accentuations which change the older material. Exegesis cannot neglect this aspect if it wants to do justice to the intention of the statement, or more precisely, to the majority of viewpoints in a series of statements which follow upon one another. And exegesis cannot neglect this aspect if it wants to make accessible the kerygmatic riches of the text's final form which are articulated as a word from various transmission witnesses from different Old Testament times. Therefore, one has to trace the course of a writing's developmental history in the viewpoints changing within the text.

It is possible that transmission historical analysis demonstrated that the text goes back to an *oral* transmission form (old individual narratives) or to an *oral* speech form (individual sayings or cultic texts). Further, one may have to account for a subsequent transmission phase, still within oral tradition, which arranged or collected these units and provided them with new accents of meaning. If so, then one calls upon the *transmission historical synthetic* approach to elucidate this process, as we noted in §5. As we saw, it appears extremely difficult to make progress toward this oral prehistory of the components of

Old Testament writings and to encounter historical findings which are even plausible within that prehistory. Today this difficulty is recognized even in those places where one must undoubtedly account for a prehistory, unlike the times which euphorically utilized *form criticism* under the supposition it could almost access the original biblical act of proclamation. To backtrack behind the formative material of a text's formulation is much more difficult than one thinks, but if necessary, one must do so hypothetically, using careful, reasoned deductions.

By contrast, one encounters relatively firm ground with the developmental phases of a text in an Old Testament literary work on the *written* level— phases (3) and (4) in our ideal pattern. Here, as literary criticism analytically elucidates, one encounters fixed formulations and literary contexts for the individual text. Here one sees linguistic and material inconsistencies within the individual text itself or regarding its immediate or its wider context. Fixed vocabularies may be separated from one another and arranged chronologically in relation to one another, possibly even in a single literary unit. Here, even with a literarily homogenous text, one may often observe during the writing's developmental history, that the text comes to stand in diverse contexts with different accentuations. Redaction history concerns itself with the area of written transmission, above all with the analytical materials from literary criticism. It envisions these analytical materials synthetically as elements of a historical, transformational process within the framework of a text's developmental history—hence the component "*history*" in redaction history. The component "*redaction*" in redaction history implies that a linguistically preexisting text would be revised in this process, in the sense of a changed construction. Thus, one discerns the character of the redactional measures. Preexisting text material (also now newly integrated) or several literary entities are joined into a new whole, by means of reordering (composition) and/or the redactor's own, new, textual inscriptions. As a rule, these measures have also been carefully conceptualized. The new is therefore constructed by constitutive joining to the old, or relatedly, in keeping with the old. Correspondingly, redactional and pre-existing material form a newly understood *whole* in the resulting writing. In this respect, redaction is a text-bound shaping which is characteristically differentiated in method and perspective from a writing's more original formulation.

Such changing, redactional processes of revision appear in different ways with widely divergent literary horizons. *Several important cases of redactional proceedings are mentioned here as typical examples.*

1. When formerly orally transmitted material is first written down (*"first written version"*), it may already involve meaningful redactional processes. These processes are evident in the deliberate ordering in which the transmitted material has now been incorporated. They are evident in the revision of the formulations by which the transmitted

material is acclimated to the entire writing and its sequence of statements. As a result, the transmitted material is now only understandable within the framework of the writing as a whole. These procedures are evident in new redactional formulations which were first formulated for the developing writing without a transmission historical basis, and which may directly express the redactional intention. These new expressions range from small, commentary-like insertions into small sections of a text, to more comprehensive new formulations (such as superscriptions and subscriptions) which have the entire writing in view and which serve to structure that writing.

2. If an Old Testament writing already exists, then its *"continuation"* (*"Fortschrei-bung"*) can appear subsequently, for example in the following procedures:

a. Occasionally, individual commentary-like additions are utilized in light of small text sections. These additions range from glosses (linguistic or historical) to speech formulas and to additions of content and theology. They are attached to the immediate context linguistically and/or by content. Over time, such additions, whose *horizons are limited to the immediate context* instead of the entire writing, can develop further with particular themes. They may be attached in clusters onto passages of the original literary entity. However, if it is not recognizable that additions are components serving an expanded restructuring of the whole (!) writing (that is, if they are treated as isolated additions), then the redaction historical approach finds application only in the narrow framework of the addition's immediate context.

b. In the text being exegetically treated, *more recent additions*, which literary criticism elucidates, can also be *part of the total redaction of the writing*. This is the case when corresponding additions are found elsewhere in the writing. Included among these corresponding additions are those which are alike in content, in the redactional method, or which come from the same historical period. They shed new light on the received writing as a whole. In this case, the task of the redaction historical approach is expanded to determine what the continuation found in this particular text wants to contribute to the total redactional profile.

c. As a rule, only one variety of (b) constitutes *literarily homogenous additions*, frequently somewhat larger in size. They not only represent an expansion of a pre-existing immediate context, but also have been *formulated specifically for the writing as redactional productions*. These additions were already mentioned under section 1). They are of greatest significance for the redactional profile because here the concerns of the redaction can unfold freely through new accents or detailed material expansions. Precisely because these newly formulated statements also wish to revise something, it is not astounding that they take up many formulations from the entire writing, pointing backwards and forward. They refer to other redactional formulations in the writing. They restructure and reaccent the context with older formulated material. And thus they provide direction to the reader for the entire writing in its redactional sense. Also, one should observe the position of the specific formulations. They often have a materially structuring function for the whole.

d. The redactional revision of a writing can also be accomplished with or without additions to the text by *restructuring the entire* received writing. This restructuring changes the perspective by shedding a different light upon the text being treated because, in some cases, a writing's newly available macrostructure (realigned into structured sections) wants to understand the text differently (as well as the associated text).

e.   Finally, in addition to cases in which the redaction historical process not only continues the existing writing by restructuring and by specific formulations, one must also
account for those cases which *connect pre-existing transmitted material from else-*
where with the given writing to produce a new entity. This pre-existing material may
be of a type which is oral or written. Conjoining two writings into one new redactional whole can provide a new dimension of meaning for each text component in
both writings when the conjoining occurs with deliberation and with redactional
structuring.

The preceding list of possibilities manifests the redactional processes of revision. It
seeks to make clear what must be taken into account in this methodological stage. It is
a broad field in the true sense of the word.

> The beginner should not become discouraged with this breadth, and should
> limit himself/herself more precisely to potential redactional manifestations *within*
> *the assigned text.* For the most part, additions and the immediate context
> are the working horizon. For the wider literary horizon of the assigned text
> (the redactional development of the Old Testament literary work from which
> this text originates), the beginner may rely primarily upon information from
> Old Testament introductions, upon recommended secondary literature, and
> upon directions from the instructor. The task of independently investigating
> texts redaction historically in the framework of the history of development for
> an entire literary work requires a precise knowledge of this work down to its
> particular formulations. And it involves tedious, detailed concordance work.
> Practically, it can only be undertaken with special concentration in the discipline
> of the Old Testament in the concluding phase of one's studies. The following
> comments for this area can only be given as initial instructions.

Here are three delimiting remarks to close this introduction into the redaction historical approach:

First, both the revising and that which is revised belong to "redaction".
Accentuations which have been incorporated in the redaction process, do not
allow themselves to be elevated to the point that one investigates only the revising interventions (restructurings, new formulations). Rather, these interventions are constantly placed in relationship to that which was revised. Its
meaning must therefore be determined *as the new understanding of the revised.*
That which is revising certainly directs how that which is revised is now to be
understood and to be read. The redactors of Old Testament writings were
generally not of the opinion that their redactional statements invalidated the
older, revised statements. For them, the writing *is valid* in the totality of all
of its statements. The redactional statements show the reader, however, that
the older (now revised) text now has only a partial validity which is limited
concerning time, persons, and/or content. For example, older judgment statements and redactional salvation statements can stand side by side on the redactional level of a prophetic writing. However, the revised and the revising
material do not stand out from one another by the typeface used in the devel-

opment of an Old Testament writing. Then how did an ancient reader recognize the redactional meaning? The ancient reader recognized the redactional meaning by continuous reading of the writing, above all, in the macrostructural and in the microstructural *position* in which the redactionally revising statements are placed. These statements are recognized especially at the beginning and end of the writing, the beginning and end of the major section of the writing, or the beginning and end of the individual pericope. All of this has implications for exegetical praxis, namely, that the meaning of redactional additions must be determined in relationship to the pre-existing text element which was revised. (See footnote 205 below.)

Second, it is necessary to offer a warning against the opinion that one can, or even should, limit oneself solely to exegesis of the *final form of the text* reached in BH and thereby avoid the hypothetical inquiry into older stages. In numerous cases, the final form of an Old Testament text indicates complex, even contradictory statements which must be clarified. Therefore, these statements force one to diachronic analysis (literary criticism, see §4) and synthesis (redaction history). Of course, the meaning intended in the final form must also be determined. However, it is only discernible if one can grasp the productive reaccentuation of the last hand. This task, however, presupposes clarification of the previous stages which have the same status as the final form of the text in the riches of the Old Testament witness. A so-called "holistic exegesis" must ask itself how it will avoid exegetical arbitrariness without diachronic textual perspective.

Third, the redaction historical approach may also be perceived thoroughly as an approach to the problem of the *history of reception* (cf Chr. Dohmen, see D below). However, one must be sure to keep in mind that exegetical interest is not limited to the reception, the productive appropriation. Alongside the reception, of equal value, stands the question of the older material's own meaning, of the meaning of the received. Both must be seen in relationship to one another in order that a text's productive transmission process releases a movement of meaning (see § 10 C II).

In keeping with the exegetical praxis within one's studies, the following development of the redaction historical approach concentrates primarily on the redaction historical processes within the framework of a specific text to be treated.

A. THE TASK

With the redaction historical approach, exegesis continues the transmission historical work, in regard to its synthetic aspect, but for the realm of *written* transmission. It thereby concludes the investigation of the productive transmission process of the text in the Old Testament.[78] This approach traces the text's history from its first written form through its expansion, or relatedly commentary, by means of additions. It also traces a text's history through its incorporation into larger complexes all the way up to its final version in the current literary context. This approach thereby determines the operative historical factors and the intentions of the statements.[79]

The redaction historical approach as such brings into focus the course of the development and the positioning of a text within a writing by the *relative* chronological order of the redactional actions. The approach thereby works through the older text phases, new relationships, changes in formulations, and changes in context. The redaction historical approach understands these elements as redactional process. The procedural steps of §7 and §8 will then contribute form critical and tradition historical perspectives which further clarifies this process. The procedural step of §9 will also attempt to pursue *absolute* chronological, historical necessities and intentions for the redaction historical development as described. As with the procedural steps of §§3–9 as a whole, all of this preparatory work is undertaken for the final, decisive procedural step of §10. In §10, determining the historical meaning is undertaken for the individual redactional text stages (see §10 C I) as well as for the course of the redaction history as such (see §10 C II).

B. COMMENTARY ON THE APPROACH AND METHOD

I. Relationship to Literary Criticism

The redaction historical approach works closely with literary criticism and evaluates its results. Both exegetical steps concentrate upon the *written* stage of transmission. Literary criticism processed partial conclusions on the analytical level. Redaction history now has the specific task of *synthetically* coordinating those partial conclusions with the aspect of the historical progression. As already accented at the end of §A, the *goal* is therefore to comprehend the merging of the materials separated by literary criticism; to pinpoint the signals of processing which were likewise designated by literary criticism; and to trace the material motives and intentions in this redactional processing. In the latter aspect, redaction history lays the groundwork for determining historical meaning (§10) under the particular perspective of the assimilation and processing of older material. Redaction history is thereby contrasted with the earlier widespread negative evaluation of additions and redactional work ("secondary" in the derogatory sense). It utilizes the redactional history of a text and the new interpretation bound to it precisely because of its notable characteristics.

---

[78] See above, § 4 A I (p. 47f).

[79] Redaction history also yields a close correspondence to the procedure of determining the historical setting.

Redaction history also comes into play with a literarily homogenous text. Even in this case one must ask in which phase of the writing's developmental history the text's formulation took place. One must ask how the text relates to other redactional measures of the same phase. One must ask how it stands in its relationship to immediate and broader context. And one must ask how its statements are changed as the writing grows into its final form. Moreover, in the case of the first written version, one has the task of determining the material relationship to the oral transmission material which is now written down.

II. Redaction Historical Processes

1. Processes for the Initial Recording of Oral Transmission[80]

We begin, so to speak, with the case of the oldest recoverable redactional process, the written registry of material previously transmitted orally. The fact that an *oral* transmission phase precedes is suggested by fundamental observation as follows (see §5): The text to be treated is comprised of a "small unit" or it forms a small unit along with the context; the text is presented as a string of such units; or the text contains such a unit when liberated from additions. In order to validate this unit, it must stand by itself, formally and materially, and not require the surrounding text as an originally planned context necessary to the understanding.

At the same time, these small units are not given to us by themselves. Rather they are encountered on a larger literary level within a written context. For example, they are encountered as neighboring psalms, wisdom sayings, legal sayings, ancestral narratives, woe oracles, or salvation speeches (e.g. Isa 41:8–13,14–16,17–20). The creation of this juxtaposition/compilation, by its structure and occasionally by its formulations, is a formative act on the *written* level which is fixed for posterity. Therefore, it is a subject for the redaction historical approach. If the first written version productively shapes older transmission, then the first written version could also be seen as the last step of the transmission history. If so, it naturally leads to the new status as written material. That new status now leads into the field of redaction history.

---

[80] The fact that Fohrer (*Exegese*, p. 140) does not ascribe the term "redaction" to this process is, in part, a terminological problem. We perceive even compositional literary processes (like those noted below in "a") to fall under "redaction." Fohrer differentiates here between "composition" and "redaction" (*Exegese*, p. 139–142). However, when Fohrer eliminates the revision of oral transmission that is undertaken with the act of writing (described below in "b") from redaction criticism, it raises the question in which methodological step he then perceives this process, which is by no means a process of "pure literary creation" (*Exegese*, p. 140). For us, *"composition"* means the entire available context and the purpose of the statements which possibly grow out of that context. This context, in which a particular text stands at the developmental phase of the writing, may be preliterary or literary. The synthetic approach, transmission history and redaction history, concentrates upon the creation and extent of a composition, or of an intended text sequence in its respective totality. With regard to the entire work, it concentrates on each of its developmental stages.

a. The first written version can be pure *codification*, in which the form of the first written rendering of the specific section corresponds precisely with the final oral stage. In this case, one asks the redaction historical question only with regard to the function of this text. If necessary, one also asks about the implicit change of the text's meaning within the pertinent literary context, insofar as the text enters into such.[81]

b. By contrast, the first written version of pre-existing oral transmission can also signify its extensive (or more limited) reformulation and *rewording* by the author of the written material.[82] This rewording is recognizable by the linguistic characteristics as well as the convergence of the relevant literary context with the redactional profile (to the degree that the text enters a literary context with the first written version). The problem of "tradition and redaction" then presents itself, namely differentiating older transmission elements from the portion belonging to the transcribing author and determining the motives for adopting the transmission piece.

c. In this regard, one should note that when differentiating between "tradition and redaction" one should by no means expect the tradition to consist only of transmission pieces which are clearly defined, detachable, and which previously were transmitted independently. One should not expect that traditions are limited to the transmission historical prehistory of the text as already elucidated. Rather one should consider that an author who is reconceptualizing by using older transmission pieces can also articulate the redactional intention and conceptions with additional educational elements. These ele-

---

81 Examples: Individual legal sayings as in Exod 21:18ff in the growing literary frame of the Book of the Covenant and of the Sinai pericope (before the Priestly, Deuteronomic, and finally Pentateuchal material); individual wisdom sayings as in Prov 15 in the frame of the book of Proverbs introduced by Prov 1–9 (wisdom as a living person!); individual cultic texts like Pss 46 and 47 in the frame of literary collections of psalms and finally of the theologically structured Psalter.

82 Contrary to current opinion, this process appears to be of greatest significance for understanding the recording of prophetic transmission. With prophetic literature, it is insignificant, from a methodological standpoint, that the author of the oral material and the writing redactor may be identical. Compare especially O.H. Steck, *Wahrnehmungen Gottes im Alten Testament*, ThB 70, Munich, 1982, p. 171–186 (particularly pages 179ff on Isa 7:3–9). In addition, see H.-J. Kraus, ZAW 85 (1973): 39 to the woe-sayings of Isa 5:8–24; Barth, *Jesaja-Worte*, p. 10f, on Isa 28:7b–22. Working on Hosea, J. Jeremias has produced ground breaking insights into the processes of the first written version of prophetic speeches. He shows how the older material has been arranged into a planned, structured composition using redactionally available parallel forms, thematic expositions, catchword connections, cross-references (backward and forward), bridge statements, abbreviations, and, through the written formulation, by concentration upon larger material subjects in the context under the presupposition that the reader of the prophetic writing already knows the preceding material. The first written version incorporates the older material into a form which is only understandable for a reader by observation on the entire written context because of its cross-referenced words, word plays, and patterns of construction. Cf. in its entirety, J. Jeremias, *Der Prophet Hosea*, ATD 24/1, Göttingen, 1983, and also his Hosea studies from 1979 and 1981 mentioned on page 10 of that book.

ments can have represented mobile, isolatable *material known by the author*.[83] These procedures will be studied further in the frame of tradition history.

d. The composition of a pre-existing oral transmission into a larger work by a revising author presents its *redactional profile* variously. On the one hand, the redactional profile presents itself when it selects, orders, and coordinates the old transmission as well as when it reformulates and rewords the old transmission (see above, "tradition and redaction"). On the other hand, working out the intentions of the redactor should especially rely upon the purely redactional components of the work (i.e. reformulated components without basis in transmission *pieces*).[84] These redactional components appear mostly in the following:

— Framing Formulations (introduction and conclusion)
— Connecting pieces
— Speeches and prayers (concentration of central theological points)

> Based on the transmission historical investigation, if a text under consideration suggests itself as the first recording of oral material, then it is entirely sufficient for an exegetical exercise (like an exegesis paper) to pursue two questions in this difficult field:
>
> 1. Regarding the text form of this phase, *what* could be *attributed to the first written version?* One should ascertain redactional measures which consolidate, structure, and adapt a text to the framework of a literary entity. Indeed one should ascertain these measures by extracting a carefully deduced oral form of the text, and by ascertaining agreement with similar measures in other places in the same writing. More recent secondary literature should point to these places.
> 2. What *material intentions* are expressed in these *redactional measures of the first written version* in view of the total ordering, actualization, and accentuation of the transmission as now shown? Again, parallel

---

[83] Thus the Yahwist, when forming the paradise narrative (Gen 2:4b–3:24), used an older paradise story which entered Gen 2:4b–3:24 as a clearly defined transmission piece and therefore belongs to the *transmission historical* prehistory of Gen 2:4b–3:24. Alongside this older story, he also used knowledge such as the concept of creation lying behind 2:7 or the concept of the tree of life. Undoubtedly, he also learned these materials through the medium of texts, but he did not bring these texts into his paradise narrative with their original contexts. As a result, they can only be methodologically perceived on the *tradition historical* path (cf. Steck, *Wahrnehmungen*, p. 48–51).

[84] Examples: Gen 6:5–8 + 8:20–22 and Gen 32:10–13 (Yahwist); 1 Sam 23:14–18 and 26:25a (author of the History of the Ascendancy, cf. R. Rendtorff, "Beobachtungen zur israelitischen Geschichtsschreibung anhand der Geschichte vom Aufstieg Davids," in *Probleme biblischer Theologie*. Festschrift Gerhard v. Rad, 1971, p. 428–439 especially 431 footnote 17).

appearances in the same writing, at the same initial literary layer, serve a substantiating function.

2. Subsequent Stages

Insofar as a text has a further literary history after its first written compilation, then one should ask the redaction historical question anew for each of the text's redactional stages.

The directions given for the first written version apply correspondingly to the redactional processes which play a role in the redactional stages. When creating a literary context, a redactor can simultaneously incorporate written texts alongside oral transmissions. In some circumstances, this new usage represents a second redactional stage.[85] A redactor can unite two or more individual texts (or relatedly complexes), which already exist in written form, into a larger entity. These transmission pieces may be combined either by *interweaving* the accounts,[86] or by *attaching* them to one another in blocks.[87] Finally, the redactional activity can manifest itself in pre-existing written texts which may be expanded and revised by the redactor's own formulations. This activity may occur in the procedures already noted but may also occur independently of the formation of larger literary compositions (or relatedly literary works).[88] If redaction history is directed toward an extensive text complex of several literary layers, then it seeks to recognize connections between the redactional work of each individual text. From that recognition, it seeks to reconstruct entire redactional *layers* and to situate these historically and theologically.[89]

In the redaction historical treatment of a text's stages which are subsequent to the first written version, it is best to differentiate between those texts which present themselves analytically (according to §4) as literarily composite and those which are literarily homogenous.

85 Example: The incorporation of the memorial of Isa 6–8* into a more extensive collection of Isaiah transmission (see Barth, *Die Jesaja-Worte in der Josiazeit*, 282–284).

86 For examples, see above footnote 29.

87 For examples, see above footnote 28.

88 For examples, see footnote 30. For the classification of glosses (small, clarifying additions which, in certain circumstances, may be only a single word), see G. Fohrer, "Die Glossen im Buche Ezechiel," *ZAW* 63 (1951): 33–53. In those places where the redactional work stands in the context of the first written version of an extensive work (especially a narrative), then that which was said in "1d" above, p. 83, applies. For example, in the case of the Deuteronomistic History, compare the position and the type of redactional formulations in Josh 1*; Judg 5:31b; 1 Kgs 8:14ff; 2 Kgs 17:7–23; 22:1f; 23:24–30, etc.

89 Examples: Isolation of Deuteronomistic redactional layers in the complex of Deuteronomy—2 Kings (cf Kaiser, *Introduction to the Old Testament*, §16); a Deuteronomistic redactional layer in Amos (by H.W. Wolff, *Joel and Amos*, Hermeneia (Philadelphia: 1977 [1969]) or relatedly the Deuteronomistic material in Jeremiah (by W. Thiel, *Die deuteronomistische Redaktion von Jeremia 1–25*, 1973). Isolation of a redaction of the Isaiah transmission in the time of Josiah (by Barth, *Die Jesaja-Worte in der Josiazeit*). Isolation of redactional layers which produce a connection between Isaiah 1–39* and Isaiah 40–62* (by O.H. Steck, *Bereitete Heimkehr*, SBS 121, 1985).

a. Literarily Composite Texts

Let us examine the case in which a written text (first written version) later receives *further additions and changes*. If these additions and changes do not derive from the same literary level, then, in conjunction with literary criticism, one seeks to determine their relative sequence. In order to profile the redaction historical process, the following illuminating questions are asked *for each stage which has been extracted:*

- In which *position* is the change/addition placed in the text? Does it exhibit a material function toward the pre-existing text which is structural, amplifying, correcting, and/or connective?
- *How* is the change/addition formulated? Does it take up formulations from the immediate context for reference, mooring, strengthening, or reaccentuation? Does it work with formulations which are found in the immediate or broader context in order to create intentional relationships to the pre-existing text and to direct the reader to notice these relationships? May one understand the change/addition as a conscious, amplifying counter-formulation to these formulations from the immediate or neighboring context? Concordance work is indispensable for this task. It should consider characteristic words and word ensembles. The goal of this aspect is again: What new accent, and in what manner, does this redactional change bring?

Because of the interdependence of the methodological steps, the methodological approaches of §§7–10 must also be included to clarify these questions. This fact is self-evident here as elsewhere.

More far-reaching are the aspects which pertain to the *ordering* of these redaction historical manifestations found in the text under consideration. During a student's exegesis, these aspects should only be traced with support of secondary literature:

- Does this change/addition revise only the specific text and, if need be, its immediate context from the same literary level? Does it therefore concern only a specific disruption whose horizon is a limited context? Are there related manifestations from the same literary level? How does the literary work appear when it receives these specific additions?
- Or is the change/addition to the text a cornerstone for an expanded reformulated literary work as a whole? In other words, is it an element of a comprehensive redaction of this work? This possibility is suggested, for example:
  — if the redactional disruption gives the text a prominent position in the macrostructure of the writing (e.g. the addition of Isa 51:11 = 35:10), or if a bridging function between larger sections of the writing should be observed;
  — if the redactional disruption makes the text stand out as the bearer of a material concern of the redaction which provides significance for other redactional disruptions in the writing;

— if the text thus produces unintelligible trains of thought regarding the text's formulation and its sequence of statements, but these thoughts point beyond themselves and produce their function in reference to the total redactional profile of the writing.

An essential criterion for an assignation of this type, as for all redactional manifestations, occurs when the text concerns processes which do not stand alone. Rather, these processes expressly serve the purpose of accentuating a larger literary entity which is thus being revised. This purpose is similar to superscriptions, structural blocks, and larger, coherent, redactional formulations.

The formulation of concepts or word ensembles can also offer help in recognizing redactional measures on older text material when it can be demonstrated that they are also characteristic for a writing's redaction. Deuteronomistic formulations in the Deuteronomistic History and in Jeremiah present a striking example of this aspect. However, one must guard against overvaluation at this point. In non-Deuteronomistic prophetic redaction the same line of thought from the same literary layer may be formulated quite differently because the language is bound to the existing immediate context (for example, cf. Isa 11:11–16 to 27:12f; and Isa 35 to 62:10–12!).

Insofar as possible, one should attempt to situate a text's redactional manifestation with reference to its position and function in the redaction of the entire writing and the writing's compositional structure. Insofar as possible, one should also attempt to gain more detailed historical determinations about this redactional layer according to §9.

b. Literarily Homogenous Texts
Two cases should be considered:

In an Old Testament literary work which has experienced a multi-layered development into its final form, the procedures of §§4–6 can establish *that a text had probably already received its literarily homogenous form with the first written version.* More recent disruptions do not appear in the text even though the writing to which it belongs has grown considerably after its initial phase. If so, the redaction historical approach is not profitable for this particular text in regard to subsequent developmental stages. However, the redaction historical approach does prove helpful by asking whether the position and function of the integrated text have subsequently changed with the growth of the writing (by restructuring, expanding, or recreating the context of the writing). Even after its initial inscription, contextual reaccentuations of an Isaiah text like 5:8–10 can thus be traced through all stages of the developing Isaiah book.

The second case is more important. A literarily homogenous text has no background in orally transmitted material before the writing originated, nor has the text been incorporated as written material during any stage of the writing. Rather, the text has been composed in its entirety, from the beginning, for some phase of the continuation of that writing. The text is thus a *redactional formulation.* This phenomenon was already mentioned in the introduction to §6, and it appears that, until now, not enough consideration has been accorded to this facet in Old Testament research, especially in the area of the Prophets, but also the Psalms. In certain circumstances, it causes one to reexamine the literary critical analysis once again. Many texts appear to be composites because one observes them in isolation, and because one does not take into account a unified redactional text's diversity of perspective over the entire revised writing. One must therefore consider whether a literarily homogenous text is really a redactional formulation.

Section "a" spoke of changes/additions which literary criticism uncovered within a literarily composite text. If these changes/additions exhibit a redactional character related to the whole work, rather than just a narrow contextual horizon, then the redactional formulation is differentiated from them. The redactional formulation is differentiated by the fact that it does not appear as an intrusion into the older text. Rather, the text represents an original, unified text created for the redaction of the writing. On a large scale, the redactional formulation functions in the framework of the entire revised writing like the addition/change functions in an older text on a small scale.

If one represents the received literary material from an earlier phase of the writing by using an empty box, and the new redactional additions by a shaded box, then the following schematic drawing results:

| 4 | 1 | 2 | 3 | 1 |

1 = Redactional addition to older texts   3 = Redactional formulations
2 = Older texts without redactional intrusion   4 = Superscription

What characteristics could suggest a *redactional formulation?*

- Such texts prefer literary seams. They occupy an explanatory position in the total structure of the writing. They have an explanatory, bridging, or concluding function in view of the entire revised work. Not infrequently, several of these texts refer to one another.
- As with all redactional formulations, these texts do not stand on their own. They constantly stand in relation to the literary surroundings which are being revised and in relation to the entire writing which is being structured.
- These texts coincide with redactional accentuations which the writing also demonstrates in this layer as a whole and in other redactional places. They do so in structure, sequence of statements, and subject profile.
- Regarding their function in the entire revised writing, these texts serve to structure and enrich the whole in the sense of precision, reaccentuation, correction, and later expansion.

Therefore, what facilitates the acceptance of a literarily homogenous text as a redactional formulation?

- The literarily homogenous text apparently represents a "text for the book" according to those characteristics already mentioned. It shows itself *from the outset to be created for a larger literary framework*. The text gains its function solely from this framework. Correspondingly, when observed in isolation, it is not really understandable. One comprehends better, however, if one sees it in connection with the entire literary work for which it was created. Also, one can see how the text, in the mind of the redactor, wants to direct its appropriate reader reception. Redactional formulations are directed toward the continuing reader reception of the entire writing. The determination of a redactional formulation therefore presupposes insight into the origin and construction of the relevant redaction for the entire writing. Also, it gains essential support by demonstrating corresponding redactional intrusion in other places of the writing.
- Redactional formulations are differentiated from new formulations which are not bound to the transmission of a writing, because the redactional formulations are *correlated to the literary entity* which they revise. This conscious referencing is expressed in the contextual position in which it is placed, but especially in the thoughtful creation of references to the context of the writing (preceding and/or subsequent). The latter is true even though the redactional formulation (depending on the scope of the amplifying intention) must by no means consist solely of these references.

  The character of these references is at first ambiguous. Perceiving them as a literary device can only be accomplished through foundational concordance work. Hence a series of perspectives come into view:

  — Does the text's formulation point to *interrelationships with other formulations* in the frame of the same work? With heuristically exposed evidence, the following comes into view: literally repeated formulations (unintroduced quotes), characteristic word ensembles, characteristic words, allusions, counter-formulations, and references to content.
  — *How do these interrelationships operate?* Which is the older, contributing text? Which is the more recent, receiving and assimilating text?
  — If the text is to be treated as a redactional cross-reference (i.e. a conscious literary cross-reference) which serves the reader reception, then *three alternatives* must be *eliminated*:

    1. One must eliminate the possibility that the reference is only a widely used, traditional phrase. For example, the messenger formula in a prophetic writing is not, by itself, a literary cross-reference in this writing.
    2. One must eliminate the possibility that the references are not treating stock language within the scope of small units in the pre-literary phase. For example, these appear in various psalms, and inside Isaiah—or Deutero-Isaiah—logia.
    3. One must eliminate the possibility that the reference simply draws upon knowledge of the older reference without implying that it must presume a literary/redactional adoption within the framework and within the service of a book's cohesion. For example, do the cross-references of Trito-Isaiah demonstrate on occasion, that Trito-Isaiah knows Deutero-Isaiah, or do they mark redactional connections in the framework of a literary continuation?

— The following can serve as evidence that the *redactional character* of a *cross-reference* operates within the frame of the literary work:

1. The redactional adoption must be shown to be literarily dependent upon the older (or at least redactionally contemporary) contributing text within the framework of the writing's developmental history.
2. The redactional adoption also implicitly presupposes the contributing text's literary position and context for the redactor and reader.
3. The receiving text elsewhere exhibits characteristics of a redaction text.
4. The reference is reconciled with the procedure and the material concept as manifested in this redactional layer elsewhere in the writing.
5. The reference produces its meaning for the author, and the reader (!), in connection with the contexts of the redactional formulation and with the structure of the revised writing. Also, it consequently presupposes the continuing reader reception of the redactional work as a whole.

One must therefore think literarily and, for the benefit of a redactional formulation, one must continually ask the basic questions: In order to understand this text do the redactor and reader presuppose the writing's preceding or subsequent context? And should this text structure and illuminate the entire writing?

— Here, as elsewhere, it is methodologically important to eliminate other options. Constellations of the alternatives (2) and (3), mentioned above, do not lead to redaction texts relating to the entire writing. Rather, they lead to "smaller units," that is to texts without an original relationship to the context, texts which stand alone, texts which are understandable by themselves, and which are self-contained literary transcriptions of texts which were orally transmitted.

It is self-evident that when determining redactional formulation one may only gain sufficient certainty by means of a redaction historical investigation of the entire literary work. This literary work must also have gained a clear picture of the redactional process, structure, organization, and subject profile of the redactional phase for that writing in whose composition these redactional formulations have their setting. According to §9, more detailed historical determination must also come into play at this point regarding the redactional layer from which this formulation derives. Also, redactional formulations can be influenced by other elements, apart from their internal references to the book (traditions according to §8, knowledge of formulations from other writings, influence of neighboring canonical books, etc.).

III. Summary of the Redaction Historical Procedure

The redaction historical approach investigates the internal (literary criticism) and the external (context) processes which may be observed from the text's development during the written transmission. The time period covered by the investigation stretches from the first written version of orally transmitted material until the last productive change of a text and/or its context at the conclusion of Old Testament writings. When treating the realm of the first written version, the redaction historical approach begins with the results of §5 (transmission units and, if necessary, the joining of these oral units). The approach turns to the productive process of the recording of these transmission units in relationship to formulation and/or organization. When treating the remaining stages, the redaction historical approach begins with the results of §4 (literarily homogenous or literarily composite text).

Redaction historical investigation can be guided by the following questions:

For the *first written version*:

a. Did §5 determine that the text had already essentially been formulated in *oral* tradition? If so, then one does not expect a significant portion to be redactionally formulated, or redactional formulations are minimal. The redactional portion may then consist of the codification, and after that, the collection and ordering of the material if this had not already occurred in oral tradition (catchword connection, transitional formulations, superscriptions, and subscriptions).

b. Did §5 determine that the text's formulation could, in practical terms, hardly be gleaned exclusively from oral tradition? If so, then the text essentially results from and for the first written version (homogeneity over against the redactional profile of the entire literary context). It is then necessary to determine more precisely the significant redactional portion in the formulation, collection, and ordering in light of the pre-existing material.

For the *remaining stages*:

c. Did §4 determine that the text was a *literarily composite* text? If so, then one must evaluate two possibilities:

   aa. Does the text indicate that written materials of diverse origin have been redactionally united into a single entity (e.g. the compilation of sources) and then joined (or compared) using redactional transitions, etc.?

   bb. Does the foundational text exist in a written form which has been expanded by particular formulations preceding the text, within it, or concluding it? Do these formulations concern individualized glosses and additions which are solely focussed on the narrow horizon of the immediate context? Or are the additions part of a redactional continuation of the entire writing (concurrence with other redactional formulations, and with the construction and the macrostructure of the same layer)?

In either case, for each developmental stage, one should highlight the *type of compilation leading to the current text* in its entirety (revising and [!] revised). If the processes are redactional, then they should be placed in relationship to parallel manifestations and to the composition of the redactional layer (setting of the text in the whole).

d. Does §4 determine that the text is *literarily homogenous*? If so, then one should again examine two possibilities:

aa. Is the text a component of an older written transmission whose formulation was not changed even to the final form of the writing? If necessary, this written transmission could have had oral tradition background as described in (a) and (b). If it was part of an older written transmission, then redaction history should determine the original literary context of this text along with the text's setting and function in that context. The same is true for all other contexts in which the text is used in the course of time, and the indirect changes which the text *de facto* experienced as a result of the change of context. During these context changes, the text becomes revised.

bb. Is the text of a type which has been written just for its literary context, for the purpose of continuing, orienting, or structuring the work being formed? If so, redaction history should determine the entire redactional level in which this contribution is admitted to a redaction of the writing. Further, redaction history should determine the redactional attributes which characterize this redaction text. It should also specifically determine the compositional and material function of this type of text for the whole. In this case, the text belongs to the revising component of a writing. If there are more recent, productive developmental phases of the entire writing, then naturally the revising text of an earlier phase itself becomes part of that which the more recent stage revises.

The literary horizon in which a unified text was *first* formulated is most pivotal for the redaction historical investigation.

A redaction historical investigation *constantly* has to ask:

1. Do redactional processes manifest themselves by the *formulations* and/or the thoughtful *composition* of the context (immediate and entire)?
2. From these processes, what belongs to the *same literary layer*, that is to the same redaction of the work (correlation with §4)?
3. What characterizes this redaction regarding the *way it works* and its *material traits*?
4. To what degree do the redactional processes signify a change of the *whole*, even of the work's revised *text material*?
5. If different redactional processes follow upon one another (in the text and/or its context), which changes show this *progression as such*?

C. RESULTS

I. Insight into the Changes of a Text in Written Tradition

That which was said for transmission history in §5 C I also applies to redaction history.

II. Redaction History as Actualizing Procedure

That which was said for transmission history in §5 C II also applies to redaction history.

III. Redaction History as the History of Israel's Faith

That which was said for transmission history in §5 C III also applies to redaction history.

D. LITERATURE

I. INTRODUCTION, FOUNDATION, AND OVERVIEW

J. Barton. "Redaction Criticism." ABD, Vol. 5, p. 644–647.
G. Fohrer. Exegese, § 9B.
K. Koch. The Growth of Biblical Tradition. p. 57–67.

II. EXPANSION AND CRITICAL ALTERNATIVES

H. Birkeland. Zum hebräischen Traditionswesen (see § 5 D II).
Chr. Dohmen. Rezeptionsforschung und Glaubensgeschichte. TThZ 96 (1987): 123–134.
M. Fishbane. Biblical Interpretation in Ancient Israel. Oxford, 1985.
H. W. Hertzberg. Die Nachgeschichte alttestamentlicher Texte innerhalb des Alten Testaments. In: Werden und Wesen des Alten Testaments. BZAW 66. Berlin, 1936. p. 110–121. (also in: Hertzberg, Beiträge zur Traditionsgeschichte und Theologie des Alten Testaments. Göttingen, 1962. p. 69–80).
Chr. Levin. Die Verheißung des neuen Bundes in ihrem theologiegeschichtlichen Zusammenhang ausgelegt. FRLANT 137. Göttingen, 1985.
S. Mowinckel. Prophecy and Tradition (see § 5 D II).
G. v. Rad. Old Testament Theology. Vol. 2, p. 33–49.
W. Richter. Exegese, p. 165–173.
O.H.Steck. "Prophetische Prophetenauslegung." In: H.F. Geißer, et al, eds. Wahrheit der Schrift—Wahrheit der Auslegung. Zürich, 1993. p. 198–244.
R. Wonneberger. Redaktion. Studien zur Textfortschreibung im Alten Testament. FRLANT 156. Göttingen, 1991.

Works Dedicated to the Discussion of Intertextuality
U. Broich and M. Pfister, eds. Intertextualität. Formen, Funktionen. Anglistische Fallstudien. Tübingen, 1985.

K. Nielsen. "Intertextuality as Biblical Scholarship." ScandJOT 2 (1990): 89–95.
D.N. Fewell, ed. Reading Between Texts: Intertextuality and the Hebrew Bible. Louisville, 1992.

For the "Canonical Approach," see:
J. Barr. Holy Scripture: Canon, Authority, Criticism. Oxford, 1983.
B.S. Childs. Old Testament Theology in a Canonical Context. Minneapolis, 1989.
_____. Biblical Theology of the Old and New Testaments. Minneapolis, 1993.
G.T. Sheppard. "Canonical Criticism." ABD, Vol. 1, 861–866.

Compare also the contributions to JSOT 16 (1980).

III. ILLUSTRATIVE EXECUTION

H. Barth. Die Jesaja-Worte in der Josiazeit. Israel und Assur als Thema einer produktiven Neuinterpretation der Jesajaüberlieferung. WMANT 48. Neukirchen-Vluyn, 1977.
T. Collins. The Mantle of Elijah. The Redaction Criticism of the Prophetical Books. BiSe 20. Sheffield, 1993.
F.L. Hossfeld and E. Zenger. Die Psalmen. Psalm 1–50. NEB. Würzburg, 1993.
De Vries, S.J. From Old Revelation to New: A Tradition-Historical and Redaction-Critical Study of Temporal Transitions in Prophetic Prediction. Grand Rapids, 1995.
J. Jeremias. »Ich bin wie ein Löwe für Efraim . . .« (Hos. 5,14). In: H. Merklein and E. Zenger, eds. »Ich will euer Gott werden«. SBS 100. p. 75–95. Stuttgart, 1981.
_____. Hosea 4–7. Beobachtungen zur Komposition des Buches Hosea. In: A.H.J. Gunneweg and O. Kaiser, eds. Textgemäß. Festschrift E. Würthwein. p. 47–58. Göttingen, 1979.
R.G. Kratz. Kyros im Deuterojesaja-Buche. FAT 1. Tübingen, 1991.
J.D. Nogalski. Literary Precursors to the Book of the Twelve. BZAW 217. Berlin: 1993.
_____. Redactional Processes in the Book of the Twelve. BZAW 218. Berlin: 1993.
M. Noth. The Deuteronomistic History. Sheffield, 1981.
_____. The Chronicler's History. Sheffield, 1987.
I.W. Provan. Hezekiah and the Book of Kings. BZAW 172. Berlin—New York, 1988.
O.H. Steck. Bereitete Heimkehr. SBS 121. Stuttgart, 1985.
M.A. Sweeney. Isaiah 1–4 and the Post-Exilic Understanding of the Isaianic Tradition. BZAW 171. Berlin-New York, 1988.
G.H. Wilson. The Editing of the Hebrew Psalter. Chico, CA, 1985.

IV. HISTORY OF RESEARCH

K. Koch. The Growth of Biblical Tradition. p. 64–67.

§7 Form Critical Approach

A. THE TASK

I. The Overarching Question of the Presuppositions of a Text or Its Stages

Anyone who has investigated an Old Testament text, several verses in length, according to §§4–6 will have gained a reasoned picture of its *developmental history*. Either, one will be able to confirm this by the interdependency of the methodological approaches in the procedural steps of §§7–9, or one must revise the picture. This picture can certainly take different forms. The text can manifest itself as literarily homogenous, with or without earlier stages in oral transmission. If so, one or two developmental stages stand out in particular. However, the text can also consolidate several developmental stages, namely, when the text is literarily composite and thus receives formulations from several authors at various times. In any case, the investigation of §§4–6 demonstrated that the text components can be isolated from one another according to the developmental stages. As a rule, these may be isolated in formulations within the text. The preliterary oral stage constitutes a significant exception. On the one hand, with narratives, one can only ascertain the subject matter and outline, not the precise expression. On the other hand, prophetic logia constitute an exception where the oral form has been condensed and changed into the existing written version for the purpose of further transmission.

The methodological steps of §§7–9 now treat each of a text's developmental stages which have been separated. Depending upon the conclusions ascertained in §§4–6, these steps each begin with the oral transmission stage, then move across stages of literary growth to the existing final form with its own linguistic character.

*   *   *

What is the *material basis* for the *approaches of §§7–9* for each of the text's developmental stages?

No one works on a text entirely in a vacuum. This is true for the one who drafts a narrative, and especially for the one who formulates a legal saying, a cultic song, a wisdom saying, or a prophetic logion. It is also true for the one who appends something to a formulation, for the one who later conjoins two different older formulations, or the one who inserts a redactional formulation into an existing text. One selects the *means of expression* which one's *language provides*. One draws upon textual patterns which already exist in one's linguistic world (e.g. legal saying, prayer, hymn). Anyone wishing to formulate something comparable (§7) works with catchwords or word associations from *intellectually pre-fashioned linguistic fields* which are familiar to the author and to the author's addressees (§8). Last but not least, the author's formulation addresses *elements from the concrete-historical world* in which the author lives (§9). All of these elements are *existing*, supra-individualistic *materials* which are significant for the one who formulates. A text contains presuppositions which an author shares along with conscious or unconscious knowledge and culture. One must clarify these formulations and simultaneously illuminate the dynamic path to formulation in order to determine what one formulates, why it was formulated in precisely this manner, what the author means and intends with these formulations. Only in this manner can one bring to light those places where an author creatively adapts these materials (e.g. deviations from text patterns, or a breach of linguistic fields). This insight is indispensable for determining the profile of the formulation and the specific intention of its statements.

With §7 we encounter once again a field of closely related methods which all treat the presuppositions of a text, or each of the text's ascertained stages, in its own respective world. Form criticism (§7) determines the setting of a text in its existing *linguistic* world. Tradition criticism (§8) determines the setting of a text in its *intellectually pre-fashioned world*. The historical setting (§9) determines the setting of the *concrete historical* world.

II. Starting Point

In form criticism, the text is divided into each of its developmental stages. Each is then investigated regarding its *linguistic shape* in order to recognize the clues for meaning which manifest themselves from the linguistic shape. Therefore, one must know how this text's linguistic shape came to be. The author, as with the author's addressees, shared a *pre-existing linguistic world*. From that world, already available patterns and possibilities are adopted in order to communicate what the author wants to say. And sometimes the author deviates from them as well. One may differentiate various levels regarding the relationship which the linguistic shape of the author's statement exhibits to the existing linguistic world. Progressing from the specific to the whole, these levels include: the *tonal level* which observes the sound of the statement; the *word level* in which the individual words of the text should be investigated; the *sentence level* treats the individual sentences, and finally the *text level* treats the text as a whole with its sentences and words. The normal elements constructing the language, such as the lexically understandable vocabulary or the syntactical rules, are all considered part of the existing linguistic pattern and possibilities for the *level of sound, words, and sentences*. Further, stylistic devices like alliteration, assonance, metaphorical speech, or *parallelismus memborum* are also considered part of the linguistic pattern. The fixed speech patterns are of particular significance for the *text level*. They provide the linguistic contour to the text as a whole. Exegesis calls these text types genres. We also know genres of this type in our own linguistic world: official birth announcements, wedding announcements, obituaries, job applications, prescriptions, recipes, menus, memos, etc.[90] To a large degree the linguistic utterances during the time period of Old Testament transmissions were formulated neither freely nor capriciously. Rather, they were formulated in connection with existing, fixed text patterns.

The selection of the linguistic pattern and the possibilities for formulating a text in antiquity were likewise neither accidental nor arbitrary. They depend upon which perspective the author wants to use to state and to communicate the facts (*statement's outlook*). They depend upon the intentions which the author associates with this linguistic utterance (*statement's intention*). Therefore, one must pay attention to the life process in whose framework the linguistic utterance takes place (*life setting, Sitz im Leben*). One example from our linguistic world will illustrate. Someone who wants to communicate the death and funeral of a relative publicly, will compose an obituary according to a pattern of formulation which is fixed even down to the vocabulary and sentence construction. The same death is also reported in other text patterns when different types of conventional procedures treat the event and change the corresponding perspective and intention. These include: the official, medical confirmation of the cause of death, the death certificate, the personal, tactful, sympathetic note which gently notifies a relative, and the eulogy, etc. In addition to the form, each of these vary in sentence formulation and vocabulary. They also follow diverse patterns. Thus, in view of the stated facts, there exists a certain *correlation* between the specific linguistic shape of a text and the specific outlook and intention of the statement.[91] Someone speaking today knows which

---

90 Compare numerous examples in Lohfink, *The Bible: Now I Get It! A Form-Criticism Handbook*.

91 Richter (*Exegese*, p. 32,41–43) presupposes that the aspects of form and content can be different for a linguistic utterance. The fact that the substance of this utterance cannot be properly appreciated without determining their form also corresponds to our understanding (*Exegese*, p. 38,42f,114,119). However, profound differences exist in two respects. The first concerns the

linguistic form must be utilized in order to state something from a certain perspective and intention. One's listeners participate in the same linguistic world and can therefore recognize the intentions of the speaker by the form of the statement. As readers of an Old Testament text, we must also inquire in this direction about the correlation. The author's outlook and intention must be deduced from the linguistic shape. However, since the linguistic world of ancient Israel is no longer intimately familiar to us, this deduction can only occur in the *process of form critical reconstruction*. In summation: Whoever works form critically on the Old Testament, must observe the concrete Hebrew (or Aramaic) linguistic shape in which a text brings a specific condition into view. One must deduce the intentions which are expressed by this form.

One must consider, of course, that our insight into the markers and the rules of this structure and into the use of the Hebrew (or Aramaic) language is

---

determination of the concepts form and content. For Richter, the formalized expression of the linguistic utterance (including the formalized state of its contents) stands over against everything related to the contents, together with the substance (*Exegese*, p. 32,41f). This manual, however, understands form as the linguistic utterance in its existing, contoured shape, without regulated formalization. This understanding includes fashioned contents (cf. below, p. 101f). The second difference concerns the *function of the distinction* of form and content for the beginning and the execution of the method. Richter applies the exegetical process as a whole in such a manner that in a first part (literary criticism to redaction criticism) every beginning point should be excluded by content to resist arbitrary entries. For Richter, the exclusive starting point should be exacted from the formalized expression of the linguistic utterance in order to delimit the investigation of the content discerningly and in a controlled manner (This investigation follows in a second part). By contrast, from the beginning, this manual takes into consideration the insoluble connection between form and content in respect to form criticism (and thereby for every transmission stage of a text, to the degree that they are subject to form critical investigation).

As previously demonstrated above (in footnote 32 for literary criticism and footnote 63 for transmission history), one should also ask whether Richter's starting point, based solely on the formalized expression instead of a more comprehensive historical starting point, does not lead to faulty conclusions and faulty judgments. And one should also ask whether one's starting point does not demand more from the structural analysis than that analysis is able to perform for determining the contents of a historical statement. When a linguistic utterance arises, *material intention and linguistic shape* stand in *conjunction* from the beginning. Exegetical analysis may not tear this connection apart and split them up into a methodological sequence. If one disregards the impression of the local content and the thematic direction of the linguistic utterance, and if one concentrates solely on the phenomena which can be formalized, then what is a structural analysis, or a determination of form? What is a form critical work in that case? One must vigorously contest the idea, which Richter staunchly accepts, that the *starting point* of the content must inevitably succumb to the danger of inappropriate entries. Topical analysis of form criticism and especially of tradition historical work (see §8) demonstrates the presupposition that controllable, verifiable determinations of the statement's contents are possible from the beginning. In some circumstances, results of the structural linguistic science can be arranged according to a historically applied form critical method. This may be done to the degree that the results are proven sound in the historical realm of Ancient Israel and of the dead language of Biblical Hebrew. However, by no means, may the implications of these results detract from the comprehensive historical starting point of form criticism which corresponds to the historical subject.

limited. Even the original pronunciation of Hebrew remains unknown to us. The findings from the spoken level (tone, rhythm, meter) are therefore to a large degree uncertain.[92] Further, research into the linguistic pattern and its significance is still in its beginnings. This limited knowledge is true for works in the area of Hebrew syntax (e.g. tenses) and style (e.g. different narrative styles). If, in the future, these lead to significant, convincing conclusions, then certainly form criticism would gain new *possibilities for inquiry*. Within the framework of this book, we limit form criticism to investigating those linguistic characteristics and those means of formation whose structural markers can currently ascertain meaning with sufficient clarity by the consistent context.[93] Traditionally, this determination occurs especially with the question of the linguistic pattern on the text level (genres). However, today, the following are also progressively gaining in importance for good reason: the description of the linguistic shape of individual sentence, the sentence order of the text, and the ascertainment of the meaning of this syntactical and stylistic finding.[94] One can encounter the form's typical construction elements with this linguis-

[92] Compare also Koch, *Formgeschichte*, 299f (5th edition, 281f; this postlude is not in the English translation).

[93] In recent years, attempts to subject Old Testament texts to a painstaking linguistic investigation have grown dramatically. It has not always been clear, however, that the investigation should treat a linguistic world in its historical character and in the service of ascertaining the intended accents of a statement. The linguistic investigation stands in close connection with other approaches of historical-critical methodology. The formulation of an Old Testament text is a process of life which has a subject oriented intention. One must consider this fact over against the objective scientific appearance of lavish, linguistically formalized structural plans for texts. Linguistic manifestations are important for exegesis when they illuminate the process by contributing to our current state of knowledge about the subject intentions of Hebrew linguistic phenomena. Examples of intensive linguistic investigations of Old Testament text in the German-speaking world are especially the works of W. Richter and his followers which appear in Eos-Verlag of St. Ottilien. In the French-speaking world examples include the works of P. Auffret treating wisdom texts and psalm texts. For the English-speaking world compare the overview by R.C. Culley, "Exploring New Directions." In methodological introductions (see §2H) corresponding sections are found in Fohrer, *Exegese*, §6 (G. Wanke); Koch, *Formgeschichte*, 298–342 (5th ed. 271–324; not in English translation), and Schweizer, *Biblische Texte verstehen*.

[94] In distinction to Fohrer (*Exegese*, §6) and Kaiser (*Exegetical Method*, section 4), we also treat the investigation of the linguistic shape of a text, not in a separate section, but under the larger concept of form criticism together with the question of form. This investigation is necessary prior to and concurrent with the determination of genre. In practical terms, the semantic analysis (compare in particular, Wanke, in Fohrer, *Exegese*, 76–78; and Koch, *Formgeschichte*, 316–330, 5th ed. 298–312; not in English translation) should, for the most part, already have taken place during the first preliminary translation (see above p. 6 and 11) to the degree that it belongs to the work of form criticism. This semantic analysis should be attributed to the analysis of the text's *linguistic* shape under a methodologically theoretical perspective. To the degree that additional contents crystalize around a concept in the framework of a more comprehensive conceptual complex, the semantic analysis crosses over into the tradition historical work (see below, p. 126).

tic finding.[95] This finding can, however, also treat the text's formal markers which are independent of the genre. On occasion, these markers can be incorporated precisely for the linguistic deviation of the genre.[96] In formulations not influenced by genres (e.g. additions, redaction texts) the form of the sentence and the sentence order represent the most important linguistic clues for the desired meaning, along with traditional linguistic fields ascertained in §8 and their use in the text.

III. Determination

In exegetical practice, form criticism primarily elaborates the particular *linguistic shape for a specific text* (no matter what size), or if necessary, for each stage of its growth that has been ascertained.

In so doing, form criticism pursues two main tasks:

1. In each case, form criticism comprehends the linguistic shape of the text *inside the individual sentence and for the sentence progression*. It also highlights the *material aspects* which are indicated by the syntactical and stylistic form in the individual text and the text as a whole.
2. When they present themselves in the text, form criticism determines (for parts and/or for the entirety) when the text level adopts and utilizes *genres*. Also form criticism determines the life setting to which they belong. Certainly, for this task it must rely upon other independent examples of the genre.

Form criticism aims toward a methodologically pertinent understanding of the construction and intention of the encountered text to the degree that the character of the linguistic formulation can be recognized. This aim even includes the choice of the genre under whose perspective the expressed contents should be seen and for whose purpose they were formulated.

Form critical work does not just constitute the investigation of the linguistic shape of an *individual* text and the parallel examples which appear during the investigation. Although clearly beyond expectations for beginning students, the task of form criticism also includes, in principle, research into the Hebrew (or Aramaic) *linguistic world as a whole* and illumination of the history of text patterns (*genre history*). In this case, work on individual texts is not the goal but is the means and the material of the investigation.

---

95 Examples: the sentence type "command" in an admonition or the stylistic device of *parallelismus membrorum* in the wisdom saying.

96 Examples: In Isa 7:4–9, the element in 7:9b, which is perceived as a conditioned threat, supersedes the genre "salvation oracle to the king." Also it accentuates the correspondence between behavior and circumstances by the use of the paranomasia *ta'ămînû/tē'āmēnû*.

IV. Terminology

1. "Form" and "Genre"

The term "form" is used in the discipline in different ways. Occasionally it is used synonymously with "genre,"[97] but more frequently its is differentiated from genre in various ways.[98] In this workbook, "form" is understood as an interchangeable term for "linguistic shape." It is thus not something which can be investigated apart from the expressed content. Form and content cannot be separated within a linguistic utterance. However, the content is constitutive to a linguistic pattern by various concrete features. When the levels of linguistic utterance are more elementary and simpler, then it is easier to generalize their contents. Tonal forms, stylistic figures, or sentence types are very general in terms of content because of their broad usage. By contrast, formulas or genres (and especially not the assigned text as a whole) cannot be separated from concrete contents by their form. The term *"form"* thereby designates the *existing linguistic shape of a text*. It also designates the genre(s) incorporated into the text with their characteristic and determining form markers. It also designates linguistic threads or art forms (*parallelismus membrorum*, among others) which are not determined by the genre. These acquired facts about the use *and* deviation of given linguistic patterns are expressions of meaning.

2. "Formula"

The term "formula" should be differentiated from "genre." A formula is a short, fixed word association.[99]

3. Form Criticism and Genre History[100]

"Form criticism" and "genre history" are also used with a certain promiscuity (in connection with the corresponding use of form and genre). However,

---

97 Compare, for example, C. Kuhl, *RGG*[3], vol. 2, col. 996 ("Form"/ "Gattung").

98 Compare, for example, H.-J. Hermisson, *Studien zur israelitischen Spruchweisheit*, 1968, p. 138, footnote 1; Crüsemann, *Studien*, p. 13f, footnote 1; Richter, *Exegese* 33,74,126f,131ff; Markert in Fohrer, *Exegese*, p. 86f; and Kaiser, *Exegetical Method*, p. 20–22.

99 Examples: "With a strong hand and with an outstretched arm" (*bĕyād ḥăzāqâ ûbizrôaʿ nĕṭûyâ*) for the powerful actions of YHWH (e.g. Deut 4:34; 2 Kgs 17:36; Jer 21:5); and "I am YHWH (your god)" (*ʾanî yhwh*) for the self-presentation of YHWH (e.g. Exod 20:2; Lev 18:2; Ps 50:7).

Richter, *Exegese*, 99–103 (taken up by Kaiser, *Exegetical Method*, p. 17; modified by Wanke in Fohrer, *Exegese*, p. 73), wants to differentiate further between "formula" and "fixed expression" (with the latter limited to *a specific* literary work).

100 **Translator's note:** As evident from the following paragraph and footnote, English usage does not adequately distinguish between the German terms *Formgeschichte* and *Formkritik*. The former literally means "form history" and the latter "form criticism." In English, however, common usage has long established "form criticism" as the standard translation for *"Formgeschichte,"*

"form criticism,"[101] the conceptual understanding of half of the method, should relate to the method as a whole, while "genre history" should remain the name used for the history of a specific genre.[102]

B. COMMENTARY ON THE APPROACH AND METHOD

I. Constituent Questions

The form critical investigation of a text can be subdivided into four constituent questions:

1. What form markers does the text show, and how does one designate the text's linguistic shape, in part and in whole (*the question of the linguistic shape*)?
2. Is the text shaped, in whole or in part, under the influence of a genre (*determination of the genre*)?[103]
3. In this particular instance, how does the genre imprint fit into the history of that genre (*genre history question*)?
4. To which external life situation does the genre belong, and which of that setting's requirements and regularities appertain to the genre? And how is the origin of the text related to this life situation (*question of the life setting*)?

---

which makes it impossible to distinguish *Formgeschichte* from *Formkritik* in anything other than an arbitrary manner. Thus, for purposes of the immediate discussion the German terms "*Formgeschichte*" and "*Formkritik*" will be used when necessary to enable distinctions. Normally, however, the English term "form criticism" will be used as the standard translation of *Formgeschichte*. Similarly, the term "*Gattung*" is distinct from the German word "*Form*". Where necessary, the translation uses the English (i.e. French) term "genre" for "*Gattung*" in order to distinguish it from "*Form*."

101 "*Formgeschichte*" and "*Gattungsgeschichte*" have a special meaning in connection with the terms "*Formkritik*," "*Gattungskritik*," and "*Formgeschichte*" for Richter, *Exegese*, p. 120–125, 149–151 (see the discussion in the 2nd–7th German edition of this workbook, p. 97f., and the addendum in the 8th edition, p. 74–76). Markert, in Fohrer, *Exegese*, p. 86f, does away with the term "*Formgeschichte*" and designates the various steps with the terms "*Formkritik*," "*Formenkritik*," "*Gattungskritik*," "*Formengeschichte*," and "*Gattungsgeschichte*."

102 One should note that Koch, *Growth of Biblical Tradition*, 38,53,57,77, perceives "*Formgeschichte*" as the summary term for all exegetical methods, in contrast to the term distinctions used here.

103 The separation of the two aspects (linguistic shape and genre imprint) into two independent constitutive questions, as we have done here, makes allowance for the fact that the formation of a text should not be understood solely as formation by existing genres and their related associations (see discussions above, p. 96 and 99f). The distinction between a text's genre imprint and its genre-dependent linguistic shape is correctly accented in the newer discussions of method, first by Richter (*Exegese*, p. 33,74,126f,131ff) and then also in the methodologies of Schreiner (*Einleitung*), Fohrer (*Exegese*), and Koch (*Formgeschichte*, 3rd ed. [German only]). In attempting a more detailed development they contrast with the widespread trend of reducing form criticism to the genre question.

II. Concerning the Question of the Linguistic Shape

Anyone who has followed the guides of this manual to this point has already gained foundational linguistic observations for the text as a whole. They have emerged from the Hebrew text, by working from the procedural step of §1 B II 2 in reference to the description of the linguistic manifestations and in reference to the possible material aspect thereby expressed.

The observational questions from that section are also the essential guiding questions for the first constitutive question of the form critical investigation undertaken here (see above pages 8–14).

However, the procedure here in §7 is distinguished from the corresponding observation phase in §1 in two ways. First, the question of the linguistic shape is no longer directed toward the entire text, as was the case in §1. Rather, it is directed toward each of the text's developmental stages as ascertained in §§4–6. This concentration has the effect of reexamination, confirmation, and/or correction regarding the text's ascertained path of development. Second, that which was observed in §1 will now be methodically reexamined and explained for the texts of the individual developmental stages. It will be reexamined with the aid of (grammatical, syntactical, and stylistic) secondary literature on the Hebrew (see remarks in §2D; §7D), as well as lexica and concordances (see remarks in §2C,E). During this reexamination and explanation of the linguistic observations on a given text's developmental elements, four approaches impacting the linguistic shape come to the foreground for each developmental stage.

1) The investigation begins by *delimiting* the established text.

Is the text a completely independent whole? Is it a self-enclosed whole with a meaningful beginning and end? If necessary, what continuation does it presuppose (previous and subsequent)?[104]

Regarding the linguistic shape, a small written unit, which can stand by itself, should be differentiated from a redactional formulation. In principle, even if not true in exegetical practice, the size of the text plays no role here (as is true elsewhere in form criticism). Form criticism not only treats small units, but also fundamentally treats collections and large literary complexes.

2) Thereafter, the question of the *structure* and the *structural components* is fundamental.

---

104 Examples: Psalms frequently stand entirely on their own (but compare Pss 42/43 and note the possibility of redactional psalms). By contrast, a given text from the Succession History can be relatively self-enclosed (e.g. 2 Sam 11:2–12:25; 20:1–22), but at the same time an episode in a larger narrative whole.

These components are recognizable, above all, in the following: scenic or functional sections, characteristic introductory or concluding formulas, connecting or dividing markings of a linguistic nature (e.g. the change of subject), the sequence of the sentences, the types of sentences (e.g. command, nominal sentence), stylistic devices (such as repetition), and the words which bind the sentences to one another (such as "because," "therefore").[105]

To classify the text one should further note the following: Which structural components are of equal weight, and which are coordinated with or subsumed under other components? The individual structural components are further categorized as independent statements (main clauses, coordinate clauses, and even parallel sentences) and subordinate statements (dependent clause, relative clause, infinitive constructions). With additions and redactional formulations, one must ask the distinctive question: How are they related to the existing literary context?

It is recommended that one should write the text in Hebrew to graphically illustrate these clarifications of the classification regarding the macro-structure and micro-structure. Also, even correspondences between individual sentence components should be emphasized (for example by using colored pens).

3) On the text level, the specific *linguistic shaping devices* have no exclusive structuring function (and in part they have absolutely no structuring function). Clarity concerning the use and the meaning of these devices cannot be fundamentally attained without deliberation on a multiplicity of texts.[106] However, these devices can perhaps exhibit important material accents which must be evaluated in the detailed interpretation (see §10).

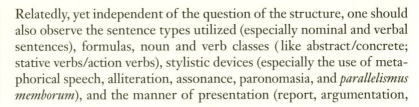

Relatedly, yet independent of the question of the structure, one should also observe the sentence types utilized (especially nominal and verbal sentences), formulas, noun and verb classes (like abstract/concrete; stative verbs/action verbs), stylistic devices (especially the use of metaphorical speech, alliteration, assonance, paronomasia, and *parallelismus membrorum*), and the manner of presentation (report, argumentation,

---

105 Example: Isa 10:5–19. The following are especially important for determining the construction and constructural components: the motivational conjunction "therefore" (*lākēn* in 10:16); the change from YHWH speech (10:5–7,12b) to an incorporated quote of the Assyrian (10:8–11,13f) which is twice used within 10:5–15 to thematicize varying aspects of the sin; and the stylistic device of the cross-reference from 10:15 to 10:5.

106 In the practical completion of one's work, the exegete should freely make use of already existing insights from the discipline by drawing upon dictionaries, grammars, stylistic studies, Old Testament introductions, etc.

instruction, etc.; scenic dualism, intertwining character). One should also determine their function in the entire text.[107]

4) Finally, one must ask about the *reference point of the author concerning the subject/facts* and the audience. In a linguistic investigation, the perspective concerns what is formulated, and what is not formulated? Why, for whom, and for what purpose was it formulated precisely in this manner and not in another way? Thus:

How do the expressed conditions specifically present the perception, experience, and thinking at the time of the statement's formation? On what specifically does the statement's author place major emphasis (e.g praying, cursing, teaching)? What does the author leave out? What could also be of interest by itself, in association with the statement?[108] For the author's purpose, what is the relationship of the hearer/reader to the statement or to the conditions expressed (perhaps different in historiography from popular narratives or in statements of praise from lists)? What does the author wish to tell the reader/hearer (purpose of the statement)?[109]

Summary of the Procedural Steps

The investigation of the *linguistic shaping* may thus be summarized according to II 1–4 in the following procedural steps. These steps reexamine and clarify the linguistic observations of §1 for each developmental stage of the text:

1. The question of the *delimitation* of the established text controlling the results of §§4–6.
2. The question of the *construction* and the *constructional components* of the established text, again controlling the results of §§4–6.

---

[107] Examples: The use of alliteration and assonance to draw out the conclusive judgment on the misdeeds of Jerusalem and Judah in Isa 5:7b (*mišpāṭ/mišpaḥ ṣĕdāqâ/ṣĕ'āqâ*); use of the nominal sentence to express the *existing* divine protection for Zion in Ps 46 (46:2,6a,8, etc.). In light of narratives, compare the famous stylistic comparison between Homer and Gen 22 by E. Auerbach, *Mimesis*, ⁵1971, p. 5–27 (especially 9ff) and the analysis of Gen 28:10–22 by Fohrer, *Exegese*, p. 185–195 (with §6).

[108] This approach is particularly suited to recognize the special aspect from which a text speaks: What is said in Ps 6, or a related complaint song, concerning the underlying affliction, and what is not said? What is said in Isa 7:1–17 concerning the decisive political situation of Ahaz, and what is not said?

[109] Since Richter (*Exegese*, 75–78,128–137,183) rejects non-formalized contents as a starting point, the perspectives named here do not come into play, for him, in the framework of the methodological steps seeking the form and genre. Relatedly, when determining the genre, those perspectives which are associated with the (non-formalized!) genre topic also do not come into play. By contrast, compare footnote 91.

3. The question of the *linguistic shaping devices* (stylistic, syntactical) used in the text's sentences and sentence order.
4. The question of the *linguistic* indices of the *author's perspective* on the text's *subject/facts* and its *addressees*.

III. Determining the Genre

1. The Process of Determining the Genre

It is much more difficult today to determine a text's genre than it was in the period of classical form criticism because Old Testament texts can no longer be seen simply as the record of small, oral speech units. What we have before us are written texts within the framework of more or less expansive literary works. Thus, one should primarily have to ask the question of the *written-literary* (!) genres in ancient Israel which has scarcely been considered to this point. By no means are all Old Testament texts simply the codification of oral transmission material. Even in those places in which this is the case, one must account for modification during the process of recording. In other words, the jump into the world of living, oral communication in ancient Israel via form criticism is hardly possible any longer. As with §5, only cautious deductions concerning the influence of *preliterary spoken genres* reveal themselves on occasion. Determining the genre in this conventional sense is then best employed today in those texts which literary criticism and redaction criticism nevertheless do suggest that the text is a small unit whose origin lies in oral transmission. Above all, one could consider cultic texts, wisdom texts, legal texts, prophetic logia (but beyond their recording in written form), and the structuring of independent narratives. Naturally, one should by no means exclude the influence of oral genre patterns on texts which were first formulated on the literary level. This influence may occur in the reformulation of transmitted material which has been shaped by oral genres or it may occur in the secondary literary usage of genres for redactional passages with a correspondingly large distance from the genre's primary oral usage. Still, the modification which results must be considered constantly.

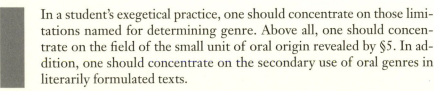

In a student's exegetical practice, one should concentrate on those limitations named for determining genre. Above all, one should concentrate on the field of the small unit of oral origin revealed by §5. In addition, one should concentrate on the secondary use of oral genres in literarily formulated texts.

This concentration is suggested because the discipline still scarcely offers preparatory works for the question of literary genres (exceptions include annals, lists). Therefore it is recommended that one ask about the genre for each developmental stage of the text separately. The ancient oriental realm represents an important field, which has been too little investigated. It represents an important field for the recognition of genres and of stereotypical life situations which lead to genres. In certain circumstances, the ancient oriental realm allows deductive suppositions concerning corresponding realities in Ancient Israel.

Only by *comparing other texts* can one determine whether or not a text, or text complex, follows the linguistic shaping of an existing text pattern for a specific life process (and if so, in what manner). A genre presents itself when several texts, literarily independent of one another,[110] possess a common foundation in respect to structural elements, topics (specific words, contents, and constellations typical for this genre[111]), and form markers.

How should one *proceed in detail* when determining the genre of a given text?[112]

> The perspective and purpose of a statement became recognizable within the framework of the question of the linguistic shape in light of concrete circumstances (e.g. prayer, legal saying, cultic rationale, historical narrative). This perspective and purpose indicate in which Old Testament text realm one should seek correspondingly shaped texts for precedence. (One works primarily with an English bible, but controls these observations by using the Biblia Hebraica.)

From there, with the help of a Hebrew concordance, one can identify and examine other texts which include the same words as the text under investigation and which are significant for the structure and for the statement's intention (as, for example, with the use of "because" [*ya'an*] or "therefore" [*lākēn*] in the judgment prophecy, or with the use of "how long?" [*'ad mātay*] or "hear/answer" [*'nh*] with the complaint psalm).

> If correspondingly shaped, literarily independent texts are found in this manner, then one may *more precisely determine* the *markers of the underlying genre* by comparative observation. Simultaneously one may also determine the individual deviation of the various examples.

By doing so, this process, in some cases, provides important specifications and corrections regarding the linguistic shape of the established delimitation,

---

110 The concurring formation of texts can rest upon a literary dependence which imitates the model at hand. The dependence can also be traced back to the hand of a single author who shapes the unity (compare Markert, in Fohrer, *Exegese*, p. 92, footnote 97, for the framing pieces of the book of Judges).

111 Example, a burial song: code word 'êk, contrast between then and now, laudatory presentation of the dead, and others. The genre topic of many psalm genres is especially abundant (cf. for example, the complaint song of the individual in H. Gunkel and J. Begrich, *Einleitung in die Psalmen*, 1933, p. 184ff).

112 For the practical completion of the work, the exegete should here also make use of the currently available insights of the discipline (see above, footnote 106). The exegete should take up the genre determinations mentioned in Old Testament introductions or in commentaries and examine them critically (cf. also Markert, in Fohrer, *Exegese*, p. 94f; Kaiser, *Exegetical Method*, p. 25f). Compare the literature suggestions below in D II.

structure analysis, and determination of the dominant perspective. However, if one finds that the text's characteristics, which were observed during the investigation, are limited to this text, then as a rule, it is not possible to speak of a specific available genre shaping the text. It may also be proven, however, that the text under investigation is just one component of a genre.[113] In order to understand more quickly, it is recommended that one follow the terminology established by the discipline for the name of the genre.

2. Variations and Deviations in Genres

The shaping of linguistic utterances according to existing text patterns does not simply signify their schematic duplication because of the dynamic nature of the language. From the outset, one should therefore naturally expect differences among individual examples of a genre and the division of a genre into genre categories.

> However, stronger deviations and reformulations of the genre must be understood as one of the following: They may be understood as indicating a change in the genre during its history.[114] The change may also be understood as a clue to particular contents which arise from the possibilities of the text-type. And/or the change must be seen as the expressed peculiarity of the author(s).

In the last instance, the deviations frequently provide clues to the specific intention of the statement for the encountered passage.[115]

3. Consolidation and Mixture of Genres

A linguistic unit is frequently shaped according to a single genre.

> However, one must also take into account that, within a text, a genre can appear in the framework of another genre, covering a larger text. The former would thus be called a "*component genre*" and the latter would be called the "*framing genre*" (K. Koch).[116]

Further, one frequently encounters the consolidation or mixture of genres. The age of these linguistic entities has not yet been decided from this fact. The hypothesis that a genre type has developed from a simple type of the genre to a complex type of the genre is problematic. Still, one must, as a rule, see the mixture of genres within one text as the sign of secondary usage, to the degree that they do not arise from the same life setting (see below, section V 1).

---

113 Example: With regard to its genre, Gen 39 is only a component part of the genre of the novella, which exists in the Joseph narrative as a whole.

114 See below, section IV.

115 Example: Isa 7:4–9 (see above, footnote 96).

116 Koch, *Growth of Biblical Tradition*, p. 18–20. The work by F. Stolz, *Psalmen im nachkultischen Raum*, Zurich, 1983, is instructive for the question of mixed genres in the psalms.

IV. The Question of the Genre History

1. Starting Point

A genre is seldom distinguished in the individual examples by duplication of the linguistic shape. More often changes and deviations appear. Reasons for these differences can be found in conscious deviation of the markers typical for the genre when adopting the genre.[117] They can also point to developments and changes to the genre in the course of the long history of its use. The starting point for the question of genre history appears especially in the latter phenomenon. Every genre has a history for the period it was in use. To that degree, an existing genre sample, for a text's specific transmission stage, can be characteristically differentiated from other expressions of this genre, both forward and backward in time.

2. Material for Comparison

Within the Old Testament and the environment of Ancient Israel, the manifestations of the genre in question offer the material for investigating genre history. Genre historical manifestations ensue from the observation of those changes which result from the development of genre elements, and not simply from the one time modification of an author using the genre. (This statement is true unless those modifications themselves effectively change the genre.) Genre historical investigations, as a rule, arise in the form of a monograph.[118] They are possible only in a very limited form within the framework of an exegesis paper on a specific text.

Summary of the Steps

The question whether a text, in whole or in part, is shaped under the influence of a *genre*, may thus be summarized in the following steps:

1. Starting point with the text
   One should proceed from insights into the *linguistic shape* in reference to the text's construction and constructural elements. In so doing, one should pay special attention to the syntactical form of the content of the statement. On occasion, the contour of these findings indicates use of a genre pattern. The facts, linguistically conceived under a specific perspective and intention, indicate in which arena a presumed genre pattern belongs (e.g. legal regulations, life wisdom, prophetic speech, song prayer, etc.)
2. Search for genre parallels
   If a genre pattern impacts the shape of the text, then the devices of linguistic shaping, which are themselves fixed component ele-

117 Compare above B III 2, p. 108, and below B V 3, p. 112.
118 Compare, for example, Crüsemann, *Studien*, p. 210–284, for the individual song of thanksgiving.

ments, ensue from *literarily independent examples of texts with corre-sponding text patterns*. These devices are made known in asso-ciation with typical words, contents, and conceptualizations. They are, in principle, located by concordance work in which the Old Testament is searched for linguistic manifestations corresponding in form and content. In practice, one will have to rely primarily on the compilation of genres in secondary literature for the presumed arena of usage (see below D II). Cult, cult poetry, wis-dom, law, royal court, death rituals, and prophetic activity pri-marily come into play. One should note that formulas, idioms, etc. are not genres (for these, compare §8).

3. Expression of the genre in the text

If a text pattern influences the text or if component and framing genres appear together, then one must more closely investigate the *concrete* expression of the genre in the text *at hand*. Various consid-erations are important in doing so:

— Is the expression of the genre in the text practically identical with other examples?

— If not, from whence does the deviation arise? Does it stem from the internal change over the course of the genre's history? Or does the change stem from the adaptation of the genre under-taken by the author?

— How is the genre's structure related to the linguistically marked structure of the text? Do both serve the same purpose? Or must one revise the text's linguistic analysis of the structure based on the influence of the genre? Or does the author deviate from the structure of the genre?

4. Consequences of the genre finding

What does the finding of 3) mean for the material perspective, the purpose, and the line of thought? What does it mean for the life setting and the communication setting of the text? Is it possible to deduce the original use of the text in the oral arena? What mate-rial accents does the genre influence contribute to the level of the written record of the text? For the author and the reader, what does the genre contribute to a text originally conceived as a written text within a literary context?

V. Regarding the Question of the Life Setting

1. Clarification of the Term

As a rule, form critical investigation, as practiced in Old Testament exege-sis, treats those genres which allow a specific linguistic pattern to be associated with specific *socio-cultural conditions and realities* (life setting). One may only speak of this arrangement if the genre is so rooted in a life process that repetition of the genre itself recalls the process.[119] A genre's occasional employment in another realm by no means signifies a new life setting.[120]

The expressed life process designated by the life setting is related to a specific topic to which other life processes can certainly be related. In this case *very different genres* also concentrate on this topic. These genres look upon this topic from different perspectives. Thus, fixed linguistic utterances are bound to *one and the same topic*, that of a military campaign, but they belong to the following genres: oracular inquiry, oracular response, sayings for purification rituals, vows, orders, call to battle, instructions to the herald, victory song, lists of booty, royal thanksgiving song, campaign report, stela inscription. These genres represent different processes relating to the military campaign but see one and the same event from characteristic perspectives.

Form criticism is also a *socio-literary* means of inspection when considering the aspect of the life setting. One should not confuse form criticism with a timeless morphology which phenomenologically describes an aesthetic world of forms.

By way of limitation, however, one must add that the rooting of genres in a specific life setting does not mean that it is always possible to deduce the cultural and institutional framework from the text's linguistic shape as fashioned by the genre. For one reason, genres can leave the life setting from which they arose (see below, V.3.). For another reason, several genres reflect their life setting so imprecisely that entering the socio-cultural conditions and realities to which they belong is not possible from the linguistic shape of texts formed in that setting.

At any rate, one must observe that deducing oral genres of speech, and their rooting in concrete areas, will always remain an inferred conclusion for the Old Testament. This statement is true because we only have examples in written form which represent a secondary usage. Such an inferred conclusion is not self-evident. It must be suggested by a positive text finding according to §5, in connection with socio-historical correspondences which can be deduced for Israel directly or indirectly from ancient oriental sources.

2. Methodological Entry

If the given text exhibits genre influence, then one must explain the *arena of life* to which the genre belongs from the outset. One must explain this origin apart from the usage in the text. Methodologically, the relationship

---

119 Examples: The dirge is rooted in the funeral procession (2 Sam 1:17–27). Or the liturgy of temple admission is rooted in the process of the pilgrims' entry into the Jerusalem temple (Ps 15).

120 Example: The use of animal and plant fables in Ezek 17 and 19 (for details, see W. Zimmerli, *Ezekiel 1*, Hermeneia, Philadelphia, 1979, see locations).

between the life setting and the applicable genre(s) must be illuminated from two directions:

a) Proceeding from the *genre* (text examples):
    In order to recognize the life setting, one must ask the following questions in light of the genre markers as well as the context in which the genre appears:

> "Who is the speaker? Who are the listeners? What mood dominates the situation? What effect is sought?"[121]
>
> From the perspective of the one speaking, does the statement presuppose the exercise of a specific function, or a specific "competence"?[122] Can the interests and concerns of specific persons or groups of persons be seen?
>
> Do the style and type of presentation (e.g. a folk-tale or theologically reflective narrative style) allow deductions concerning the socio-cultural roots?
>
> To which ordered life processes in Israel do the genre's structure, form markers, perspective, and contents point?[123]

b) Proceeding from the *socio-cultural conditions and realities*:

> Here it is necessary to obtain knowledge concerning the Israelite and ancient oriental history (economic, social, cultic, and religious), to the degree that their acquisition is possible at this point.[124] They comprise the material from which the life setting can be conceived and delineated.

3. Relationship between Genre and Life Setting

In the simplest case this relationship is *an immediate one.* The genre is used in the framework of its life setting. In the Old Testament writings, this case is possibly presumed in written literary genres. It can be deduced with oral genres if the text can be traced back into oral transmission. However, the relationship between genre and life setting in the Old Testament *often* presents itself *more complexly,* which creates special problems for form criticism:

121 Gunkel, *Reden und Aufsätze,* p. 33.

122 Compare Kaiser, *Exegetical Method,* p. 27.

123 Example: Individual song of thanksgiving: the introductory *tôdâ* formula (Isa 12:1) or the naming of the thanksgiving offering in the course of the psalm (Ps 116:17) point to the process of presenting the *tôdâ.* The bi-polarity of the speech can be recognized in two directions (Ps 30:2–4,7–13/5f). On the one hand, in the process of the *tôdâ,* the one praying transfers the offering to YHWH with direct *address* to YHWH. On the other hand, the one praying reports *about* YHWH's deed to those participating in the sacrificial meal; compare Crüsemann, *Studien,* p. 282–284.

124 For literature, see above, §2 K,L.

a. A genre can be used *outside of its life setting*. Either, it can be used ad hoc in another arena without becoming strongly rooted in that arena,[125] or it can become an integrated component of another arena and thereby enter a new life setting. This new setting can be grounded in the change or the withering away of the original life setting.[126]

In the Old Testament these secondary usages of genres can already appear in the oral transmission. For example, such secondary usage can be seen in prophetic logia which are influenced by non-prophetic genres, or in psalms which are impacted by wisdom genres. Above all, however, the influence of oral genres upon the written level consistently represents a secondary usage.

b. If a genre makes a transition from the realm in which it derived into another realm, then certain *changes in the genre* appear which stand out in every genre's history (e.g. its topic, consolidation with other genres or genre elements[127]). These changes can be noted especially in the numerous cases of ad hoc adoption. In the end, these changes mean that one can no longer speak without qualification about one and the same genre. As a result the following may be noted:

1. The current understanding that a single genre can traverse *several life settings* is problematic.
2. Even though widely presupposed in current understanding, defining the term life setting solely as the place of use for genres of very diverse background is unsatisfactory. It fails to take into account that a new arena (life setting) produces substantive changes when it adopts a genre, as shown above. The *term life setting* must therefore be understood more *narrowly*. It must be determined as a formulatively effective arena only for those genres which are rooted in that arena and which are consistently used there. Genres which are rooted in another life arena, but which appear in the shaping arena, will then be assimilated (in altered form) into that arena and its genres, as a result of its shaping power.

c. If a genre is taken from the arena from which it derived into another arena, its original *characteristics* are not entirely lost, in spite of the fact that the life setting is no longer present and that the genre has changed. The very fact that the genre has been selected is apparently grounded in the specific intention and purpose of the new statement. The new statement was articulated by borrowing from a foreign genre. As a result, it is imperative that one observe a genre's markers and goal, even when a genre which is used for a different function than its original life setting. This is necessary

---

125 Examples: Use of the wisdom genre fable (see above, footnote 120) or the instruction to the herald in prophetic pronouncements (Isa 40:9–11; Jer 46:14; etc. Compare Crüsemann, *Studien*, p. 53f.)

126 Examples: The *prophetic* dirge (Amos 5:2; Isa 1:2ff; 14:4b–21; for further examples and indication of the character see H. Jahnow, *Das hebräische Leichenlied im Rahmen der Völkerdichtung*, 1923, 162ff.); saga traditions as a component of the Yahwistic work. The last instance concerns the transition into the setting in literature (setting in the book). "But a question then immediately arises: What is the *Sitz im Leben* of this literature itself, that is, for what public or semipublic reading of it, and where and by whom?" (Kaiser, *Exegetical Method*, p. 26).

127 Examples: The consolidation of herald instruction with the imperative hymn in Isa 48:20; Jer 31:7; or the consolidation of the dirge with the judgment prophecy in Isa 1:21–26. In both cases there is a corresponding change in the genre topic.

if one wants to perceive the intent and perspective of the new statement which was formed using that genre.[128]

The situation changes only in those cases where a genre is brought over solely to reproduce certain contents, or conceptualizations, which are associated with it.[129]

Summary of the Steps

If the text under investigation is influenced by a genre, then one must raise the question of the genre's *life setting* in relationship to this text. The following steps may be summarized:

1. Deducing the genre's stereotypical situations

   The genre pattern was ascertained from the text under investigation and additional parallels in the framework of the second component question (B III and IV). One must inquire into the *stereotypical situation* which this pattern requires and in which it belongs. In doing so, one must combine inquiry into the text indices with ascertaining corresponding historical realities (according to V 2). In practice, one must essentially examine form critical secondary literature to see what it offers.

2. Illustrating this situation from Old Testament (and ancient oriental) sources

   If one has ascertained a life setting for the genre pattern, then one should acquire *the most graphic picture possible*, historically speaking, concerning the processes within this framework, especially the linguistic processes. In this manner, one can illustrate how the linguistic pattern functions for this genre within this framework. One can identify the speaker, the listeners, the actions and processes which shape the frame. One can identify the intention of this fashioned linguistic act, and the subject's accents and perspectives which are selected and highlighted.

3. Relationship between the situation from which the text arises and the situation of the genre

   After this inquiry, one returns to the *text under investigation* and to the impact of its genre. One considers how the origin of this text relates to the situation which gave rise to the genre (life setting). For this task, one should examine the possibilities of V 3 for the text. When there is an immediate relationship between genre and life setting, one should strive to deduce concretely visible implications for its original usage, according to "2". In all other cases,

---

[128] See Fohrer, *Introduction*, p. 28f,333.

[129] Examples: The use of a natural onomastic list in the theophanic material of Job 38ff where God is encountered at the end of the Job dialogues. .

 meaning when there is secondary usage, one must ask what the original life setting contributes materially to the genre's new usage. For example, adopting a wisdom genre in Isa 1:2f and a priestly genre in Isa 1:10–17 can show that it is now the prophet who claims the authority and the function of the wisdom instruction and the priestly instruction. He does so by critically distancing himself from the original speakers of these teaching utterances.

VI. Area of Usage

Form criticism is not limited to a specific text or to a specific transmission stage. Rather, form criticism is meaningful in several aspects simultaneously. Form criticism is meaningful in oral as well as written transmission stages, for a text (component genre) within a larger section of text (framing genre), and for an independent text. It is meaningful for a small unit as well as a more comprehensive text complex (such as the Yahwistic work or the Deuteronomistic History).

C. RESULTS

I. Result of the Question of the Linguistic Shaping and the Determination of Genre

Presenting the results of these two component questions can proceed together because they concurrently investigate the revision of an existing linguistic pattern and the possibilities in a text. In addition, determining the genre more precisely continues the question of the linguistic shaping for the text level.

1) In light of a multitude of possibilities, clarifying the devices of the *linguistic shape* (by form and content) provides thoroughly important clues for the special (!) statement profile for this (!) text in whole and in part. It also provides indicators of the desired material meaning (compare examples above in A II and B VI).

2) Analysis of the linguistic shaping and of the genre provides the relevant *division* of the linguistic utterance into its structural components and their material relationship to one another.

3) A text's uniformity, formally and according to genre, is an indicator of its *unity* and can signify its original *independence*. This independence is especially important for the area of oral transmission.

4) Further, the uniformity allows the pertinent *delimitation* over against the context, and thus leads to the identification of the units of meaning which are foundational for interpretation.

5) The *statement's purpose and perspective* can be perceived more precisely by recognizing the linguistic shaping, and then by recognizing the shaping of the genre.[130]

II. Results of the Question of the Genre History

The results of the question of genre history for the exegesis of a specific text lie in the following:

1. Only with such an investigation can one specify, with historical precision, the genre as it existed for the text's author.
2. The intention and purpose for the existing use of the genre can be sketched and profiled by distinguishing between that which existed in the genre history and ad hoc changes.
3. Such an investigation makes deductions possible regarding the historical classification of the individual text, or its different transmission stages.[131]

III. Results of the Question of the Life Setting

1. Those linguistic utterances utilizing a genre within the life setting from which that genre stems, provide *important clues* for understanding the text. It provides clues *regarding the text's intention and the limit* in respect to a specific audience and speaker, as well as in respect to the directions of specific social and cultural stages of development.
2. The meaning of form criticism for the *exploration of historical processes* in Ancient Israel rests on the relationship between genre and life setting. The genre allows a deduction concerning historical and communal relationships. Genre history reflects changes in these relationships. However, it is not methodologically permissible to convey genre history directly onto the historical level of progress. Genres can still continue to exist in a kind of inactive state long after the disappearance of their life setting.[132]

---

130 It is pertinent to differentiate between the *function* of the genre for a linguistic utterance and the author's *intention* when fashioning that utterance. However, "the results of genre criticism" may not just "provide important clues for the intention of a speaker or the author of a written piece." Rather, determining the genre (or relatedly, its concrete usage in a given text) and perceiving its author's intention stand in an *indissoluble* interrelationship. Determining the intention of a linguistic utterance without deductions and orientation from form critical conclusions (or against these conclusions) cannot be performed in a manner which is methodologically verifiable. It must therefore remain out of consideration. See H.W. Hoffmann, *ZAW* 82 (1970): 345f; and H.W. Hoffmann in Fohrer, *Exegese*, p. 157–160, where, on p. 160, the above-cited quote appears (emphasis ours).

131 Compare above, B III 3 (p. 108).

132 Compare Koch, *The Growth of Biblical Tradition*, p. 34–36.

D. LITERATURE

I. INTRODUCTION, FOUNDATION, AND OVERVIEW

J. Barton. "Form Criticism." ABD, Vol. 2, p. 838–841.

K.-H. Bernhardt. Die gattungsgeschichtliche Forschung am Alten Testament als exegetische Methode. Aufsätze und Vorträge zur Theologie und Religionswissenschaft. H. 8. Berlin, 1959.

G. Fohrer. Exegese. § 6 (G. Wanke) und § 7 (L. Markert).

H. Gunkel. Die Grundprobleme der israelitischen Literaturgeschichte. In: Gunkel. Reden und Aufsätze. Göttingen, 1913. p. 29–38.

_____. Die israelitische Literatur. Leipzig, 1925 (Darmstadt, 1963).

A. Jolles. Einfache Formen. Halle, 1930 (Tübingen, ⁴1968).

O. Kaiser. Exegetical Method. p. 28–43.

K. Koch. The Growth of Biblical Tradition. p. 3–38.

G. Lohfink. The Bible: *Now* I Get It!: A Form Criticism Handbook. New York, 1979.

F. Stolz. Das Alte Testament. Studienbücher Theologie. Altes Testament. Gütersloh, 1974. p. 43–93.

G.M. Tucker. Form Criticism of the Old Testament. Guides to Biblical Scholarship. Old Testament Series. J.C. Rylaarsdam, ed. Philadelphia, 1971.

II. EXPANSION AND CRITICAL ALTERNATIVES

D. Greenwood. Rhetorical Criticism and Formgeschichte: Some Methodological Considerations. JBL 89 (1970): 418–426.

J. Muilenburg. Form Criticism and Beyond. JBL 88 (1969): 1–18. Also in: P.R. House, ed. Beyond Form Criticism: Essays in Old Testament Literary Criticism. Winona Lake, 1992. p. 49–69.

J.H. Hayes, ed. Old Testament Form Criticism. San Antonio, 1974.

W. Richter. Exegese. p. 72–152.

H. Schweizer. Form und Inhalt. BN 3 (1977): 35–47.

_____. Biblische Texte verstehen. p. 40ff.52ff.

M. Weiss. Die Methode der »Total-Interpretation«. VT.S 22 (1972): 88–112.

Compare also the following categories.

For *individual genres*, compare the summaries of:

O. Eißfeldt. The Old Testament: An Introduction. §§ 2–16: p. 9–127 comprehensively (also the supplements, p. 722–739).

G. Fohrer. Introduction to the Old Testament. §§ 7–14, 38–41, 47, 53: 51–100, 256–278, 311–317, 347–358 (also the supplements, 518–519, 524, 526–527).

O. Kaiser. Introduction to the Old Testament. Oxford, 1984. §§ 5, 6, 25, 28, 29, 34.

K. Koch. Formgeschichte. p. 271–275 (Bibliography not in English edition).

A. Ohler. Studying the Old Testament from Tradition to Canon. Edinburgh, 1985.

W.H. Schmidt. Old Testament Introduction. §§ 5, 9, 13, 25, 27.

J. Schreiner. Einführung. p. 194–231. (Forms and genres in the Old Testament)

See also: I. Lande, Formelhafte Wendungen der Umgangssprache im Alten Testament, Leiden 1949.

Dedicated to *Semantics:*
B. Kedar. Biblische Semantik. Eine Einführung. Stuttgart, 1981.

Dedicated to *Stilistics:*
L. Alonso-Schökel. A Manual of Hebrew Poetics. Rome, 1988.
W. Bühlmann and K. Scherer. Stilfiguren der Bibel. Ein kleines Nachschlagewerk. Mit einem Anhang von O. Rickenbacher: Einige Beispiele stilstischer Analyse alttestamentlicher Texte. Fribourg, 1973.
E. König. Stilistik, Rhetorik, Poetik in Bezug auf die biblische Literatur komparativisch dargestellt. Leipzig, 1900.
W.G.E. Watson. Classical Hebrew Poetry. JSOT.S 26. Sheffield, 1984.
Compare also the literature mentioned in § 2 D; § 3 D I (Hebrew Poetry).

On the Discussion of *Linguistics and Exegesis*[133]:
W. Dressler. Einführung in die Textlinguistik. Tübingen, 1972.
E. Gülich and W. Raible. Linguistische Textmodelle. Munich, 1977.
X. Léon-Dufour. Exegese im Methodenkonflikt. Munich, 1973 (French, 1971).
K. Koch. Formgeschichte. p. 289–342 (not in English translation).
_____. Reichen die formgeschichtlichen Methoden für die Gegenwartsaufgaben der Bibelwissenschaft zu? ThLZ 98 (1973): col. 801–814.
K. Koch and others. Amos. Untersucht mit den Methoden einer strukturalen Formgeschichte. 3 parts. AOAT 30. Kevelaer—Neukirchen-Vluyn, 1976. Especially part 1, p. 1–89.
W. Richter. Exegese, especially p. 21ff, 27ff.

For the *Current State of the Discussion:*
R.C. Culley. Exploring New Directions. In: The Hebrew Bible and Its Modern Interpreters. Chico, CA, 1985. p. 167–200.
R. Knierim. Criticism of Literary Features. In The Hebrew Bible and Its Modern Interpreters. Chico, CA, 1985. p. 123–165.
H.-P. Müller. "Formgeschichte/Formenkritik, I. Altes Testament." TRE XI (1983): 271–285.
H.D. Preuß. Linguistik—Literaturwissenschaft—Altes Testament. (See above, footnote 9).
See §1CV.

III. EXEMPLARY EXECUTION

J. Begrich. Die priesterliche Tora. In: Werden und Wesen des Alten Testaments. BZAW 66. p. 63–88. Berlin, 1936. Also in: Begrich. Gesammelte Studien zum Alten Testament. ThB 21. Munich, 1964. p. 232–260.
M.J. Buss. Form Criticism. In To Each Its Own Meaning: An Introduction to Biblical Criticisms and Their Application. Louisville, 1993. p. 69–85.

---

[133] An evaluative summary of W. Richter's method is found in the 8th–11th German edition of this workbook, p. 74–76.

F. Crüsemann. Studien zur Formgeschichte von Hymnus und Danklied in Israel. WMANT 32. Neukirchen-Vluyn 1969.

W. Groß. Lying Prophet and Disobedient Man of God in 1 King 13: Role Analysis. Semeia 15 (1979): 97–135.

The volumes of the commentary series: The Forms of the Old Testament Literature, which have appeared since 1981. R. Knierim und G. Tucker, eds. Grand Rapids.

IV. HISTORY OF RESEARCH

J. Barton. "Form Criticism." ABD, Vol. 2. p. 838–841.

H.F. Hahn. Old Testament in Modern Research. Chapter 4: Form Criticism and the Old Testament, p. 119–156. Philadelphia, 1954.

W. Klatt. Hermann Gunkel. Zu seiner Theologie der Religionswissenschaft und zur Entstehung der formgeschichtlichen Methode. FRLANT 100. Göttingen, 1969.

H.-J. Kraus. Geschichte der historisch-kritischen Erforschung des Alten Testaments. Neukirchen-Vluyn, 3 1982 (see the index under »Formgeschichte«, »Gattung«, »Gattungsforschung«).

§8 Tradition Historical Approach

A. THE TASK

I. Starting Point

The avenues in §§4–6 have already investigated a text's *pre-text*. This investigation asked about the previous stages of the text under investigation, in the sense of fixed textual components from which the text was formed over time until it reached its final form. Thus in typical pattern an oral transmission piece served as pre-text for the first written version. Written text versions, together with their literary contexts, then served as pre-texts for additions and redactional expansions in the text. Form criticism and tradition history also treat phenomena which are presupposed in the text and to which the text refers. However, form criticism and tradition history do not inquire along the lines of §§4–6 which sought phenomena which had been integrated into a text in the course of its transmission and, relatedly, could be isolated analytically as fixed textual components.

Instead, form criticism and tradition history have another starting point regarding a text's presuppositions. They share a common underlying insight, namely that the statements of Old Testament texts are not solely the expression of an isolated author. Rather, even when they are first constituted at the beginning of their development, statements were formed under influences and with shaping devices which provided the author the prerequisites of possible linguistic utterances. From §7, the treatment concentrates upon the *pre-text of the "world"* in which an author and the author's addressees live. It is a linguistic (§7), intellectual (§8), and concretely historical (§9) world in which a formulation and its original understanding were taken as self-evident. One could speak of the *aura of unrealized resonance in the formulation* about which the exegete must later inquire and determine if he/she wants to participate in the original understanding of a text.

As we saw in §7, form criticism treats the *linguistic* pattern and possibilities presumed in the linguistic realm and the socio-cultural world. Form criticism thus investigated *how* a statement is *shaped linguistically,* and what may be gleaned from that knowledge which impacts the perception of the statement's reference and purpose. In other words, one asks about the presupposed linguistic world, its concrete matrix, and how this statement transcends that linguistic world.

Tradition history proceeds from the perspective that an author lives concurrently in an *intellectual* world of *facts* which are presupposed and fixed. Tradition history asks *the degree to which* the *contents* of the author's statements are *determined* by pre-existing elements from the author's intellectual world, the degree to which the statements can only be understood from their background, or the degree to which the author has deviated from that intellectual world.

The assertion that one must take account of the influence of facts from the existing intellectual world when trying to comprehend the formulation and the original understanding of Old Testament texts is not simply a postulate. An overview of the assertions of the Old Testament itself forces one to this conclusion. It is shown by certain *concurrences* scattered across the Old Testament or which are characteristically bundled together. These concurrences *do not stem from transmission historical or literary dependency of texts.* There one again encounters the same *thought structures* (such as the correspondence between deed and condition), the same *fixed images* (such as the comparison of human life with grass), the same *fixed themes* (such as Jerusalem as a city which the waters of chaos and the nations of chaos cannot conquer), and the same *thematic ensembles.* Last but not least, one encounters the same *word ensembles* which appear to belong to a fixed technical language. These ensembles were formed in particular institutions and scholastic circles such as wisdom, cult poetry, priesthood, legal concerns, the royal court, and over time, also prophetic tradents. These manifestations always appear in formulations or they direct those formulations and may be labeled by the summary term *"fixed contents."* It is chosen because, in part, these manifestations lie behind the formulations (thought pattern, religious convictions). Also this term was chosen because, in part, the manifestations are not fixed in formulations (knowledge, material), and because, in part, they appear in varying formulations even though with similar words (compare the varying formulations in assertions concerning the mastery over the primordial sea). These manifestations are thus primarily encountered in fixed words, in vocabularies, and formulated structures[134] in the tradition arena of institutional language (scholastic and specialty). Tradition history treats these influences which offer more precise meaning to the formulation of an Old Testament text and to the original understandability of that formulation.

---

134 Here in §8, genre is no longer considered among the consistent linguistic elements. Existing, fixed contents were not just transmitted in connection to a single genre. Rather, these contents could enter very different genres. A relatively strong association between genre and existing, fixed contents only appears when the association appears with the genre as the topic of that genre. Tradition history concerns intellectual influences on the formulation which can be shown in the text even without genre influence.

Existing, fixed contents from a specific intellectual world influence the assertions of an author living in that world. This influence, investigated by the tradition historical approach, is not just an ancient phenomenon. Today, for example, two commentators might look back over the economic development of Western Europe in the last decades. If one commentator speaks of "market fluctuations" while the other speaks of the "capitalistic world rocked by crises," the difference is not explained by reference to individual, spontaneously different impressions. Rather, the difference can only be explained by reliance upon the very different, effectively fixed, intellectual world of each of the commentators. One example of the constitutive affiliation of a single expression with an identifiable intellectual world, can be found in the expression "advertising costs." By itself, the expression has a clear meaning (costs associated with advertising). This meaning, however, does not by any means incorporate the intonation of the word which is certainly intended but not stated. This meaning is provided by the fact that the expression is a set, fixed term from the intellectual world of fiscal matters and can only be used and understood in dynamic relationship to this intellectual world. Another example: How should one understand the following sentence? "Saul's claim of founding a national state is elevated by the Davidic conception of a territorial state." What does "elevated" mean? Does it mean "raised," "dignified" or "exhilarated?" The meaning of the word may only be deduced by the one who knows the precise usage in the fixed, intellectual world of Hegel. Numerous other examples could be readily brought forth to illustrate the problem we also face with Old Testament texts.

II. Determination

For each developmental stage, the tradition historical approach inquires into the particular *impact on a text by its contents (intellectual-, theological-, or religio-historical)*. The tradition historical approach thereby determines the thought patterns, contents, concepts, or conceptual complexes which are presupposed by the text, incorporated into the text, or revised by the author. The tradition historical approach does not concentrate on a theme as it would appear today (such as the image of mother in the Old Testament). Rather, the tradition historical approach concentrates on very specific criteria found in the text. These criteria indicate the fixed contents of a statement and thereby indicate its involvement in an existing intellectual world. They register these contents from the perspective of the author, and thereby evoke how the addressee would have associated the contents.

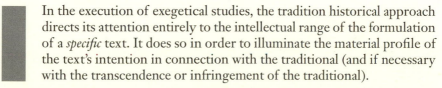

In the execution of exegetical studies, the tradition historical approach directs its attention entirely to the intellectual range of the formulation of a *specific* text. It does so in order to illuminate the material profile of the text's intention in connection with the traditional (and if necessary with the transcendence or infringement of the traditional).

Parallel to the inquiry into a specific text, yet transcending that task, the tradition historical approach also concentrates upon the *context itself* (both the *intellectual* context and the context in the *history of theology*). The tradition historical approach concentrates especially upon the history of various concepts and how they are brought together in the framework of a larger, contoured conception.[135] For the most part, these tradition historical investigations are available as specialized studies, as was the case with studies of genre history. One should consult these studies for tradition historical clarifications concerning findings in the text.

The tradition historical approach's inquiry into the text's traditional contents must be distinguished from the question of the history of the text itself (transmission history and redaction history) and from the linguistic shape of the text (form criticism). It must also be distinguished from the history of a text's reception which originates with the statements of a text.

III. Terminology

The term "tradition historical approach" is anything but uniformly understood in exegetical literature as a result of the ambiguity of the expression's first word. Frequently, "tradition" is understood as *traditio* (the process of transmission), and related to the transmission process of a text. It is then used synonymously with transmission history, or with transmission history and redaction history combined.[136] The nomenclature used by us, in agreement with other exegetes,[137] defines the tradition historical approach from *traditum* (that which has been transmitted; tradition[138] as transmitted contents). The nomenclature relates to the appearance of fixed contents in texts, and it relates to the history of these contents and concepts. Lacking an adequate term, the nomenclature only attempts to stabilize terminology in order to improve the possibility of closer agreement.

---

135 For examples of this type of investigation, see below under D III. Consult recent investigations such as, J. Day, *God's Conflict with the Dragon and the Sea* (Cambridge, 1985); C. Kloos, *YHWH's Combat with the Sea* (Amsterdam—Leiden, 1986); J. Jeremias, *Das Königtum Gottes in den Psalmen* (Göttingen, 1987).

136 Compare above, p. 64f. By contrast, R. Bach (in *Probleme biblischer Theologie*. Festschrift G. v. Rad, 1971, p. 19f, etc.), even uses the German equivalent of "transmission history" for that which we designate as "the tradition historical approach"! For a discussion of the confusing terminology, compare the synopsis of R. Knierim, "Criticism of Literary Features, Form, Tradition, and Redaction," in: D.A. Knight and G.M. Tucker, The Hebrew Bible and Its Modern Interpreters, p. 146ff.

137 Compare, for example, Fohrer, *Introduction*, p. 29f,31; Fohrer, *Exegese*, p. 27 (Hoffmann), p. 119 (Wanke); F. Stolz, *Das Alte Testament*, Studienbücher Theologie, 1974, p. 114f. Koch, *Was ist Formgeschichte*, p. 71,326ff (neither passage appears in the English edition), treats the tradition historical manifestations under the term "special linguistic phenomena which require semantic methods for their illumination." For further discussion of the problem, see below, footnote 163.

138 "Tradition" in this broad sense designates the entirety of the fixed contents into which the tradition historical approach inquires. This definition also forms the basis of our designation of the method as tradition historical. With this independent term, "tradition" is conventionally bound to a narrower meaning. "Tradition" is then synonymous with conceptual complex or the context of the concept.

B. COMMENTARY ON THE APPROACH AND METHOD

I. Differentiation from the Transmission Historical Approach

The terminological ambiguity of the terms "transmission history" and "tradition history" proceeds variously with the mixing of contents to the point that both aspects can be treated with the same term.[139] The tradition historical approach proceeds from its constitutive finding that fixed contents constantly reappear in various texts without implying literary dependence is provable or is even probable. Fixed contents reappear without implying that this appearance is connected with the adoption of a specific transmission piece. From this starting point, it follows that the tradition historical approach should not simply be identified with the transmission historical approach.[140] Those pre-existing elements, toward which the approach is directed, are by no means taken up into the text as a fixed transmission piece.[141]

II. Areas of Tradition Historical Inquiry

The fixed contents, about which the tradition historical approach inquires, are not all of the same type. One must therefore differentiate the following areas of tradition historical inquiry:

1. An Israelite author, as well as the author's addressees, lives in an intellectual world and is shaped by it. If one relates that intellectual world to the *entire* cultural realm of Ancient Israel (and of the Ancient Near East) as a whole, then, in tradition historical respects, one must consider a particular *world view together with its specific thought patterns*.[142] In this context, the problem of a particular "Hebrew thought" presents itself.[143]

139 Compare, for example, E. Zenger in: Schreiner, *Einführung*, p. 135f; W. Zimmerli, "Alttestamentliche Traditionsgeschichte und Theologie," in: *Probleme biblischer Theologie*. Festschrift G. v. Rad, 1971, p. 632–647; Rast, *Tradition and History* (see above, §5 D I), especially p. 59ff along with p. 1ff.

140 Compare the detailed methodological discussion by Steck, "Theological Streams of Tradition," in *Tradition and Theology in the Old Testament*, p. 183–191; and Steck, *Schöpfungsbericht*, p. 26ff, 272ff.

141 Examples: A tradition historical investigation of Jer 7:1–15 must ask about the concept of the imparted protection in the Jerusalem temple which is presupposed in 7:4,10. By contrast, transmission history asks about the previous stages of the current Deuteronomistic version of the text in Jer 7:1–15 itself. In Judg 4, the tradition historical question treats the concept of the exclusive activity of YHWH in the attainment of victory (4:14f), while the transmission historical approach inquires into the oral prehistory of the oldest literarily homogenous version of the text of Judges 4. In both cases, the tradition historical approach concerns the concepts which have naturally obtained linguistic shape in specific, concrete texts (and are still ascertainable only in these texts). However, these concepts have not entered *as* one of these concrete texts in Jer 7 or Judg 4.

142 Examples: the concept of a cause and effect relationship (cf. Koch, *Vergeltungsdogma*).

143 See especially, Koch, *Formgeschichte*, p. 333–336 (bibliography, but not available in the English translation).

2. Fixed contents of the kind presented below are also situated in a *particular* intellectual world inside Ancient Israel (and the ancient orient): in specific geographical realms, with specific social groups, at specific locations, institutions, and even with a specific circle of persons.

    Even here, one should primarily take characteristic thought patterns into consideration. These patterns reflect religious and theological *convictions* which determine the perception of reality and the experiential and intellectual processing of reality.[144]

3. Further, the reservoir of *knowledge and awareness* belongs to the fixed contents which stand at the author's disposal as a component of the author's education. This reservoir is known to the author from individual tradition pieces, and these might even occur to the author, but they are not integrated into the author's statement as a tradition piece.[145] Naturally, this reservoir includes more extensive *material* which the author knows and considers when formulating a text. As a rule, the vocabulary and the structure of formulation of these background contents are seldom fixed. For this reason, they are freely shaped when they are adopted into a text. This free shaping makes the contents more difficult to perceive methodologically.[146] The constancy of the formulation is greater with *fixed images and comparisons, idioms, and linguistic conventions.* These elements must also be considered here.

4. Within a particular intellectual world, *terms* can attract a special meaning which greatly surpasses the lexically perceived meaning.[147] Here, as already mentioned, *scholastic language and specialized language*, with their characteristic words and word associations which were shaped by Ancient Israel, play an important role. Above all, one should mention the royal court, the military, legal concerns, priesthood, temple poetry, wisdom, the Deuteronomic/Deuteronomistic school's language, and a developing prophetic language. At times, even a single characteristic term may desire to

---

144 Examples: the conviction that seeing God leads to death (Gen 32:31; Exod 33:20; Judg 6:23, etc.) or that the world is divided into an arena of the clean and the unclean (cf. Num 19:11–13; Hag 2:11–13).

145 See above, p. 82 + footnote 83, and examples from Gen 2:4b–3:24. Further, see Steck, *Schöpfungsbericht*, p. 28f, and passages concerning Gen 1:1–2:4a (e.g. the statements about the realities before the creation in Gen 1:2. *Schöpfungsbericht*, 228ff).

146 A store of knowledge, awareness, and materials is then methodologically observable if one inquires into the statement's contents. Then one can see whether those contents reflect training and education or whether they concern knowledge which the author gained from experience. This is especially significant with materials when literarily independent parallel texts can be found which suggest the employment of a broader circulation of common contents, in spite of a different formulation and usage.

147 Examples: *gʿr*, rebuke (cf. Gen 37:10; Jer 29:27 with the references in Ps 104:7 and Isa 17:13 which stand in the framework of a larger conceptual context); *maḥseh/maḥāseh*, "refuge" (cf. Ps 104:18; Job 24:8; with Ps 46:2; 61:4).

evoke associations in this intellectual world.[148] Therefore, analysis of a term can frequently not be limited to its semantic explanation in the context of its various occurrences which results from reference to lexicon and concordance. An explanation must be expanded by an "investigation of the theological, material context in which a term is anchored (vocabulary range!), as well as an investigation of the term's home and its origin".[149] Recent theological dictionaries provide important suggestions at this point.[150] As the ground breaking investigations of O. Keel have demonstrated, *ensembles of strands from ancient oriental pictorial symbols* sometimes offer absolutely essential aids for illuminating the intellectual world which shapes a text.

5. Finally, fixed contents also appear as *themes*[151] and *concepts*.[152] These themes and concepts, however, should be those which Ancient Israel itself formed, not those which were simply taken from the exegete's own world and attaches to texts. Unlike the images mentioned in "3," they are not exclusively material knowledge. Rather, these themes and concepts are compact processes of reflection which interpret reality. The vocabulary and the structure of formulation are also considerably more fixed. They differentiate themselves from the conceptually loaded terms treated under "4," which are themselves often components of themes and concepts. They differentiate themselves naturally by the scope of the thought patterns and convictions discussed in "1" and "2" by greater thematic inclusivity, stronger mental adaptation, and corresponding, fixed linguistic entities. Themes and concepts then are distinguished by a thematic point of crystallization, by a fixed subject of statements, and by the extent of their shaping in respect to vocabulary and structure of formulation. These characteristics appear even when the linguistic version continues to fluctuate within a certain frame. Concepts transcend themes by their theologically reflective elaboration, and by thoughtful differentiation. They also transcend themes by confirming a specific inclination of the state-

148 Examples: YHWH is *nôrā'* (Ps 47:3; 76:8, etc.) as an abbreviation of YHWH's victorious activity according to Jerusalem cultic theology; or *maḥăšābāh* as an indication of wisdom influence upon the formulation of the Yahwistic prologue to the flood story.

149 Steck, "Das Problem theologischer Strömungen," EvTh 28 (1968): 447, footnote 4.

150 See above, §2 M.

151 Examples: the theme of the exodus from Egypt: compare, for example, Deut 6:12; Judg 2: 12; Ps 136:10–15, which use the formulation of "bringing out" (*yāṣā'* in hif`il) of Israel, with Judg 6;13; Hos 12:14; Ps 81:11, etc., which use the formulation of "bringing up" (*ālāh* in hif`il) of Israel. Also compare Hos 12:10; Isa 10:24–26; 51:9f; 52:11f. The theme of the "day of YHWH" (cf. Amos 5:18–20; Isa 2:10+12–17; 13:2–22). The theme of "return" in prophecy (cf. Hos 5:4; 14:2ff; Amos 4:6–12; Jer 3:1–4:4; Isa 10:20–23).

152 Examples: the concept of the battle against the nations (cf. Pss 48:2–9; 76:2–7; Isa 17: 12–14); the Jerusalem concept of king (cf. Pss 2; 72); the Deuteronomistic prophetic statement (cf. 2 Kgs 17:13–17; Jer 7:25f; Neh 9:26,30).

ment and by *a* specific profile of linguistic wording.[153] The question of the concepts is an especially important area for tradition historical work when presupposed by a text, taken up into a text, or modified by a text. This question will be expressly treated below in section IV.

III. Recognizing Fixed Contents

How can one recognize whether, and in what fashion, fixed contents are presupposed, assimilated, or modified in a text? Here one must consider from the beginning that fixed contents do not manifest themselves in any text in a manner in which they are completely unveiled and explicated. It is much more characteristic for the phenomenon treated by the tradition historical approach that the intellectual and conceptual *background* of a text is taken into view. Thus the tradition historical approach treats the elements of a shaped, intellectual world which are not formulated in the text, but which, without doubt, were considered, intended, and understood along with the text. They are also inevitably indicated by explicit text elements. Thus, fixed contents stand in the text like the tip of an iceberg.

1) The best presuppositions for recognizing a text's fixed contents exist where (in a hermeneutical circle!) the intellectual world of Ancient Israel (and of the Ancient Near East), or the various expressions of an intellectual world, have already been preliminarily reconstructed and are known. These include arenas like wisdom and the Jerusalem cult theology.[154]

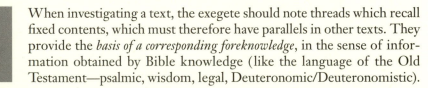

When investigating a text, the exegete should note threads which recall fixed contents, which must therefore have parallels in other texts. They provide the *basis of a corresponding foreknowledge*, in the sense of information obtained by Bible knowledge (like the language of the Old Testament—psalmic, wisdom, legal, Deuteronomic/Deuteronomistic).

Only if one can demonstrate these parallels in at least one other literarily independent text, can one speak at all about a *fixed* content.

One must differentiate sharply between these parallels and an author's *literary reference* to another Old Testament text which the author knows. Cri-

---

153 It is questionable whether one can reveal "the transmission interest of a specific tradent circle" only by the concepts or their contexts (as Huber believes, in Fohrer, *Exegese*, p. 111,115). The extensive transmission of the theme "the day of YHWH" (see Huber, p. 109) is not conceivable without the interest of prophetic circles in this theme. See section V below, "The Tradition Historical Approach as Historical Process."

154 Along with theological dictionaries for catchwords, compare the bibliographic references to monographs, especially those mentioned in Old Testament introductions and surveys. Further, text books and monographs on Old Testament theology and on the history of Israelite religion (see above §2 N) prove valuable. An orientational overview may be gleaned from my sketch, "Theological Streams of Tradition." See also the chart in Steck, *Arbeitsblätter*, 6 (see above, §2 F).

teria for the latter case are: (1) The agreement exists only in these two places. (2) The author also demonstrates knowledge and use of this writing in other places. (3) The reference is not an expression of a more broadly disseminated concept, but is a singular statement. If these literary references are directed toward references in the same book, then they could indicate the character of a redactional continuation.

2) *Concordance work* is the foundational means for tradition historical analysis in a text. This is true for both the investigation of a text in an exegetical exercise and for the expansive task of attaining a synthetic image of Israel's intellectual world and its history of theology. Likewise, concordance work also serves to evaluate the hypothetical discussions of this expansive task.

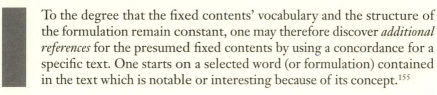

To the degree that the fixed contents' vocabulary and the structure of the formulation remain constant, one may therefore discover *additional references* for the presumed fixed contents by using a concordance for a specific text. One starts on a selected word (or formulation) contained in the text which is notable or interesting because of its concept.[155]

The more specialized question of the recognition and history of concepts will be treated in more detail subsequently, in section IV.

3) Finally, many texts already

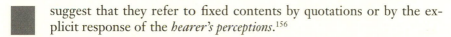

suggest that they refer to fixed contents by quotations or by the explicit response of the *hearer's perceptions*.[156]

IV. The Concept History Approach

The question of the concepts and the history of concepts is an especially important area of the tradition historical approach. It can be separated terminologically as the concept history approach and it can be seen as a special segment of the tradition historical question.

1. Recognizing a Concept

A *concept* is distinguished by fixed vocabulary, characteristic formulation structure, specific conceptual contour, and a typical train of thought (material logic). These concepts may be subdivided into various conceptual *elements* and again into individual conceptual

---

155 Example: By using the concordance in Isa 52:12, the notable formulation *(yṣ') bĕḥippāzôn*, "(to go forth) in a fearful hurry," can also be found in Exod 12:11 and Deut 16:3. This leads to the theme of the "exodus from Egypt" which stands in the background of Isa 52:11f.

156 Huber draws attention to this phenomenon, in Fohrer, *Exegese*, p. 113f. Further examples: Mic 3:9–12 (verse 11); Jer 7:4,10.

factors. One should observe that some situations require a certain breadth of variation in respect to the vocabulary and the consistency of formulation.[157] Several concepts form a *conceptual complex* or *conceptual context*, when present in a thematically centralized composite and a reflective relationship. If this conceptual complex perceives the experiential world from a self-enclosed perspective, then it can be qualified as a *conception*. For example, in the Old Testament, these conceptions are offered by Jerusalemite cult theology, Israelite wisdom, and also the intellectual framing entity of the Deuteronomistic view of history with all of its implications explicated elsewhere (e.g. Deuteronomy).

2. Perspectives on the Question

a. Does a text rely upon pre-existing concepts?

This approach fans out via various individual questions. The comparison with other texts using a concordance is unavoidable.

- Does the text indicate a *vocabulary* (e.g. a vocabulary range[158] or word ensembles) which is encountered in other literarily independent texts?[159]
- Is a fixed *structure of formulation* thereby maintained? (For example, one should consider active or passive verbs, transitive or intransitive verbs, a statement's characteristic contents as subject or object.)
- Do characteristic *conceptual contents* recur which on occasion fall into invariable elements and factors?
- Are these bound to one another in a stable construction, and do they agree in typical, equivalent material logic, or in a demonstrable *train of thought?*
- With the same structure of formulation, the same conceptual contents, and the same train of thought, are there also *variations of formulation* for the concept using related types of words?[160]

---

157 Example: The texts mentioned above in footnote 152 concerning the concept of the battle of nations, where the attacking powers are cited as *mĕlākîm* in Ps 48:5, as *'ăbîrê lēb/'anšê-ḥayil* in Ps 76:6; and as *'amîm/lĕ'ummîm* in Isa 17:12. Likewise, there are differences in the formulation of the activity of YHWH and in the subsequent reaction of the attackers. Kloos (see footnote 135), 75ff,191ff,198ff, provides an example of the breadth of this variation for a concept's formulation with respect to the formations for the chaos battle.

158 This phrase does not mean the linguistic scientific term of the semantic range (cf. Koch, *Formgeschichte*, p. 321f) or the word's setting (cf. Koch, *Formgeschichte*, p. 327f—neither of these references appears in the English translation). Rather, it means the stock of words and word associations which are typical for a concept.

159 Example: in the thematic unit of Mic 3:9–12, circulating around Zion/Jerusalem, the formulation that YHWH is in the midst (*bĕqereb*) of the inhabitants of Zion (3:11) points to the concept of the protective presence of YHWH on Zion (cf. the corresponding formulation and the context in Ps 46:6; Jer 14:9; and Zeph 3:15,17).

160 Thus the power opposing YHWH in the chaos battle can be called the primordial sea, the sea, water, billows, Leviathan, *rāhāb*, and *tannîn*. Also YHWH's mastery and victory appears in different, but related action verbs.

Also, for the most part concordance work already leads to these references because they maintain characteristic terms. The varied formulations raise questions: Do the variations stem from the breadth of the tradition itself? Do they reflect historical changes in the concept? Or should they be attributed to the author because they agree with the author's particularity.

█████   b. What is the larger association of the concept?

If a pre-existing concept is mediated, then one must also ask to which larger conceptual association (conceptual complex) it belongs, and whether it is actually a component of a conception.

- Do the comparisons of the parallels indicate that the consistent concept is also bound to a *constant conceptual context*?
- Do material relationships and overlaps demonstrate that this constant conceptual context represents a *materially self-enclosed conceptual association* or, on occasion, a conception?
- How does one determine the center, the *thematic crystallization point*, or the core of this conceptual association?
- Is this conceptual association distinguished by characteristic terminology (*principal terms*) which are concentrated in it?
- Is this conceptual association typically characterized by the extent of its contents, train of thought, thought structure, or the *special perspective* on the experiential world?

█████   c. Where is this conceptual association naturally situated?

The formation of concepts into conceptual associations presupposes substantial processes of reflection. These reflection processes are condensed into a more or less stereotypical terminology, but one which has its own characteristic stamp. For this reason, the setting of these conceptual associations can only be sought in *sites of explicit education*. As a rule, these are attached to *long-standing institutions*. One should mention the Jerusalem cult, the royal court, or wisdom education. These sites are also tied to characteristic functions which are represented by bearers of that function (e.g. wisdom teacher, royal offices, temple singers) and by characteristic genres.

█████   d. Which indices point to the presence of an intellectual world in the text?

The presence of an intellectual world to which a text is conceptually related is primarily recognizable from the *text's formulations* when compared with independent parallel formulations (cf. "a" and "b"). Even examples from the present time show that one must consider an intellectual world if *genres* are used which belong to this sculpted world (cf. "c"). With the genre "tax return," the intellectual world of fiscal matters is also present. Relatedly, characteristic terms from this world appear, like the example of "advertising costs" which we used above. These terms appear when treating various related genres (tax return, tax laws, tax guide, tax assessment). The same is true for the Old Testament. The entire intellectual world of Jerusalem cult theology stands behind every Jerusalemite cultic genre (hymns, genres concerning the plight of the king and the individual), even when that world is only formulated in parts. This intellectual world is visible in the topics of these genres by their characteristic formulations (YHWH as king, refuge, protection, deliverer from the waters of chaos, etc.).

However, the presence of a recognizable intellectual world can also be given by a minimal number of characteristic formulations when a *representative* of this intellectual world speaks or acts. In our modern example, the term "advertising costs" is also clearly defined, even without a supporting context or a characteristic genre, when it is used by a financial officer who represents competency in fiscal matters. Relatedly, in Ancient Israel, one would have understood the appearance of representatives of sculpted worlds (such as lawyers, wisdom teachers, temple singers, priests, etc.) as self-evident embodiments of the world they represent. When Isaiah or Jeremiah speaks to the priests, or when Micah speaks to the Jerusalemites, the respective intellectual world must be seen as the background of their speech. It must be seen as a contemporary world for the speaker and for the hearers, even when expressly formulated indices are not extensively present in the text.

Thus, the tradition historical approach essentially inquires into what a statement presumes, intends, and insinuates.

 e. Where necessary, how does a text transcend its given intellectual world?

The distinct deviations which an author adopts in existing concepts demonstrates that tradition is by no means always taken up homogeneously. These deviations include the author's use of concepts, and the author's departure from the train of thought, thought structure, and extent of the conceptual association. These transcendencies are *of great significance* for *determining the intention* of the text. They may not, however, lead to the erroneous conclusion that an author could be totally divorced from his/her own intellectual world and that only these new statements are characteristic of the author.

3. Dimension of the Concept History Approach

It has already become clear that concept historical work is completed in various degrees and dimensions. It can relate to an *individual conception*, along with its pertinent conceptual complex. It can also relate to the stock of traditional concepts in a *specific text*. Finally, concept historical work can relate synthetically to the progression of *theological streams* and the concepts characteristic for those streams.

As already noted, comprehensive inquiries into the concepts, conceptual complexes, and theological streams which transcend the specific text must remain specialized treatments. As a rule, the exegesis of a specific text can only investigate the assimilation of a concept in that specific text. Nevertheless, the methodological framework of the entire approach is presented below in abbreviated fashion:

a. Investigating Individual Concepts

Investigating the history of individual concepts and their respective conceptual complex is fundamental. This investigation transcends the specific text. One may speak of a *concept's history* when the same concept is found in literary utterances within the biblical realm in multiple instances from different time periods, but when no immediate literary dependency is present. However, dynamic, historical transmission must be taken into account as the means of mediation (tradent, location).[161] During this transmission, individual concepts, or individual parts of a conceptual complex, can change completely within the framework of their homogenous world (e.g. the notion of chaos within Jerusalemite cult theology as a dragon or as "sea"). Even the language of the tradition is not stereotypical, uniform repetition. Rather, it is the expression of a living, intellectual process.

b. Investigating a Specific Text

The concept historical question can be directed meaningfully toward a specific text under the following condition: It must be based upon the background of investigations which transcend the specific text, and then it must evaluate the material these investigations provide. Their purpose is the more precise ordering of the fixed concepts and the conceptual associations (traditions) appearing in the text, whether explicit or implicit, and their deviations.

c. Theological Streams

The synthesis of concept historical work exists by illuminating the theological streams and the intellectual realms of biblical times. This synthesis is comparable to research into the history of theology. These intellectual realms are generally characterized by a fixed conceptual complex which crystallizes the guiding conception of other theological statements and genres. Also these realms may connect other conceptual complexes characteristically. The resulting entity can be called the *store of concepts*, and the realm of their transmission can be called the *arena of tradition*. Even if the research into the illumination of these tradition arenas and theological streams stands in the beginning stages, it still contributes a great deal. It shows that the various theological streams are not only related to special carrier groups, but that they are also related to specific geographical realms in characteristic fashion (Northern Kingdom: covenant, people of God; the city of Jerusalem: cosmic conceptions; Judean countryside).[162]

V. The Tradition Historical Approach as Historical Process

Tradition historical work does not inquire into characteristically shaped thoughts and their history by an abstraction of historio-social conditions.

---

161 Example: The history of the Deuteronomistic statement about prophets, or relatedly, the entire Deuteronomistic view of history (for both, see Steck, *Israel und das gewaltsame Geschick der Propheten*, especially p. 79f, 193–195, 278f, and 184–189, 312f).

162 Compare my discussion above in footnote 154.

Thus, it does not present a process concerning the development of ideas divorced from the course of history. More precisely, it provides the disclosure of those processes which enable the real historical *mediation* of fixed contents.[163] The tradition historical approach thus asks the following:

> Who are those responsible for transmitting these thoughts?
> What interest do they have in these thoughts?
> What is the historical setting of the carriers?
> What experiential aspects of the world are characteristic for them?

The criterion of the real historical mediation generally protects against too hastily recovering conditions between the texts of Ancient Israel and the history of religion. The question of the influence of the *history of religion* on Ancient Israel's texts (essentially influence from the Ancient Near Eastern environment) is an important part of tradition historical work. However, this work must be performed strictly according to the methodological viewpoints which are valid for this question.

VI. The Tradition Historical Approach and the History of Motifs

The term "history of motifs" appears in Old Testament research with "the tradition historical approach," either used in association or synonymously with it.[164] The history of motifs strives for the history of the smallest thematic building block in the text. One should consider the following to understand the validity and value of investigations of the history of motifs.

1) The history of motifs is not recommended as an *independent method*. It always runs the danger of correlating adopted themes with diverse elements and with historically unrelated elements. In addition, it tends to transcend the constitutive context by inappropriately isolating motifs.[165] As tradition his-

---

[163] As already addressed above, p. 130f, this statement is especially true in view of concepts and conceptual complexes. The perspectives on the concept historical analysis mentioned there naturally presuppose conditions in the historical realm. It must be possible that the intellectual contents and thought movements were transmitted *in that type of fixed and consistent* form. One must consider, from a broader perspective, whether the socio-cultural conditions presumed by the concept historical phenomena were first present in the framework of a courtly/stately culture which divides labor. One must also consider whether sites arose in which the contents and language of concepts were consistently shaped and transmitted. In prior times, the store of these fashioned concepts would have been considerably smaller, but one could especially imagine phrases from ritual proceedings and juridical entities.

[164] For example, compare Fohrer, *Exegese*, p. 27 (Hoffmann), p. 102ff (Huber), p. 199ff.

[165] This tendency is demonstrated by Huber, in Fohrer, *Exegese*, p. 106f, when he uses the designation of YHWH as rock (*ṣur*) in Ps 28:1; 31:3 as a motif. He then divorces the constitutive context of this conceptual element from Jerusalem cult theology (cf. Steck, *Friedensvorstellungen*, p. 37, footnote 87).

torical work demonstrates, these smallest of thematic building blocks very frequently represent fixed concepts or conceptual elements which stand in inseparable relationship to larger conceptual contexts. They are transmitted within this framework, and they receive characteristically formulated meaning and contour within this association. Work on the history of motifs fails at the unavoidable task of showing that the dynamic nature of a motif which appears in different places, is historically mediated. Also, it fails at the task of making that motif understandable. Recourse to consistent structures of consciousness is a designation of the problem, but not a solution.

2) The *material basis* of the history of motifs approach lies in the fact that specific conceptual elements can appear as such in new associations and contexts. However, this isolation of individual concepts must be raised as a problem. One must ask to what degree its genuine conceptual context should still be considered with the specific concept. From that point, the motif's expression is used for further manifestations, such as meaningful numbers or specifying narrative topics (e.g. selection of the man who is good for nothing as far as one can tell). Precisely in this last case, it is often difficult to distinguish between motifs of a genre and freely roaming motifs.[166]

VII. Steps of the Tradition Historical Investigation of a Text

Confirmation of the Approach:

The tradition historical approach puts forward that which is *presumed by a text* based upon the text's intellectual surroundings. The tradition historical approach proceeds to the degree that the presupposed material is not a preliterary or literary developmental stage of the text itself (§§4–6), or to the degree that literary reference or genre influence (§7) does not exist. Rather, the tradition historical approach is directed toward *elements of the intellectual world* in which the author, and listener, of each developmental stage of the text move self-evidently. These elements represent that which is linguistically indicated but not expressly formulated. It represents that which is thought, intended, or necessarily associated along with these elements. The manner in which an author uses these elements (whether used consistently or in topically deviated fashion) is fundamental to a relevant historical understanding of the text's formulation.

However, the *indicators* of these elements from the intellectual world appear in a text's linguistic shape in various degrees and directness. These indicators must be demonstrated by multiple, literarily independent, occurrences in the Old Testament (or the Ancient Near East).

This recognition has implications for the execution of the specific steps. Simplified for practical reasons, the following stand in the foreground:

---

166 Cf. Koch, *The Growth of Biblical Tradition*, p. 56f.

Guiding Questions:

1. Thought Patterns

> Does the intended logic of a sentence, paragraph, or text demonstrate that a thought pattern which is not expressly formulated shapes the statement?

For example: A consequence results from every deed. Deed and effect stand in (precise) relationship to one another. Especially for the beginner, the necessary means of help is found in the secondary literature.

2. Fundamental Convictions

> Do the text's words demonstrate specific religious, theological convictions in association with the logic of the immediate context? Do these fundamental convictions lie beneath the statement inexplicably?

For example: blood as the setting of life, seeing God is fatal, childlessness as shame. The necessary means of help is here theological dictionaries under the catchwords and their synonyms.

> All further steps must be executed with *concordance work and theological dictionaries for the Old Testament* because they are concerned with fixed linguistic worlds in the formulation of the text. The starting point is always the existing formulation in the text itself. Along with the formulations in the context of the text, the formulation points to specific (!), particular tradition backgrounds about which one should inquire. By no means should the tradition historical approach project the entire range of meaning for the words into the formulation at hand!

3. Images, Phrases, etc.

> Are fixed images, comparisons, phrases, formulas, linguistic and conventions adopted in the formulation? From which arena of use do they stem? What do they signify? What do they intend?

4. Pregnant Meaning for Individual Words

> Do individual words or word associations in the text have a pregnant meaning which more precisely narrows the lexical breadth of meaning in regard to the material context, speaker, listener, or life situation to which the text relates?

5. Word Ensembles as Reference to Traditional Concepts and Conceptual Contexts

> What does an investigation of *parallel examples* provide for the word ensembles in the sentence, paragraph, and the text? If these only appear in formulations of the same author or if they can be established as *literary references* on the author's part, then further tradition influence on this formulation cannot be established directly.

In other cases, the parallel should be investigated more precisely in the sense of the questions in IV 2, because they provide reason to believe that one encounters elements of *traditional* concepts, conceptual contexts, and even conceptions. The contents, scope, and logic of these elements resonates even though not expressly stated. Even individual characteristic terms can be intended, and have impact, as associations of a more comprehensive intellectual creation. Here a series of subsidiary questions present themselves:

a. Origin of the word ensemble:
   From whence does this word ensemble derive? In which traditional text arena of the Old Testament (or ancient oriental culture and religious history) does the concordance show examples which are literarily independent, unchanged, and fully accumulated? Is one pointed to fixed linguistic fields of Ancient Israel (court, priesthood, legal entities, cult poetry, wisdom, Deuteronomic/Deuteronomistic tradition, prophetic language)? Already the articles in theological dictionaries are sometimes arranged accordingly.

b. Shape of the concept in the tradition
   How does the concept noted by the word ensemble appear in the tradition? Does the parallel statement offer necessary expansions which resonate in the text under investigation? Is one directed to a larger conceptual context which stands behind the text formulation under investigation? How does this conceptual context appear? To what does it belong? What does it accomplish? What is the setting of the concept noted in the text?

c. Content and intention of the concept
   What does this concept intend to signify in its traditional framework? What does it presuppose by way of experience, thought, and the history of religion? What view of the experiential world does it release? What does it exclude? What logic, train of thought, and insight does it intend?

d. Concept history
   What can one say about historical changes inside the intellectual world?

The means of help for answering the subsidiary questions of "a"–"d" may be gained from the literature references in footnote 154.

6. The Use of the Traditional in the Text under Investigation
   With these findings of traditional influences upon the text under investigation, one must finally return to this text *itself* and *its* use of the traditional.

a. With thought patterns, basic convictions, images, phrases, etc.:
   In light of positive findings for steps "1"–"3," one should now
   ask what the tradition background, now more clearly understood, accomplishes for the content, perspective, and intention
   of the formulation *at hand*. What should one incorporate for
   the historical understanding of the statement because it was
   manifestly associated and bound to that formulation by the
   author and the addressee? One should also expressly inquire
   whether the author's own accents are added to the existing formulation by adapting the tradition by means of linguistically or
   materially shaping the statement, or even by using an ingenious
   language and conceptualization. What should these accents indicate? Agreements with the author's profile in other places and
   differences in the language and the flow of thoughts stemming
   from the tradition can provide clues for the function of its formulation.

b. With the influence of fixed linguistic fields:
   This approach is more important when one receives positive
   findings for steps "4" and "5" because they point to the influence of fixed linguistic fields. In this case, the entire text of a
   developmental stage should be compared with the mediated,
   traditional linguistic field, or even with various, influential linguistic fields. As a result, various possibilities are conceivable
   and should be probed:

α. The text conforming to tradition
   The author's expression coincides entirely with tradition. This conformity is shown by the identical, corresponding, or related formulations,
   as well as by agreements in the extent of the content and the train of
   thought. The conformity is present even when the author only silently
   presupposes individual conceptual references that are essential for the
   material logic, or when the author addresses these references only
   in abbreviated fashion. A tradition historical comparison of Ps 48 with
   Ps 46 or of Prov 7 with Prov 9 would lead to this result. The author of
   the text at hand is thus seen simultaneously as a representative of the
   tradition, such as the Jerusalemite cult theology or theological wisdom.
   Confirmation is also provided when the statement's selected genre
   comes from the same arena according to §7.
   In this case, the tradition represents the intellectual framework during
   a specific historical phase. It also represents the background of the text
   at hand. For the author and hearer, the tradition establishes its plausibility. One should then primarily determine which detail and accent the
   author particularly emphasizes, by the express formulation, from that
   which is possible for the tradition.

β. The text continuing tradition

The author's expression operates within the framework of tradition by drawing upon that tradition. Perhaps the tradition historical investigation indicates that the author even belongs to the same, or closely related tradition arena (wisdom/temple). However, the author may continue that tradition independently (for example, the Job dialogues or Qohelet continues the wisdom tradition). Or the author may limit the tradition reflexively by another tradition arena (for example, post-exilic prayers limited by wisdom influence in the Psalms). Here one must distinguish that which is guided by tradition from that which transcends the tradition in concrete texts.

γ. The text changing tradition

The author uses tradition when formulating, but no longer simply emanates from this tradition arena. Rather, the author changes traditional concepts or conceptual contexts by deviating from accents or formulations, or by changing the train of thought even to the point of reversing that tradition. This case appears especially in the statements of prophetic transmission which take up legal, cultic, and wisdom tradition, but transform this tradition into a new prophetically topical statement. Here one must determine, as precisely as possible, why, on the one hand, traditional material is taken up in the service of new material statements. One must determine why traditional material is selected, thereby stimulating certain associations which, additionally, must be made audible to us as accompanying intellectual overtones. On the other hand, one must determine where the accents are rearranged, where they deviate, and where they are transfigured in comparison to the tradition. This determination must be made for the individual statement as well as for the entire text. For their part, even the transformations may draw from tradition, like prophetic tradition.

For example: The prophetic adaptation of the concept of the heavenly court assembly of YHWH. Why does the concept appear in 1 Kgs 22:19–22 and Isa 6 as an event, but scarcely appears in Isa 40:1–11, and does not appear in Isa 42:1–4? Why are the acting participants called spirit in 1 Kgs 22, seraphim in Isa 6, and voices in Isa 40?

The goal of this step when investigating an *specific text* is not to trace tradition historical ancestors as an end in itself. Rather, one seeks to understand the text in its peculiarity. Here one seeks to understand the text in the tradition historical approach in light of the tradition incorporated into the text and utilized by it. This orientation of the approach upon the specific text is not designed to pay homage to ideals of originality, but in order to make clear the special features and peculiarity of this text!

The tradition historical approach gradually makes possible a glance into the intellectual *processes* which lie at the root of this text's formulation if the texts provide the possibility of prominent data for insight into the profile and intention of the text!

All of this proves that the tradition historical approach provides the most important preliminary work for determining the contents and profile of the statements of the assigned text, as it will be undertaken in the interpretation (§10).

C. RESULTS

I. Comprehending the Text's Profile

A linguistic utterance can not be sufficiently understood by itself. It must be understood *in conjunction* with the historical situation in which it is made.[167] It must be understood in the framework of its socio-cultural conditions and realities.[168] Last but not least, the linguistic utterance must be observed from the background of *the theological stream and of the intellectual realm* in which it stands and operates. This ordering according to specific concepts, theological conceptions, and a fixed thought world is unavoidable if the profile of a text is to become clear. This ordering is unavoidable if one is to comprehend how to conceive a linguistic utterance, or from which fixed perspective one should perceive the contents. It is unavoidable if one is to comprehend the lines along which the linguistic utterance argues, and in which frame of thought it was understood by its hearers and readers. This ordering is also valid (and how!) in those places where traditional elements have been changed and where it can be determined where a linguistic utterance transcends its traditional roots into a specialized statement. The outermost tip of this *deviation* then appears if a text critically takes up a traditional concept and reverses it.[169] The understanding of this type of text is unalterably bound to the fact that its polemical point, and the critical delimitation which it accomplishes, are noted in the course of the tradition historical investigation.

II. Insight into Connections

Tradition historical work in the comprehensive sense attempts to illuminate the theological streams and the intellectual realms of the biblical time. Thus, it aims toward a *history of theology for Ancient Israel and early Judaism.*

---

[167] See below, §9.

[168] See above, §7 B V (p. 110ff) and §7 C III (p. 116).

[169] Example: Deviation of the concept of the battle of the nations in Isa 29:1–7 (in 29:1–5bα YHWH attacks *against* Jerusalem while leading the nations).

Where this research already has reached productive results in some areas, informative connections have been found between texts and text groups which had previously appeared unrelated. Or, these results have provided supporting arguments for the presupposition of these connections which had been presupposed for other reasons. On the one hand, this recognition of larger connections is advantageous to understanding the specific text. On the other hand, it is the starting point for acquiring the connection between the Old Testament and the New Testament, thereby preparing a biblical theology in a historically relevant manner.

D. LITERATURE

I. INTRODUCTION, FOUNDATION, AND OVERVIEW

G. Fohrer. Exegese, § 8 (F. Huber).

O.H. Steck. Israel und das gewaltsame Geschick der Propheten. WMANT 23. Neukirchen-Vluyn, 1967. p. 18f (additional literature), and 107, footnote 4.

_____. Theological Streams of Tradition, in: Tradition and Theology in the Old Testament. D.A. Knight, ed. Philadelphia: Fortress, 1977. p. 183–214, especially 183–191.)

II. EXPANSION AND CRITICAL ALTERNATIVES

G. Fohrer. Tradition und Interpretation im Alten Testament. ZAW 73 (1961): 1–30 (also in: Fohrer, Studien zur alttestamentlichen Theologie und Geschichte [1949–1966]. BZAW 115. Berlin, 1969. p. 54–83.

H. Gese. Essays on Biblical Theology. Minneapolis, 1981.

O. Keel. The Symbolism of the Biblical World: Ancient Near Eastern Iconography and the Book of Psalms. New York, 1985.

_____. Wirkmächtige Siegeszeichen im Alten Testament. OBO 5. Freiburg (Switzerland)—Göttingen, 1974.

D.A. Knight. Rediscovering the Traditions of Israel. SBL Dissertation Series 9. Missoula, 1973.

K. Koch. The Growth of Biblical Tradition, p. 70f; Formgeschichte. p. 326–342 (not in English translation).

H.P. Nasuti. Tradition History and the Psalms of Asaph. SBL Dissertation Series 88. Atlanta, 1988.

G. Pfeifer. Denkformenanlyse als exegetische Methode. ZAW 88 (1976): 56–71.

W. Richter. Exegese, p. 75f (footnote 11), 136f,153–155,178,182f (concerning »Motiv« and »Stoff«).

Tradition and Theology in the Old Testament. D.A. Knight, ed. Philadelphia 1977.

G. Wanke, Die Zionstheologie der Korachiten in ihrem traditionsgeschichtlichen Zusammenhang. BZAW 97. Berlin 1966. See especially p. 39f, 64ff, 109ff.

For literature on linguistic science and exegesis, see § 7 D II.

III. EXEMPLARY EXECUTION

M.E. Biddle. "The Figure of Lady Jerusalem: Identification, Deification, and Personification of Cities in the Ancient Near East." In: The Biblical Canon in Comparative Perspective. K.L. Younger, Jr., W.W. Hallo, B.F. Batto, eds. Lewiston, NY, 1991. p. 173–194.

K. Koch. Gibt es ein Vergeltungsdogma im Alten Testament. ZThK 52 (1955): 1–42. Also in: Um das Prinzip der Vergeltung in Religion und Recht des Alten Testaments, K. Koch, ed. p. 130–180. Darmstadt, 1972. (the question of a particular world view [cause and effect conncection]).

H.-M. Lutz. Jahwe, Jerusalem und die Völker. WMANT 27. Neukirchen-Vluyn, 1968. p. 47–51,155–177. (Tradition historical investigation of a specific text [Isa 17:12–14]).

G. v. Rad. Wisdom in Israel. Nashville, 1972.

W.H. Schmidt. Königtum Gottes in Ugarit und Israel. BZAW 80. Berlin, [2]1966. (Religio-historical investigation)

_____. The Faith of the Old Testament: A History. Philadelphia, 1983.

O.H. Steck. Israel und das gewaltsame Geschick der Propheten. (Tradition historical investigation of a concept and its association with other concepts [Deuteronomistic view of history]).

_____. Das Problem theologischer Strömungen in nachexilischer Zeit. EvTh 28 (1968): 445–458, especially 445–448.

_____. Friedensvorstellungen im alten Jerusalem. Psalmen-Jesaja-Deuterojesaja. ThSt(B) 111. Zürich, 1972. (Tradition historical investigation of a conception [Jerusalemite Cult theology]).

_____. Der Schöpfungsbericht der Priesterschrift. FRLANT 115. Göttingen, [2]1981. (Question of the knowledge and educational condition)

H.W. Wolff. Hoseas geistige Heimat. ThLZ 81 (1956): 83–94. Also in: Wolff, Gesammelte Studien zum Alten Testament. ThB 22. Munich, [2]1973. p. 232–250.

_____. Amos' geistige Heimat. WMANT 18. Neukirchen-Vluyn, 1964.

§9 | Determining the Historical Setting

A. THE TASK

Old Testament texts confront us today as a collection of the faith transmission of Ancient Israel. This collection belongs to the unity of holy scripture which becomes current again in each generation. In their origin, however, Old Testament texts were all rooted *in a particular historical situation*. They are promulgated in a specific time, in a specific geographical realm. They have authors of various social stations and various intellectual-theological shaping. They speak to specific addressees, each with their own particular experiential horizon and world view. They presuppose particular political and social realities, incisive social changes, and formative historical events. Understanding these texts is impossible without a historical view of the conditions and components which these texts include. The procedure of the historical setting therefore has the task of comprehending[170] the given text's roots in a specific historical setting, for every stage of its development.[171]

B. COMMENTARY ON THE APPROACH AND METHOD

I. Dating a Text

Dating a given text, or the layer in which it appears, is fundamental for the procedural step of the historical setting. Which observations allow one to determine the text's time of origin?

---

[170] More than with any other procedural step, exegetical work must draw upon available research results (above all in the areas of "Old Testament Introduction" and the "History of Israel") and the corresponding literature (see above, §2 G, J–L).

[171] This statement results from the fact that the historical setting is very closely associated with the literary critical, transmission historical, and redaction historical approaches. See above, footnotes 32, 69, and 79.

Several reference points deserve mention here:[172]

1. The presupposition, or mention, of contemporary events or events from the past.[173]
2. Social, constitutional, or cultural realities which mark historical boundaries.[174]
3. Dating a specific text[175] or the entire text complex to which it belongs.[176] (Of course, this must be critically examined.)
4. The presupposition or treatment of other, datable texts from the Old Testament.[177]
5. The classification of the history of a genre,[178] a concept, or a theological stream.[179]
6. The relative relationship to the other transmission or redactional layers from the same text complex.[180]

II. The Contemporary History and Social Environment of a Text

Once the given text has been more or less precisely dated, then one must more precisely determine the contemporary historical and the social realities in the environment of its origin.

---

[172] Compare also the references from Fohrer, *Exegese*, p. 147ff.

[173] Examples: Lamentations looks back on the destruction of Jerusalem in the 6th century B.C.E. (cf. 1:3f,7; 2:5ff; 4:20–22; 5:18, etc.), and stands relatively close to those events. Mic 7:8–20 presupposes, among other things, that the wall of Jerusalem lies in ruins (*terminus ad quem*: the reconstruction of the wall by Nehemiah). In addition, compare footnote 25 above on the book of Isaiah. Evaluating the corresponding reference points requires one to consider the phenomenon of *vaticinium ex eventu* differently.

[174] Examples: A text refers to the contemporary kingdom in the country (cf. Isa 8:21f). A text presupposes the domestication of the camel, iron fitted chariots, place names and their changes, designations of peoples and countries, etc.

[175] Examples: Isa 14:28–32; Ezek 20.

[176] Examples: the superscriptions of many prophetic books (e.g. Isa 1:1; Amos 1:1). Of course, these can only be evaluated for authentic words of the prophet.

[177] Examples: The books of Chronicles use Gen–Kings as a source. Isa 2:2–4 presupposes Deutero-Isaiah. Confusing tradition historical dependence with literary or transmission historical dependence can only lead to false conclusions at this point.

[178] Example: A saga style which is shorter (e.g. Gen 32:23–33) or more extensive (e.g. Gen 24). However, observe the limitation discussed above in §7 B III 3 (p. 108).

[179] Example: The position of Deut 30:1–10 inside the history of the Deuteronomistic model of history (for this, see O.H. Steck, *Israel und das gewaltsame Geschick der Propheten*, 1967, p. 140f, 185f).

[180] Example: The relative relationship of the various literary layers in Isa 10:5–27a to one another (10:5–15,16–19,20–23,24–26,27a). For discussion, see H. Barth, *Die Jesaja-Worte in der Josiazeit*, 1977, p. 17ff.

This determination occurs first in *cross section*: From which political situation in the Ancient Near Eastern realm does one proceed (e.g. the New Assyrian Kingdom as hegemony)? What special relationships exist in Israel (e.g. Judah is still independent while the Northern Kingdom has been dissolved into Assyrian provinces)? What were the momentous contemporary events? By which social orders, tensions, or upheavals was the socio-historical situation of Israel characterized at that time?[181]

This type of cross-sectional investigation very quickly requires *protracted sectioning* through political history and, as far as possible, through the social history of Ancient Israel and the Ancient Orient. The particular realities of a specific historical setting can only be understandable from the larger perspective of the previous and subsequent development.

Human *experiences* from this time should also be explored from a synthetic overview of the realities of the intellectual world of the text which were amassed in §8, and from the text's external world in §9. These experiences may result from this synthesis, from the correspondence of the text's historical world (events, social conditionings, tradition historical guidance, making oneself aware of this world, and mastering this world), and from the text itself. In conjunction with this synthesis, one should also ask which *problems* existed then which were unavoidably manifested by the contemporary experience.

III. Identifying the External Realities Mentioned in the Text

Within the framework of this procedural step, the *clarification of geographical and historical questions, as well as other realities,* ensues in the service of the historical view of the realities of origin and of a text's assertions. These realities were self-evident to author and addressee in their time, but must be re-identified today.

By realities, as the meaning of the word indicates, one means concrete, visually experienced elements and conditions: for example, a mountain, a people, wanderings of a people, buildings, clothes, animal and plant life, etc. Clarifying these realities, however, cannot disregard their *connection with specific inner process or religious manifestations of life*. Also, one must delve into other areas to the degree that they are contained in the term "realities" in its genuine meaning. The reality "cult stone" is perhaps associated with the practice of incubation.

---

181 Concerning the legitimate demand for an intensification of social history investigations, one must not overlook the degree to which we can generally reconstruct the social history of Ancient Israel and the Ancient Near East from the transmitted texts (and archaeological findings). The relatively small number, to this point, of socio-historical works does not simply indicate a blindness to the problem. See above §2 K,L for literature on the social history of Israel and the Ancient Near East. G. Theißen, "Die sozialgeschichtliche Auswertung religiöser Überlieferung, *Kairos* NF 17 (1975): 284–299, provides an important contribution to the methodological problem of socio-historical evaluation of religious transmission.

The reality "throne" is associated with certain religious concepts of power. Even here, one must again work with cross-sections and protracted sections.[182]

A special problem presents itself when the *presentation of historical processes* makes the author's own recent past or, especially, times from the more distant past, the subject of an assertion in the text, rather than when an author addresses undisputable realities which are known to all. These processes must also be identified in this procedural step. Determining what actually happened, compared with those presentations, is an unavoidable presupposition, which enables one to recognize which attitudinal perspective the text provides (e.g. selective accentuation in the processes of the succession of David in the Succession History) or even the deviating interpretation of events which the text provides (e.g. danger to Abraham in Gerar as the danger to a prophet, Gen 20). On occasion, one may even recognize interpretation which is based thoroughly on real historical experience from the interim period. In the framework of exegesis, one must naturally note the facilitating function of this historical identification. The goal of exegesis is to state how the author has interpreted these events. Determining what actually happened has an independent function in the framework of the discipline "history of Israel."

IV. Determining Author and Addressee

 Determining the *author* of a text aims less at identifying that person by name, which as a rule is seldom possible. Rather, it aims more toward situating the author in a specific religio-intellectual and social setting.

Old Testament literature is largely anonymous literature, and in addition, in those places where names are mentioned, one often deals with pseudepigraphic manifestations (for example in numerous psalmic superscriptions or in Proverbs). Even in those places where we do encounter the name of an author or an authorial group, the persons remain essentially in the dark (e.g. in the case of Amos, or even more with Micah, the Korahites, etc.). They retreat almost completely behind their statements. We are thus left with scattered, individual references in the text.[183] And we are left with form critical and tradition historical deductions, not only from the specific text but also from the literary layer as a whole to which it belongs.

 What can one recognize about the social position and function of the author based on the life setting of the individual units, or of the work as a whole,[184] and, as necessary, based on the style[185]? To which theological direction and stream does the author belong?[186]

---

182 Once again, compare specifically the reference in footnote 170.

183 Example: Isaiah. Cf. 7:3; 8:2f,16; 28:7b–22.

184 Compare for example the corresponding inquiry into Lev 1–7 and Deut 4:1–8 in Kaiser, *Exegetical Method*, p. 27–29.

185 Compare the references in Kaiser, *Exegetical Method*, p. 16–18.

186 Examples: the Deuteronomistic origin of a secondary literary layer in Amos (especially 2:4f) and in Jeremiah (e.g. 11:1–14; 19:2b–9; 44:2–6).

When determining the *addressee*, exegesis is also left with deductions from the text, except in a few exceptions in prophetic literature (e.g. 2 Kgs 1; Amos 7:10-17; Isa 7; Jer 28). Again, one must especially evaluate the results of the life setting.[187]

Recognizing the addressee provides essential clues for the particular problem, perspective, and purpose of a statement. If concrete reference points for identifying the addressee are lacking, then one can at least attempt to reconstruct imaginatively the experiential and expectational horizon of an addressee for the historical setting of the text.

V. Concerning Materialistic Historical Interpretation of Old Testament Texts

The employment of biblical text material has brought the problem of materialistic historical interpretation into the current topical discussion (for example, through the particular manner in which the text is processed and interpreted as currently seen in the works of Ernst Bloch and Stefan Heym).[188] Judgment about this interpretational starting point depends essentially upon its definition. If, by materialistic historical interpretation one means that the religious transmissions of Ancient Israel must be explained strictly *in the* socio-historical context of its origin, and if one means that the theological and social position of an author influences the tendency of the content of the author's statements, then historical critical exegesis of the Old Testament can thoroughly adopt this position. Indeed, historical criticism has always performed this task with various degrees of clarity and decisiveness.[189] However, one must decline materialistic historical interpretation if it wants to perceive Old Testament texts *from* their socio-historical setting as the fundamentally "defining moment(s) of final authority"[190] for perceiving the formation of thoughts and if it wants to determine the manner in which the interests and setting of human speech are bound to the ruling categories of explanation.[191]

187 Example: the participant in the sacrificial meal as one of the addressees in an individual song of thanksgiving (see above in footnote 123 and the literature mentioned there).

188 Cf. W. Dietrich, *Wort und Wahrheit*, Neukirchen-Vluyn, 1976, especially p. 27ff where, on p. 35f, the references to the works of Bloch and Heym appear.

189 Compare the questions concerning the life setting (above p. 110ff), the real historical mediation of texts and traditions (problem of the tradent, see above 133f), and the historical setting. Further, compare approaches analyzing tendencies such as A. Weiser, "Die Legitimation des Königs David," *VT* 16 (1966): 325–354, in light of the History of David's Ascendancy. Discussion of the agreement and difference between the David transmission and Heym's *The King David Report* (New York, 1973) is sadly lacking in Dietrich's remarks about Heym's novel (*Wort und Wahrheit*, p. 29).

190 This formulation from Friedrich Engels (quoted by Dietrich, *Wort und Wahrheit*, p. 29).

191 In this context, compare the attempts which are exegetically and hermeneutically problematic because of the primary theological intentions of reverse patronization. With the help of a

VI. Overview of the Approach to the Historical Setting

When determining a text's historical setting, one must clarify the following chief problems:

1. *Dating* the text in all its developmental stages leading up to the final form
2. The contemporary *historical environment* of these datings in cross-sectional and protracted form
3. The *realities* mentioned in the individual developmental stages of the text
4. Delimiting the *author* and *addressee* (in correlation with §§6,7,8) of the developmental stage of the text

Various fields from the world of the text's historical origin come into view according to the finding of the text formulation:

1. The historical environment of the text's origin in respect to national, political (foreign and domestic), and military processes
2. To the degree that one is able, ascertaining the historical shape of the historical influences (intellectual, religious, theological, pietistic) of the text (correlation with §§7,8)
3. Cultural backgrounds manifested in the text (every day world, morals, needs, clothing, nourishment, living quarters, livelihood, daily routine, etc.)
4. The socio-historical environment of text formulations, author and addressee (settlement history, social groups, classes, economic relationships, household, trade)
5. Geographical, climatic, botanical, zoological manifestations in the text
6. Relevant archaeological and epigraphic information for understanding the text (e.g. House types, temple lay-out, gates, cult utensils, settlement history, deductions concerning socio-historical elements)

See above, §2 I–M, for helps in clarifying details of the text in the sense of the historical setting.

---

method of materialistic exegesis they attempt to subjugate biblical texts to socio-revolutionary purposes. The freely undeniable social dimension of the biblical text is thereby caused damage if biblical water is simply conducted over ideological mills. Compare the bibliographic references above in §1 C V. M. Clévenot, *So kennen wir die Bibel nicht*, Munich, [2]1980. For method and examples, compare the considerations in W. Schottroff and W. Stegemann, eds., *God of the Lowly*, Part One: Old Testament. New York, 1984. Also Schottroff and Stegemann, *Traditionen der Befreiung*, vol 1.: *Methodische Zugänge*, Munich, 1980. Compare also R. Albertz, *A History of Israelite Religion*, Louisville, 1994; N.K. Gottwald, *The Hebrew Bible*, Philadelphia, 1985; *idem*, *The Hebrew Bible in Its Social World and in Ours*, Atlanta, 1994; W. Brueggemann, *A Social Reading of the Old Testament*, Minneapolis, 1994.

C. RESULTS

The historical setting places a text into the effective arena of historical powers, social powers and the formative experiences in which the text was fashioned, and therefore can only be appropriately interpreted historically. The historical perception of the text's author, addressee, and developmental realm is the key to understanding the particular contour of its statement, but also its limits. While critical exegesis connects the text back to its original historical setting, it thereby protects against too quickly extending the present into completely different historical situations. It shows the necessity of a hermeneutically grounded mediation in the present.

D. LITERATURE

G. Fohrer. Exegese, § 9C.
O. Kaiser. Exegetical Method, p. 35–36.
For additional literature, see § 2 I–M.

Part Three

Purpose

§10 Interpretation as Determination of the Text's Historical Meaning

A. THE TASK

The goal of all exegetical procedures, the historical exposition of the text, is accomplished and presented in a particular phase, that of interpretation, following the individual methodological procedures of the investigation.

The task of interpretation is to determine, in a scientifically documentable form, which *historical intention and meaning of the statement* should be noted in the text's concrete form *within the historical realm of origin* and in the various stadia of its Old Testament development. Interpretation as the determination of the text's historical meaning seeks to acquire and to present the extent to which the text's shape carries the meaning of the statement's contour in the text's genuine historical environment. The following are all perceived as factors of a dynamic articulation of meaning in the historical situation to which they belong: historical and social realities, intellectual predispositions, processed experience, effective impulses, the author's conceptual purpose, and the character of the addressee. They allow one to see the articulation of meaning in a concrete text and a historical life process.

The interpretation is directed toward the text in the historical course of its productive formation. For this reason, the interpretation is principally undertaken *separately for each of the text's ascertained stages of growth*.

As necessary, one should attach an *interpretation of the text's Old Testament development* as a *movement* of meaning, together with rationale, to the determination of historical meaning for each of the individual text stages. This interpretation is attached in order to envision exegetically the text's productive transmission inside the Old Testament.

Reflections can lead one to conclude how the *text's perceived historical meaning* should be presented *in light of our present time*.

The interpretation leads one to attempt an appropriate English translation of the text based on the exegesis.

A series of limitations is presupposed when determining this task:

1. "Interpretation" is used here in place of the procedural step which is often called "*individual exegesis*"[192] and /or "contextual exegesis." In order to avoid false associations, we will refrain from these common designations. Above all, one should be warned emphatically against the misunderstanding that this procedural step is solely interested in retrieving the explanation of undecided *details* in the text. Explaining details in the text is already unavoidable in large measure, if not completely, in the framework of the preceding methodological procedures. Geographical and historical explanations, as well as the explanation of other realities must result in the framework of the historical setting (§9).[193] Analysis of terms,[194] as well as other tradition historical and history of religions determinations based on individual statements, are achieved within the framework of tradition history (§8).[195]

2. The interpretation seeks to determine historically the particular contour of meaning for the text, the *material intention*, which the *text as text* had in its time. The goal is thus not simply to determine the *subjective intentions of the statement's author*, no matter how essential these are for the interpretation.[196] The interpretation should first be directed toward the authorial intentions which effectively shaped the text in light of specific addressees within a historical situation. The interpretation should trace the concrete shape of the text back to these intentions and thus perceive the text shape as a purposeful utterance of life. From that point, however, the interpretation must observe that the text mediates and actually attains a statement's content in a specific situation. This content proceeds beyond the originally intended historical horizon of the author (in contrast to that Isaiah's opinion, his announcements of judgment against Judah first come to fruition in 587 B.C.E.). Also, the content signifies more, or something other, than the author had intended (e.g. the evaluation of the ancient Elijah transmission first as an explanation of events in the subsequent period;

---

192 Compare the directions of Fohrer (*Exegese*, p. 151ff: Hoffmann) and Kaiser (*Exegetical Method*, p. 30ff) respectfully who apply a particular procedural action for this aspect.

193 See above, p. 143f.

194 See above, p. 126.

195 See above, p. 125ff.

196 Hoffmann, in Fohrer, *Exegese*, 152,155ff, exclusively addresses "comprehensive exegesis" concerning the authorial intention or, in the case of a text's development, the authorial intentions. Still, one should note the critique of this subjective term of intention in the theoretical discussion. Cf. Gadamer, *Truth and Method*, 243ff; Pannenberg, *Theology and the Philosophy of Science*, especially 208ff.

or the secondary association of the "servant songs" to Israel).[197] "*Meaning*" is thus a category of purpose for interpretation which transcends authorial intention. Meaning also takes into account that a text can mean more than the author intended with given statements, even for the hearers in the original setting, but especially in the subsequent time (e.g. Jonah 3f: The meaning of the announcement of judgment against Nineveh is different at the end than the original intention of the statement of YHWH and Jonah). In this manner, experiential constellations play an essential role, even though they are different than those which the author included. Alongside and beyond the determination of a statement's contents, interpretation seeks those experiential constellations which the author intended. It also attempts to understand a text's historical meaning beyond the subjective purpose of the author and beyond the subjective reception of the author's listener. If it does so, then it inquires (historically!) into the appropriateness and the illuminating power which a statement possesses objectively in light of the contemporary realities and the statement's experiential reality.

This inquiry is especially appropriate for the reference and for the protection of the *statements about God* regarding the pertinent experiential reality. Such determinations constitute the theological core of historical interpretation, and pertain to importance, evaluation, and critique.[198] Micah took a critical position over against the Jerusalemites' assertions about God (3:11f), which were considered orthodox in Jerusalemite cult tradition. With reference to the depth of the given experiential reality of the time, Micah's critical position appears just as effectively grounded as the manner in which the productive Isaiah transmission transcends the Isaiah words in light of the experiential reality of the Josianic period.[199] By the same token, however, one can recognize the one-sidedness of Qohelet's statements about God by these same interpretive perspectives.[200]

[197] One can only point to essential, scientifically theoretical considerations for the differentiation between "subjective intention" and "meaning." The text opens these considerations for (later) understanding. Cf. H.R. Jauß, *Literaturgeschichte als Provokation*, Suhrkamp edition 418, ²1970; W. Iser, *Die Appellstruktur der Texte. Unbestimmtheit als Wirkungsbedingung literarischer Prosa*, Konstanzer Universitätsreden 28, 1971. Compare in English: H.R. Jauß, *Towards an Aesthetic of Reception*, Minneapolis, 1982; W. Iser, *The Act of Reading: A Theory of Aesthetic Response*, New York, 1980; W. Pannenberg, *Theology and the Philosophy of Science*, London, 1976, especially, p. 195ff, 206ff.

[198] In addition to the broadly outlined scientific theory of Pannenberg, compare also Dietrich, *Wort und Wahrheit*, p. 21ff, whose critical evaluation of Old Testament texts by referring to the "center of the Old Testament" depends, however, upon whether one considers such an internal center of the Old Testament as given and determinable. We doubt this. Wanke, in Fohrer, *Exegese*, p. 161ff, seeks a path oriented toward linguistic science for a methodically determinable interpretation of the text's statements about God.

[199] Compare the investigation of Barth, mentioned above, p. 93.

[200] To undertake the possibility of interpretation, importance, evaluation, and critique by confronting the text's statement with the experiential reality of the time does not at all mean that the text's statement was itself merely the articulation of widely accessible experience. It does not mean that the text's statement simply came into existence *on the basis of* the processing of these experiences. Here one must rather maintain contingent factors. For example, these factors are presented in Old Testament prophecy as the declaration of the Word of YHWH (cf. Steck, *KuD* 15 [1969]: 281, footnote 1). Deutero–Isaiah's breakthrough of pronouncements of salvation ran

3. In so doing, one conceives exegetical interpretation as observing the articulation of the theological depth of meaning for the experiential reality in the historical realm. If so, then one takes up the text's claim in order to make meaning accessible. The more that one claims that the text does not want to be historically limited and transitory, but is instead extended to future times and actually includes our present time, then the less that the exegetical-historical discipline, as such, is capable of *articulating the demanding character of the text for today, relevantly and concretely*, and the less it is capable of legitimately expressing the relevance of the texts for the present. Here, responsible, demonstrable theological discourse is essentially directed to the work of the other theological disciplines.[201] By using one's imagination to take up the text as a component of the modern world,[202] however, the exegete can and should confront the historically processed theological interpretation of the text as a historiographical process for one's own life and our contemporary world. When considering this interpretation, references are characterized, differences ascertained, and possible impulses are specified for the contemporary experience of self, world, and God.

4. Interpretation seeks to perceive the material intention of the text as the intention of the author. From that intention interpretation seeks to deduce meaning from the experiential reality of the text's formative time. Determining the goal of interpretation should not mislead one to reduce its goal to the formulation of very general theological sentences (or even to the formulations of scope) which apparently consolidate the contents and direction of a text. The *meaning of the text* is given in a specific historical situation in the concrete structure of the text's statement. It thereby has *concrete historical and linguistic shape* from which it cannot be divorced exegetically. The interpretation should thus sketch the train of thought and the shape of the entire text's statements. It should also sketch all of the text's components as a concrete linguistic-intellectual process which illuminates meaning.

B. RELATIONSHIP TO THE METHODOLOGICAL APPROACHES

As already mentioned,[203] those *methodological steps* presented in §§3–9 are partial questions for historical understanding. They are directed toward par-

---

directly counter to contemporary experience. Prophetic judgment speeches do not simply diagnose the impending crisis of the time. Isaiah was not just a better politician. From these examples, it is quite clear, even with the power and appropriateness of statements, that one cannot contest that they remain partially in the experiential world of their time.

201 Compare Lehmann, *Der hermeneutische Horizont*; Pannenberg, *Theology and the Philosophy of Science*, p. 371ff; and §1A above. This does not exclude that the exegete must be exposed to the text's demanding character in the contemporary world even if the exegete cannot comprehensively process the text within the framework of historical-exegetical investigations. Recently, P. Stuhlmacher (*Schriftauslegung*; "Zum Thema: Biblische Theologie des Neuen Testaments," in K. Haacker, etc., *Biblische Theologie heute*, BThSt 1, 1977, p. 25–60, there p. 31f.) and F. Hahn ("Problems of Historical Criticism"; Die neutestamentliche Wissenschaft," in W. Lohff/ F. Hahn, eds., *Wissenschaftliche Theologie im Überblick*, 1974, 20–38, there pages 28ff; and "Exegese, Theologie und Kirche," ZThK 74 (1977): 25–37, correctly mention this point. Compare also Dietrich, *Wort und Wahrheit*, p. 11,21ff; Barth/Schramm, *Selbsterfahrung*, esp. p. 47f.,67ff,101ff.

202 See above, §1 B II 1 (p. 6f).

203 See above, §1 C I (p. 14).

ticular aspects of the text and are nothing more than *preparation for the inter-pretation*.[204] The procedures are in many respects interdependent and often continuous. Text criticism established the original Hebrew text. Literary criticism, transmission history, and redaction criticism illuminated the development of the text and/or they outlined the text's formative arenas with respect to influential contexts. Also, they made visible the process of the text's transmission to the point of its current version. Finally, form criticism, tradition history, and the historical setting have exposed the components of the text in the text's own world in various aspects, whether articulated or unexpressed. These components include historical, social, and linguistic elements, the history of ideas, and the history of theology. They also established those places where the text transcends the pre-existing material. If all of this has been accomplished, then the *interpretation* now addresses the text *in its entirety* in each of its productive formative arenas which are manifested in the text's mediated development. This interpretation now determines the text's meaning as text. It determines how meaning is expressed in each particular historical situation when adopting and transcending pre-existing elements.[205] For a demonstration, compare my exposition of Gen 2–3 (below, p. 202).

204 Establishing that the procedures of §§3–9 function as preparation for the interpretation (§10) has validity on the level of *theoretically defined comprehension* of exegetical work.

Another level is the *concrete flow of exegetical work*, as will be demonstrated in §11. By this flow, each person will have the experience that the various procedures of §§3–9, as we often stressed, not only simultaneously specify, limit, and even correct one another, but they also are already shaped by the goals of the interpretation. Correspondingly, these procedures already process questions about the determination of historical meaning. Therefore, it frequently appears unclear what remains to be done in the procedural act of the interpretation. However, this impression can be confronted by the specific determinations of the goal which we provide in §10. It is true that the methodological procedures are all directed toward the goal of the interpretation, but each of these only clarifies partial aspects and component questions. By contrast, the interpretation has its own approach which relates to the meaning and is therefore comprehensive. This comprehensiveness has consequences for the third level of exegetical work—the *written presentation* of the results of the work.

> One should note here that when writing the paper, not all of the results enter fully into the corresponding section when presenting an exegetical procedure, even though those results must be concretely processed in the framework of that procedure. Rather, one should proceed in such a way that one limits oneself strictly to clarifying the respective component question and the accompanying rationale. One should also reserve the specific interpretation materials, which were processed during that procedure, for the presentation of the determination of historical meaning.

205 One should energetically guard against the widely held misunderstanding that, with respect to the intention of the statements and the meaning of the text, only those text elements come into view in which the text's author says something "new" by transcending linguistic, form critical, and tradition historical pretexts. Those strands in which the author integrates these pretexts into a statement, whether verbalized or unexpressed, also belong to the statement's intention and meaning. The newness and particularity are provided from the combination of traditional elements with elements transcending tradition in the particular situation of the composition.

C. COMMENTARY ON THE EXECUTION

I. Interpreting the Text in Its Own Formative Arena

1. What Is the Subject of the Interpretation?

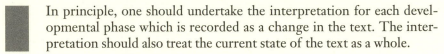

> In principle, one should undertake the interpretation for each developmental phase which is recorded as a change in the text. The interpretation should also treat the current state of the text as a whole.

The subject of the interpretation is thus the *entire state of the text for each of the steps of its development*, as analytically mediated by the literary critical and transmission historical approach. By no means is it limited to only those text elements which last entered the transmission process. Rather, it is more important to show how the new elements change the current text in its entirety, and how they shift its meaning.[206]

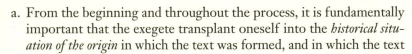

> In practice presenting the interpretation is of course concentrated, in breadth and fullness, on formative arenas which are materially profiled and extend across the text. The other stages are arranged and subordinated in the presentation. These stages can either be deduced only vaguely (e.g. a pre-Israelite site legend of Mamre in Gen 18) or they only slightly modify the meaning of the entire (!) text by smaller additions (e.g. Isa 7:8b). These stages can be coordinated and subordinated in such a way that specific interpretational elements already explicated need not be unnecessarily repeated for the more recent developmental stages. This decision can be made on the basis of findings already processed from the methodological determination of the text development.

2. Which Framing Conditions Comprise the Process of Interpretation?

> a. From the beginning and throughout the process, it is fundamentally important that the exegete transplant oneself into the *historical situation of the origin* in which the text was formed, and in which the text

---

However, simply repeating tradition in a historically changed situation can achieve that which is new and particular. Exegesis is the perception of meaning of a linguistically compressed, comprehensively historical life process. By no means can it be reduced to the elaboration of innovations in intellectual history!

206 Thus the interpretation of Gen 22 can by no means be limited to the corresponding transmission stage of the theologically interpretive elements of 22:1a,12b which entered the narrative last. These elements certainly want to show the existing narrative as a whole in a new light (a test of obedience before the divine promissory gift of the son). Likewise, one cannot interpret Gen 28:10ff only with respect to this growth the transmission stage which added the promises of 28:13–15. It is the growth of a fully received transmission which should now be seen anew in its entirety. Also, one should observe this aspect vigorously in prophetic transmission with its numerous later additions.

was directed to concrete addressees as an expression of meaning with specific intentions.

The exegete should thus construct a *historical perspective of the realities of the origin* as one already attempted to do imaginatively prior to the methodological procedures (§1B). Now, however, this perspective should be explained, corrected, and made more precise by scientific determinations from the investigation of the historical setting (§9). The author (or authorial circle), the circle of addressees, place, time, and concrete situation shall then be disclosed to the exegete according to the measure of scientific clarity. Drawing upon the results of the investigation of the intellectual preconditionings (form criticism and tradition history, §§7 and 8) clarifies how both author and addressee are directed by these traditional pre-existing elements. Drawing upon these results also clarifies how their historical world, with its demands, was then experienced. This historical perspective can thereby expose those necessities of the concrete experiential world by which the formation and declaration of the text wants to be encountered.

 b. Within this framework of historical perspective, the exegete now takes a *position with the statement of the text* itself. One attempts to sketch the statement as a living process of the expression of meaning in the historical realm in which it belongs under strict observance of its particular text form.

In distinction to the text itself and its original audience, the interpretation can of course *not* be limited to the *simple repetition of the text*. Rather, it reaches the point of expressly including the scientifically grounded modalities of meaning that were unquestionably self-evident with the origin of the text, but which were no longer self-evident to all who came later. In addition to the perspectival actualization of the realities of origin, this includes especially the endeavor of making more precise the form, contents, and intention of the text's expression of meaning. It thereby makes known the current historical understanding in the elaborated presentation of that which was connoted, intended, or even presupposed as self-evident in the given vocabulary of the text. It also enables materially proper understanding. One should particularly observe the historical appropriateness of the word associations in the vocabulary selected for the English version of the interpretation.

3. How Does this Interpretation Process Proceed in Detail for the Single Formative Text Arena (or for the Respective Text Arenas)?[207]

 a. Following a historical illustration of the realities of origin, one should next present findings concerning the *major divisions, contour, and purposive direction of the entire text* and its individual parts.

[207] In the presentation, the interpretation can begin according to the didactic principle by moving from the whole to the parts and then proceeding again to the whole. It can begin with a

This presentation should correspond to the framework as it was processed in form criticism (§7).

> Knowledge of the genre and/or its genre elements provides the concrete movement of thought for the text. As necessary, it includes (!) the author's concrete transcendence of the genre. This knowledge shows the *appropriate arrangement* of the text[208], the functional value (e.g. introduction, turning point, climax, statement of purpose), and the context of the organizational pieces within the framework of the entire text. One should arrange the descriptive interpretation, not by verses or even by sentences, but by the organizational pieces peculiar to this text which run alongside the line of thought of the text with its components.[209] Knowledge of the genre and/or the author's transcendence of that genre simultaneously manifests the *type and purposive direction* of the entire text (narrative, legal saying, teaching, annals, cult song, communal prayer of lamentation, wisdom saying, prophetic pronouncement of judgment, etc.), and its organizational parts (narrative introduction, establishment of the legal case, lament, presentation of guilt). Thus it manifests the particular perspective of the expressed conditions as well as the effect which the text intends to elicit from the hearer or reader beyond the simple reception of its contents. If no genre influence is present, then the analysis of the linguistically demonstrated macrostructure and microstructure of the text (§7) exposes the organization, intention, and perspective (compare also §8).

b. Thereafter, the *interpretation of the individual organizational parts* in the text are each processed and presented.

In doing so, one should pay attention to the following:

α. Describing the character, sectional function, and partial purpose of this *organizational section* as a part of the whole.

---

concentrated substantiation of the realities of origin and a presentation of the total contour, purposive direction, and organizing sections of the text. Next one can add the interpretive processes for each individual organizational piece, and then return to the perspective of the entirety by an interpretation of the entire text layer.

208 Some cases indicate that the author of the text at hand concretely transcended the genre(s). In those cases then one no longer simply identifies the arrangement of the text with the parts of the employed genre(s). Also, the subject of the statement, the purposive direction, and the organizational sections of the text can change in respect to the genre. Example: In the paragraph of Isa 7:3–9, the threat of 7:9b offers an essential transcendence of the genre shaping 7:4–9a which forms the climax of the statement. At the same time, this threat is of greatest significance for arranging the section and decisively changes the resulting purpose of the genre which shapes 7:4–9 in the current text. Cf. O.H. Steck, *EvTh* 33 (1973): 77–90, there p. 82 (also = *Wahrnehmungen*, p. 176f).

209 Kaiser, *Exegetical Method*, p. 37ff, describes the process and presentation of the interpretation of the whole differently. We do not accept the possibilities of choice apparently opened by the interpretation any more than we adopt the theologically excessive demand to be an attorney of the present age in confrontation with the text.

β. Describing the *content of the statement* present in this part of the text according to the intention of the author. This content is described as a purposive bundle of that which is stated explicitly as well as that which was also intended and heard. For this purpose, one must evaluate the following:

1. The *linguistic structure*. It provides the view of the expressed conditions (e.g. circumstances, action, time) and the intended reception of the hearer (e.g. to receive that which is communicated, or to consider something on the basis of questions and references) according to the results of form criticism (§7).

2. The *explicit content* according to the formulation of the text. The text's unequivocal meaning, to the degree that it can still be determined today, is provided primarily from several elements: from the context at hand, from the lexical meaning of the words and their delineation and deepening by the immediate context, by revealing the tradition historical preconditioning of the formulations (or their transcendence, see tradition history, §8). The text's unequivocal meaning may also be provided by observing its character based on the topics of the genre (or their transcendence, see form criticism, §7), and by drawing upon parallel statements from the same author and/or the original context as identified in transmission history (§4), literary criticism (§3), and the historical setting (§9). As necessary, unequivocal meaning is also provided by stylistic figures (*parallelismus membrorum*) or images, comparisons, and metaphors offered in the text. Finally, meaning is provided by contrasting statements which would also be historically conceivable or expected in this context but which are not offered.

3. The *aspect directed by subject and audience* from which the author offers the expressed content, according to the conclusions of form criticism (§7), tradition criticism (§8), and the historical setting (§9).

c. After interpreting the individual organizational pieces, one should include an *interpretation of the entire text* as a purposeful, meaningful unity within the frame of a historical life process.

In doing so, one should pay particular attention to the following:

α. Progression, contour, deliberated context, weight of the *material movement* which the author consummates when presenting the text and which the addressees allow to be consummated.

β. A dynamic view of the entire text as a life process on the part of the *author*.

—What occurrences and experiences does the author presuppose? What necessities compel the author to form the text? What tradition historical presuppositions are thereby activated and how are they reaccented? For what reasons are these presuppositions transcended by correction?

—What is new in the statement from the perspective of its situation and from the perspective of the hearer?

—What does the author want to accomplish in the historical setting of the author's hearers/readers? What boundaries and decisions does the author address in the framework of the historical possibilities of that time?

—What is singular and what is common for this text in light of other statements from the same author or authorial circle?

—What experiential reality from the author's time does the author want to clarify and influence? What incontrovertible experiences, interventions, and perspectives of reality of that time does the author associate with statements about God in particular? What attitude does the author provide regarding humanity, Israel, or specific groups and persons from that time and world?

γ. A dynamic attitude about the text on the part of its *hearers*, if the text offers starting points for such.

— What intervention does the text undertake in the world of the hearer? What effect did the text actually have on them?

—Does the actual effect differ from the speaker's intention? What are the experiential reasons for this deviation?

δ. The *historical meaning of the text* beyond the mediated intention of the author and the reception of the hearers.

Do the contents of the text signify even more than the author "objectively" intended in light of the experiential reality of that time?

One can provide an answer to the question if one situates the text in the wider context of the author's time and experiential reality beyond the concrete horizon of the situation and beyond the horizon of understanding of the author. Also, one can provide an answer if one asks what the text in this expanded framework contributes to the background of the experiential reality which enables one to understand experiential reality more appropriately, more comprehensively, or deeper. Thus, based on corresponding expressions from the background of 9th century prophecy, the statements of Amos which were publicly critical of society have the quality of an entirely new type of critical perception of Israel in its social world of the monarchial period. They even have this new perspective for Judah even though Amos, in his time, intentionally addressed the Northern Kingdom and not Judah. Determining meaning and authorial intention occur separately if the contents of the text subsequently encounter a different experiential horizon which the author never had in mind. When the original authorial intention is transcended, or even contradicted, a text's meaning can become visible precisely during the text's productive transmission. The tradents of the exodus tradition have, for this transmission, inferred a meaning for the experiential reality of Israel by the saving God. This meaning reached far beyond the partial experience of the Moses group both chronologically and spatially. This meaning explained the entire experience of the people to that point their qualified its future. Since the exilic period, the intention of the royal psalms to qualify the power of the Davidides no longer had any experientially illuminating significance. Rather, it had to live on as the deepening of meaning for Persian power or as a proleptic meaning for a future, messianic time in the future.[210] Shifts between punctiliar material intention and the meaning of a text can thus appear especially during the Old Testament development of a text in the experiential framework of more recent times.

II. Interpreting the Text in Its Old Testament Development

Suppose literary criticism, transmission history, and redaction history have demonstrated that the text has undergone a development. Or suppose they have demonstrated that, over the course of time, the text was incorporated into a broader context. In either (or both) case(s), one must discuss and interpret the path of the entire text's productive transmission within the Old Testament alongside the individual developmental stages.

Here, the *task* is to determine the material movement which is expressed in the text's transmission process within the Old Testament.

Instead of a superfluous summation of the contents of the individual transmission stages which have already been treated, one should consider their connection, which now becomes the object of the interpretation.

What remains constant during this development? What is changed? And what shows the older state of the text in a new light?

At this point, these are the elementary leading questions of this procedural step, namely the interpretation which illuminates the material, theological result of the synthetic transmission history and especially the result of the redaction historical investigation. Again, one should observe a series of aspects for the effort:

---

[210] For the changes in the movement of meaning in Psalms transmission, compare, e.g. J. Becker, *Wege der Psalmenexegese*, 1975. For the changes in the transmission of the exodus event, see P. Weimar/E. Zenger, *Exodus. Geschichten und Geschichte der Befreiung Israels*, 1975, especially p. 11ff,139ff,167ff.

G. von Rad often noted this very significant fact. He noted that this view was connected to the wider transmission of texts inside the Old Testament, texts which "could always have fresh meaning extracted from them." (*Old Testament Theology*, vol. 2, p. 45). Compare Part Three of *Old Testament Theology*, vol. 2 (p. 319ff), as well as the work, "Offene Fragen im Umkreis einer Theologie des Alten Testaments" (1963), printed in G. von Rad, *Gesammelte Studien zum Alten Testament II*, 1973, p. 289ff.

1. The task is presented in a dual perspective:

If the *text* has experienced *productive growth*, then one must understand this process as the material change of its content, whereby one must also consider the new contexts.

Example: The text of 1 Kgs 18:21ff has grown as an individual narrative, which then becomes a component of the Elijah cycle of 1 Kgs 17–19, and later becomes part of the deuteronomistic presentation of the monarchial period, as well as part of the priestly configured history of Gen 1 to 2 Kgs 25 from the post-exilic period.

Suppose the text has not experienced a development, but has been incorporated into *changing transmission contexts* as it is conveyed over time. If so, then one must determine the function changes within this context. With their respective intentions as the subject, one makes this determination to the degree that one can recognize these intentions and to the degree that they provide a coherent material profile.

2. Above all, the synthetic insights of transmission history and redaction history, along with the literary critical and transmission historical analyses, offer the essential *preparation* to which this procedure should be affixed. If the emphasis rests upon the transmission *process*, its means and motifs,

then it rests upon the *material movement* of the changing content of the text which corresponds to this transmission process.

3. One should inquire into this material movement *interpretively* with analogous *means* as with the interpretation of the individual text arenas. Thus, it should inquire into the following:

— changes in the historical environment as the text is conveyed (time, place, persons responsible for transmission, situation, experiential horizon, theological conditionings)
— form critical expansion of the text or incorporation of the text as one genre element into a more comprehensive framing genre with new contours, turning points, and purpose
— the contents of newly incorporated formulations and of the entire text within this changed framework
— the reason for abbreviating the text from earlier stages, etc.

Already the material movement inside the transmission of individual Old Testament texts can be an example of the changes, or the deepening (or leveling) of the Israelite understanding of YHWH over the course of history in the face of changing experiential horizons. The material movement in the transmission of an individual text then participates in the ebb and flow of the character of Israel's perception of YHWH as it has been comprehensively determined in the history of Israel's religion and in Old Testament theology. The insights of these two areas of work conversely demand the capacity of recognizing the movement of meaning from individual texts.

4. In particular, one must observe

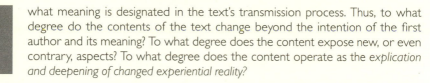

what meaning is designated in the text's transmission process. Thus, to what degree do the contents of the text change beyond the intention of the first author and its meaning? To what degree does the content expose new, or even contrary, aspects? To what degree does the content operate as the *explication and deepening of changed experiential reality?*

Suppose one thereby sees the respective meaning of the text already acquired in the individual transmission stages. Suppose one also notes the changes of the Israelite experiential world which are designated in the transmission events of the text. If so, then a *movement of meaning* becomes visible whose flow, profile, and tendency one should observe. This movement of meaning in the changing contents does not, by any means, necessarily progress continuously or even automatically. The movement of meaning makes clear paradigmatically how the perception of meaning in Israel at that time was shaped by the productive relationship between the experiential world and the transmission. In some cases, this shaping happened in different theological streams with different results. The experiential world is clarified by the transmission and the meaning of the transmission is transformed in light of changed experience. For Israel, this transformation is expressed in the fact that God is not a rigid principle and not the extrapolation of fundamental values of this world, but the "Living God". God's "being" is "in becoming" as one can recognize from the connection to historically experienced changes.[211]

An example is the movement of meaning in the transmission history of 1 Kgs 18:21ff. Elijah himself successfully sought to reclaim the territory of Carmel for YHWH against Baal. The first transmitters of the Elijah transmission had shown the meaning by the termination of the events and the return of the rain. They also confirmed that the land of Israel and its fertility belonged only to the one God, YHWH. In this substance of the transmission, later transmitters saw legitimation for Jehu's extermination of the Baal devotees. They perceived the meaning of this grave process from their own experiential world so that the meaning of the transmission extended to topical political events. This perception was quite different from Hosea's (1:4) recollection of the kingdom of his experiential world. Finally, in the Deuteronomistic History, the transmission achieves meaning in light of the catastrophe experienced by Israel. It achieves meaning as a transmission related to the people and all foundations of their well-being. Elijah was one of those who warned Israel, but who was not heard (2 Kgs 17:13). The fact that YHWH was the exclusive God in the land of Israel has now been confirmed against Israel and it

211 E. Jüngel, *The Doctrine of the Trinity: God's Being Is in Becoming*, Grand Rapids, 1976.

explains the end of its kingdom. Thus, the transmission of 1 Kgs 18:21ff participated in the constitutive meaning and the changing actualization of the first commandment in Israel's history of faith.

D. CONSIDERING THE TEXT'S HISTORICAL MEANING IN LIGHT OF THE PRESENT

In concluding the process of historical interpretation, one should attempt to establish crisp, precise considerations regarding how the results of the determination of historical meaning can be presented in our time. This attempt is performed to *introduce* the result of the interpretive process *into a theological procedure* which is responsible to the historic transmission, demonstrably reflective for the sake of our time, and no less importantly, for the exegete and our world in order to adopt the compelling character of the text which is not historically limited. The imaginings about the text as a component of today's world that were acquired before entering the exegesis[212] are thereby taken up. These imaginings are then taken further according to the text's unequivocal historical meaning, at least as approximated.

One has thus gained the following essential insight: The text does not just represent an arsenal of sentences requiring explanation. Rather, in its realization, it also represents a process of life which wants to open the processes of life. Accordingly, one must look to the corresponding realities of today: at the text's experiential foundations; at its historical, social, intellectual, and theological conditionings; at the shape of its statement; and at its contents. Where have *changes* entered the historical realities or the experiential world? Where is the theological foundation changed by the New Testament in contrast to the historical profile so that it necessary to shape the text statements further in order to assimilate them as a process of life today? On the other hand, in spite of its historical conditioning, where does the text reveal deficits in our experience of the world and self, in establishing values, or in ways of acting? Where could the historical meaning provide *impulses* for the present experience of self, world, and God? And where can these impulses be conveyed further in the work of a theology related to the present time?[213]

---

212 See above, §1 B II 1 (p. 6f).

213 See examples pertaining to how one acquires the stages of understanding and thought movements during Old Testament transmission by including the transmissions for qualifying this finding in view of our present time: In light of a specific text (Gen 32:23–33), see H.J. Hermisson, "Jakobs Kampf am Jabbok," *ZThK* 71 (1974): 239–261. For the history of Old Testament concepts, see H.H. Schmid, "šālôm. »Frieden« im Alten Orient und im Alten Testament," 1971; J. Jeremias, *Die Reue Gottes*, 1975. O.H. Steck, "Zwanzig Thesen als alttestamentlicher Beitrag zum Thema: Die jüdisch-christliche Lehre von der Schöpfung in Beziehung zu Wissenschaft und Technik," *KuD* 23 (1977): 277–299. For an Old Testament tradition, see G. v. Rad, *Wisdom in Israel*, 1972. From the

E. SUGGESTION FOR PROCEEDING WITH THE ACQUISITION AND PRESENTATION OF THE INTERPRETATION

The following suggestion is offered to stimulate the central task of §10, namely how one proceeds concretely, and how this procedure can be recorded in the *written presentation* of an exegesis paper.

I. The progression of the work begins by *bringing to mind* the framing conditions based upon the results of the methodological procedures:

1. The *basis* is the original text according to text criticism (§3).
2. What are the text's *developmental stages* which stand in succession for interpretation (literary criticism, transmission history, redaction history, according to §§4–6)? Compare §10 C I 1.
3. What are the *historical realities of origin* (expressed, intellectual, author, addressee) for each developmental stage of the text (historical setting according to §9 by resorting to form criticism [§7] and tradition history [§8])? Compare §10 C I 2.

Within the framework of the written presentation of the interpretation it is not necessary to reformulate "1" and "3". The results of §§3–9 have already been introduced to the reader in the framework of the preceding presentation of the procedural steps. By contrast, when presenting the interpretation of "2," it is recommended that one provide a brief summation of the literary critical, transmission historical, and redaction historical procedures according to §§4–6.

To this presentation one adds the particular process of interpretation which is now presented in its entirety in written form. The sequence of the acquisition and presentation is suggested as follows:

II. *Interpreting each developmental stage* of the text.

Here the ideal case is presented in which the various developmental stages are presented with the current extent of the text and the statement's tangible profile. Compare, however, the practical remarks in §10 C I 1.

1. The first developmental stage:
   a. Briefly restate its extent and the realities of its origin. (See above, I "1" and "3".)

---

perspective of a contemporary problem, see O.H. Steck, *World and Environment*, Biblical Encounter Series, Nashville, 1980.

  b. Briefly restate its overall structure, organizational turning points, and purpose (form criticism according to §7). Compare §10 C I 3a.

  c. Interpretation of the first organizational component. Compare §10 C I 3b.

  aa. translation

  bb. character, function of the part, the partial purpose of the organizational component

  cc. Designation of the contents of the organizational component

  — linguistic structure

  — expressed circumstances

  — aspects directed by the subject and addressees

  d. Interpretation of the remaining organizational components in the same manner as c..

  e. Comprehensive interpretation of the text of the first developmental stage. Cf. §10 C I 3c.

  "2," "3," "4," etc. as necessary:

  Interpretation of the text for the remaining stages analogous to "1."

III. *Interpreting* the text in its Old Testament *development*. Compare §10 C II.

IV. Pointed considerations of the text's historical meaning *in view of our present time*. Compare §10 D.

  These considerations are not obligatory for an exegesis within the academic discipline of the Old Testament.

V. *Translation of the whole text*

  Compare §10 F. This translation should be definitively formulated in line with the interpretation. It should not, however, be presented in this interpretation. Rather, it should precede the written work as a whole. Developmental stages and organization can be typographically demonstrated.

F. TRANSLATION OF THE TEXT

Only after concluding all exegetical procedures can the preliminary translation, undertaken at the beginning of the exegesis, be brought into an appropriate version based upon insights achieved since that point.[214]

---

214 Compare, Kaiser, *Exegetical Method*, 37f. In distinction to Fohrer, *Exegese*, 180, and us, Kaiser arranges the final translation act between the individual exegesis and the interpretation of

Even for today's reader to receive the creative impulse of the historical elements, the translation cannot be a modernizing, actualizing translation which transcends the hermeneutical task. Rather, today it must be just as readable as faithful to the wording. And it must be as precise as historically possible. The selection of the English words is undertaken according to those words which, by their associations, lead the reader to the shape and contents of the statement in the historically mediated sense.

G. LITERATURE

G. Fohrer. Exegese, § 10 (H. W. Hoffmann) and § 11 (G. Wanke).
O. Kaiser. Exegetical Method, p. 36–41.
W. Richter. Exegese, p. 174–190.

Literature about the *hermeneutical problem:*
R. Bultmann. Das Problem der Hermeneutik. ZThK 47 (1950): 47–69 (also in: Bultmann, Glauben und Verstehen, vol. 2. Tübingen, ⁵1968, p. 211–235.
G. Ebeling. "Hermeneutik," RGG³ III, col. 242–262.
H.-G. Gadamer. Truth and Method. New York, ²1991.
W. Joest. Fundamentaltheologie. Theologische Grundlagen- und Methodenprobleme. Theologische Wissenschaft, Vol. 11. Stuttgart—Berlin—Köln—Mainz ²1981, p. 59–72.174–212.
E. Krentz. The Historical-Critical Method. Guides to Biblical Scholarship. Philadelphia, 1975.
B.C. Lategan. "Hermeneutics." ABD, Vol. 3, p. 149–154.
K. Lehmann. Der hermeneutische Horizont der historisch-kritischen Exegese, in: Schreiner. Einführung, p. 40–80.
W. Pannenberg. Theology and the Philosophy of Science. London, 1976.

Literature especially concerned with *hermeneutics of the Old Testament:*
J. Goldingay. Models for Interpretation of Scripture. Grand Rapids, 1995.
A.H.J. Gunneweg. Understanding the Old Testament. OTL. Philadelphia, 1978.
H. Seebass. Biblische Hermeneutik. Urban-Taschenbücher 199. Stuttgart—Berlin—Köln—Mainz, 1974.
L. Schmidt. Art. Hermeneutik II. Altes Testament. TRE XV (1986). p. 137–143 (bibiliography).
F. Watson. Text, Church, and World: Biblical Interpretation in Theological Perspective. Grand Rapids, 1994.
C. Westermann, ed. Probleme alttestamentlicher Hermeneutik. Aufsätze zum Verstehen des Alten Testaments. ThB 11. Munich ³1968.

---

the whole. However, even the interpretation of the whole can still provide important insights for conveying the text in English.

Part Four

Illustration

§11 The Exegetical Process Using Gen 28:10–22 as Example

This section will illustrate, using Gen 28:10–22 as an example, how the process of exegetical work can proceed with a text using this workbook. Thus, the *process* of exegetical work is presented, not the additional act of the presentation based on this work. An exegetical treatment of this text is not attempted in light of all of its difficult problems in current research. Neither is an original contribution attempted for the exegetical discussion of this text. Rather, this section attempts more simply to illustrate the course and the interconnectedness of exegetical procedures. For reasons of space, even this task cannot take place in breadth and completeness. The attempted purpose appears to us to be achieved if the reader can see the representative illustration of this book for several procedural steps.

A. FIRST PROVISIONAL TRANSLATION OF THE HEBREW TEXT

Already the *basic attitude* with which one approaches the work is important. One must treat a well known text, perhaps one which has been familiar since children's worship services and elementary school. Appropriately, this attitude appears in the expectation that the text continues to deserve attention and every consideration. One expects that the text possibly shows meaning which one still does not know, and that it exposes a biblical impulse for explaining our life in our world.[215] This anticipatory submission to the text begins with the first penetration into its genuine linguistic world.

Thus one begins with the *initial, yet entirely preliminary translation of the text with the help of dictionary and grammar*. One becomes accustomed to unknown words and grammatical manifestations with the effect that one is able to use the Hebrew text in all subsequent procedures without difficulty. One thus has the text at one's disposal. All demonstrable exegetical observations and decisions can only be established by continually reading and considering the text in the original language.[216]

B. OBSERVATIONS

I. Concept of the Text as Component of Today's World

Perhaps the following impressions and consequences, among others, present themselves under the direction of the above mentioned determinations and questions.[217]

The narrative is all too well known. In some circumstances it is known from memories of religious training and pictures of the sleeping Jacob and the heavenly ladder. There is no evident reference to the life of one's current experiential world. Therefore, this clearly legendary story is materially neutral, although perhaps aesthetically pleasing. Upon closer examination there is much which is foreign (staircase to heaven with angel/messenger; a pillow of stone covered with oil; a place as the gate of heaven; giving of a tithe), which, like Jacob and Bethel, is taken to be legendary coloring and thus, is of no interest upon closer inspection. The main point of the story, that God appears to Jacob with promises for him, is told with incomprehensible details (God at the top of the staircase to heaven; location of the gate of heaven; why the erection of a stone?). Well intentioned, engaged Bible readers will see dynamic contact to their experience in that they will see Jacob as an example of how guidance and the protection of life is not at the disposal of humanity, but promised by God. But what about contradictory experiences?

These and other impressions and consequences (in some cases they may be expanded in conversation with others) remain, for now, collected and preserved for action at the conclusion of the exegesis. This action takes into consideration the text's historical meaning in light of the present time. The impressions and consequences are collected and preserved for further theological

215 Compare above §1 A, p. 3f.
216 Compare above, §1 B I (p. 5, cf. 8ff).
217 Compare above, §1 B II 1 (p. 6f).

work on the text following the exegesis, and for incorporating the text in a sermon, lecture, or Christian lifestyle today. These observations are important for the exegetical work to the degree that here one becomes cognizant of pre-suppositions about the character, meaning, and value of the text. Also, in attempting to perceive the text in its historical self-understanding, these presuppositions must be kept in check.

Subsequently, one attempts a historical perspective from the text in its historical realm.[218] We recognize this perspective in the following broader realm because it is recent and especially important for exegetical directions.

II. Concept of the Text as a Component of Its Historical World

The person responsible for the exegesis should be strongly encouraged to dedicate sufficient time to this imaginative traversal of the text *before* any methodologically directed, scientific investigation, without drawing upon commentaries, essays, or monographs. One should only rely upon the text of the Hebrew Bible, a reference work such as a bible dictionary, and as necessary a concordance. Also, one should again return to this imaginative traversal of the text *alongside* one's scientific procedural treatment of the text. The exegete should employ his/her current knowledge about the Old Testament (or quickly expand that knowledge concerning specific topics). The exegete should then look, look, and look again. One should make one's own observations and thus achieve a dynamic overall picture of the historical understanding of the text! The density and content of scientific-exegetical questioning, and accordingly the density and contents of the results, essentially depend upon this imaginative action. It is thus of minor importance how defensible this image remains when tested by scientific procedures. This picture will turn out differently for a beginner than for one more experienced in exegetical exercise. Also educational limits and competence will have an effect. The image of the text created from one's own observations (rather than merely arranging the secondary opinions one has read, critically) will benefit the understanding and the life of the text. Following the first historical impressions of the text, one begins with precise linguistic observations of the Hebrew text (according to §1 B II 2). These observations prepare the linguistic analysis in connection with the form critical approaches. They have been omitted here for reasons of space and of the Hebrew printing, but compare Fohrer, *Exegese*, 186–195.

1. However, a *selection of additional aspects of imagination* of the basis of linguistic observations are mentioned below:

---

218 See above, §1 B II 2 (p. 8ff).

- *The text is not complete by itself:* The reason why Jacob is in Bethel on a trip from Beersheba to Haran (Gen 28:10; where are these places?) is no more stated than whether Jacob would be protected and return safely (28:20f; cf 28:15). The text is thus part of a larger narrative context.
- Where is this *larger narrative context?* What does Gen 28 presuppose as the context? In the preceding, it does not presuppose 28:1–9 (Jacob goes to Paddan-Aram to seek a bride instead of Haran), but presupposes 27:41–45 (to Haran in 27:43, fleeing from Esau). Afterward, it apparently presupposes the departure (29:1) on the journey, staying in Haran with Laban, the return trip (29–34), and especially Gen 35 where Jacob is again in Bethel with clear reference to our text (appearance of God, protection on the journey, resolution of the vow in 35:1,3,7,14). Also, flight from Esau mentioned in verses 35:1,7 shows that the contextual connection of 28:10ff with 27:41ff is correct, even though 28:10ff does not explicitly mention the flight from Esau. Even the excluded paragraph of 28:1–9 apparently continues in Gen 35, since 35:9 again mentions Paddan-Aram (supported by the corresponding promise between 28:3f and 35:11). Thus, the text is only a slice from a larger narrative context. Gen 27:41–45 precedes and following Gen 29–34, individual (but not all) statements in Gen 35 refer back to Gen 28:10ff.
- Now return to the text again. The question of the *dominating subject* which the organization determines has to be asked. Apparently, the dominating material assertion is the appearance of God in the dream (28:12–15) and the reactions of Jacob to that appearance in the morning (28:16–22). Confirmation is achieved in the fact that Gen 35:1,3,7,14 recapitulate this subject as the center of Gen 28. Gen 28:10–11 are the introduction which establish the narrative context (journey situation) and expound the situation of the dream revelation (evening, Jacob spends the night, sleeps).
- The two parts of the dominating subjects (28:12–15+16–22) can be *subdivided* again. One should pay attention to the explicitly changing references between the members. Within the appearance of God in the dream, 28:12 expounds the scene of revelation, while in 28:13–15 the appearance of God occurs as divine speech. The reactions of Jacob are staggered. After awaking, Jacob draws several conclusions from the dream revelation: 1) 28:16, without Jacob knowing it, YHWH was here. Verse 16 refers back to 28:13. 2) In parallel fashion, 28:17 establishes Jacob's fear because the house of God and the gate of heaven are here. The last element apparently refers back to 28:12. 3) In 28:18, Jacob erects the stone that was under his head as a pillar (*maṣṣēbāh*—what is that?), which relates to 28:11aßb. 4) In 28:19 he names the place Bethel, meaning house of God, which relates to 28:17 and 28:11a (note the reference word *māqôm*/place). 5) In a final reaction in 28:20–22, Jacob makes a vow for protection (28:20f related to 28:15) on the journey, related to 28:10. In so doing, the vow itself also indicates cross references: the pillar which had been erected (28:18), the house of God (28:17,19[?]), God's giving (perhaps 28:20).
- We may capture this insight about the text's organization and internal references in a *chart*[219]:

219 Of course, these insights into the construction of the narrative have, in whole or in part, already been recognized in the research. This fact does not mean that they cannot be recognized independently by careful observation of the text. Compare W. Richter, "Das Gelübde als theolo-

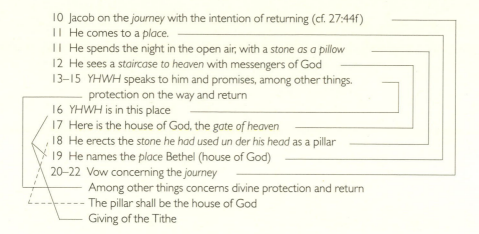

10 Jacob on the *journey* with the intention of returning (cf. 27:44f)

11 He comes to a *place*.

11 He spends the night in the open air, with a *stone as a pillow*

12 He sees a *staircase to heaven* with messengers of God

13–15 *YHWH* speaks to him and promises, among other things.

protection on the way and return

16 *YHWH* is in this place

17 Here is the house of God, the *gate of heaven*

18 He erects the *stone he had used un der his head* as a pillar

19 He names the *place* Bethel (house of God)

20–22 Vow concerning the *journey*

Among other things concerns divine protection and return

The pillar shall be the house of God

Giving of the Tithe

In spite of the fact that the text presupposes a larger narrative context, the text is a unit by itself within that larger context. It is held together by a symmetrical construction of corresponding narrative elements. The symmetrical axis lies between verses 15 and 16. The *construction of the unit* can be described more specifically. In the upper portion of the symmetry, one finds all the threads of Jacob's situation before the onset of the revelatory dream (28:10f) and the revelatory dream itself (28:12–15). In the lower portion, one finds that the narrative threads from above are taken up, in reverse order, in the form of Jacob's reactions to the revelatory dream. Indeed, they are taken up with respect to the dream itself (28:16f) and Jacob's concrete situation (28:18–22). The two-fold division of the units which has been observed is thereby confirmed again: the introductory exposition of Jacob's situation (28:10f) + the revelatory dream (28:12–15) and Jacob's reaction to his situation (28:16–22). The central material movement of the unit is thus God's qualifying and changing entry into a certain life situation of Jacob which results in specific reactions of Jacob. Various strands of this entry can thus be observed: the site of the event, the journey, Jacob after the return (land for him and his descendants, innumerable descendants who expand spatially in every direction, and the horizon of a positive relationship to all persons in the inhabitable earth).

• One must ask the unavoidable question: *Where, when, why, and from whom* did such an artfully and thoughtfully shaped text arise? The considerations which materialize here, depend entirely upon the degree of Old Testament knowledge which one already possesses.

Anyone with a basic knowledge of Genesis knows that the text takes place in the patriarchal period, that it concerns Jacob, and that he represents a semi-nomadic group of people in Palestine who own herds. They also stand at the beginning of a sedentary and agriculture lifestyle. It is less likely that the text, as it lies before us, should be situated in the last third of the second millenium, or that the text is the

---

gische Rahmung der Jakobsüberlieferungen," *BZ* NF 11 (1967): 21–52; E. Otto, "Jakob in Bethel," *ZAW* 88 (1976): 165–190, especially 172ff.

narrative material of this Jacob group. The artistic construction of the text is just as perplexing as the promises of 28:13–14 which proceed well beyond the experiential and expectational horizon of the patriarchal groups.

Precisely because of these promises one might think, at the earliest, of the end of the pre-state period, or the bitter experiences of the time of Saul. In Saul's time, these hopes had perspective and rationale. Or one could think of the early monarchial period, where the promises became reality, or even later in the time of Josiah, or the exilic period, or even the post-exilic period where such promises strengthen the expectations. In any case, it was no longer Jacob and his patriarchal group who formed the horizon of the text. Rather, it was Israel as a people whose existence, whether supposed or expressed, is grounded here in a divine promise to Jacob, the father of the twelve tribes. But, in these times would one have expressed these thoughts in the concrete form of Gen 28? At that point (!), would one expect that the narrator would simultaneously want to explain the meaning of the name Bethel? Is the protection of Jacob on his journey still a problem? Are the notable concrete circumstances of the appearance of God in this place (staircase to heaven for the messengers of God, gate of heaven, stone pillar anointed with oil, and even the house of God) still important in these later times? Since the time of Josiah and his concentration of the cult in Jerusalem, Bethel as the house of God or pillars as cult objects were out of the question! Why, analogously to the sketchier scene of Gen 12:1–4a, is a solemn promise to Jacob, as in 28:13–15, not sufficient for the experiential horizon and theological desire of these later times?

• Such considerations are achieved through affiliated knowledge from history and from the theological history of Israel. The exegete should become keenly attentive to *peculiar threads* which the text contains in spite of its symmetrical, artistic inclusiveness. These threads become visible when one returns again to the text and peacefully conceptualizes, considers, and associates its details. For instance:

The text apparently has two assertional interests. On the one hand, it is concerned with Jacob, his trip, and with his (as well as his descendants) more distant future. On the other hand, it is concerned with the manner and provisions with which Bethel was recognized and named as the place of the presence of God. Were both assertional interests bound together from the beginning?

It is also peculiar how the interest in Bethel is presented in the text. At the stony place where Jacob spends the night, he sees in a dream what this place really (!) contains which he did not previously know. A staircase to heaven is placed on the earth here. It is thus the place where God in heaven visits with the earth through messengers. It is thus the gate of heaven. Somewhat hesitantly one can also bring the "house of God" into the picture. The place is the lower entrance to the dwelling of God. It reaches from the earth into the heavens where God lives. Perhaps one thinks of the tower of Babel which provokes one to seek more information, which perhaps furnishes corresponding analogies (consult e.g., *Reallexikon der Assyriologie*, or the *Anchor Bible Dictionary*, vol. 1, under Babel, vol. 1, p. 561f, for holy *house*, holy *gate*, the tower of Etemenanki [»cornerstone« of heaven and earth] which has steps). However, how does one account for the fact that in 28:13, God visits with Jacob without messengers as mediators? How does one account for the fact that the stone erected as a pillar has no evident association with the picture in 28:12,17 (at any rate, *IDB*, vol. 3, 816, shows temple pillars)? How does one account for the highly unusual statement in 28:22 that this stone pillar shall become a house of God (!) even though Bethel is already the house of God before the erection of the pillar (28:17)? It is no less unusual that Jacob is afraid after (!) the extremely generous promise is communicated to him. Anyone who recognizes oracular language, or consults the concordance under "fear" will see that the assertion of fear precedes the oracle (cf. LXX to 28:13, one cannot recognize this in BHS, only in the irreplaceable BHK). It is really puzzling that the text as a whole thinks of a place which is not known for its solitary, complete stones, and which necessitates spending the night in the open, and yet according to 28:19, the place is already a city ('îr)!

- Anyone who looks longer at the text comes upon *additional conspicuous elements*. Many of the threads find no correspondence in reference to the narrative: the messengers of God in 28:12 but not 28:13; the erection of the pillow-stone as pillar (28:11,18) also in 28:22, but without the anointing of the stone (28:18, see however the reference in Gen 31:13 the anointing and the vow in Gen 28, also Gen 35:14 [addition of drink offering]). Also noteworthy is the change in the designation for God: YHWH in 28:13,16 (cf. 28:21) but Elohim in 28:12,17,20,22 (cf. Beth-El in 28:19). Finally, if there is a difference in the text between the appearance of YHWH and the appearance of the messengers, how does one reconcile that in 28:12 Jacob's dream is associated with the appearance of the messengers while Jacob's awaking in 28:16 is associated with the appearance of YHWH? Must one thus correct the symmetrical schema and relate the first three words of 28:16 (and then Jacob awoke from his sleep) to 28:12 (in addition to 28:17) and relate the remaining statements of 28:16 to 28:13–15? Or, because of the disruption in the flow which then appears, does the symmetrical schema only belong to the current text in its final form? Also the context demonstrates unusual elements. Jacob names Bethel in 28:19, but again in 35:7 when he builds the altar after his return with reference to Gen 28, and finally for the third time in 35:15, apparently in the framework of the other contextual line in which takes Jacob to Paddan-Aram (28:1–9; 35:9ff, especially verses 10,13,15 where God speaks ('mr, dbr).

- Combined, these peculiar threads make one wonder whether everything stands in the text because of a unifying intentional shaping. The self-critical exegete should ask by way of follow-up whether these threads are only peculiar because of the historical distance of our modern demands for a text's logic and consistency. At any rate, the text contains problems which require clarification. One can no longer answer so simply the *questions about the realities of origin*, or questions about the intention, meaning, and effect of the text, as it was first attempted when fascinated by the discovery of the symmetrical construction.

2. The beginner might cease the observations at this point and attempt to clarify them by entering into the methodological procedures and by finding insight in secondary literature. The advanced student can attempt even more observations on the text based upon knowledge about the transmission history of the patriarchal stories (individual narratives, sagas about the establishment of the cult, sagas about a place, patriarchal cycles, adoption into classic pentateuchal sources). An advanced student can further investigate the literary critical and transmission historical possibilities from the text. Without secondary

literature, the exegete can bring together *observations* which make the threads of the text at hand understandable based on its *history of development*. Examples include:

• Gen 28:13–16 (always without the first three words, demonstrated in the following with asterisks) speaks of YHWH and creates tensions over against its environment: YHWH rather than Elohim; YHWH instead of the messengers; interest in Jacob rather than the interest in Bethel; promissory speech; the vow as a reaction of the addressee following the admission of a promise is quite singular (as an overview of the patriarchal narratives in Genesis shows). There are indeed problems: the re-lationship between 28:15 and 28:20 (does 28:15 presuppose 28:20 or the other way around?); further, the problem of fear following the promissory speech. One can offer the supposition that 28:13–*16 entered the text later. Anyone for whom Gen 28:14 recalls Gen 12:3 as a characteristic image of the Yahwist will want to delve the question more precisely, because one must examine whether 28:13–*16 consti-tutes an expansion of the text by the Yahwistic pentateuchal source (J). Orientation concerning the contents and method of J are required.

• If one is already somewhat familiar with the classic explanations regarding source analysis of the Pentateuch,[220] one should attempt to progress a little further. The tan-gible style of the Priestly Writing is not found in the text. The observable alternation of the designation for God, between YHWH and Elohim, prompts one to examine whether the text represents a conflation of the Yahwistic and Elohistic pentateuchal sources. A coherent J section was already found (28:13–16*). What else belongs with it? Gen 28:21b again has YHWH, but the formulation is puzzling. In J, YHWH has been honored since Gen 4. How then can J allow Jacob to say that only if he returns safely will YHWH become Jacob's God? Since the YHWH criterion is otherwise lacking, further assignations are difficult. Now for the counter-inquiry: *What belongs to E?* Gen 28:12 offers Elohim, likewise 28:17. Gen 28:12 presupposes Jacob's sleeping, along with the dream. Thus, 28:11 (and the first three words of 28:16) belongs to E, and 28:18 refers to the sleep. Likewise, 28:20-22 (excluding 28:21b) are Elohistic because of the designation for God. Gen 28:19 remains. It is more difficult, but because of Beth-*El*, the assignation to E is more likely. Finally, if 28:10 belongs with 28:20–22, as the text observations indicate, then it is Elohistic. However, 28:10 presupposes Gen 27:41–45 which in turn belongs to Gen 27:1ff (a Yahwistic text as demonstrated by the designation of YHWH). This is suspicious. With Gen 28:20-22, E presupposes a journey account, but 28:10 is Yahwistic. Has the E-version of the journey account been "broken off" by the melding of the sources? Gen 28:11 is also difficult. Because of the dream in 28:12, as already noted, it belongs to E, but 28:16 belongs to J (Jacob awoke from sleep; this place) relates to 28:11. Is 28:11 then "mixed" from both sources? One cannot, however, achieve a division. Further, if J concludes with 28:16, then the place of this promis-sory speech would not even be identified in this source, even though it is expressly

---

220 See A. de Pury, "Yahwist ("J") Source, in *ABD*, vol. 6, p. 1012–1020; A.W. Jenks, "Elohist," in *ABD*, vol. 2, p. 478–482; and J. Milgrom, "Priestly ("P") Source," in *ABD*, vol. 5, p. 454–461.

mentioned here (28:11?,16) in distinction to the J source of Gen 12:1–3 (which is not situated). By way of summary: In this attempted explanation, J operates fragmentarily. Is it likely that two sources have been combined into a single text when balanced by the manipulations one would then have to accept?

- Anyone who has doubt and yet has not sought help in the research may want to consider another way. As a model, one may consider *older transmission* taken up into a single source.

  For the moment, set aside 28:13–*16 in the search for an older transmission. It seems to be a coherent insertion, presumably of Yahwistic origin. The remaining text is also not without problems, above all as observed in 28:19b where the place is a city which was previously named Luz. Insight from *BHH, 231 (for English, cf. ABD,* vol. 1, 711; vol. 4, 420), shows that, prior to J, Bethel and the nearby city, Luz, were separated spatially and by name. Does 28:19b, which identifies the city, belong then to a text after J? A glance in the concordance under Luz provides the following: Josh 16:2 and 18:13 also separate Bethel and Luz. Judg 1:23 is like Gen 28:19. In the Jacob story, Gen 48:3 clearly relates to the context to which Gen 28:10ff does not belong (28:1ff+35:9ff), as well as 35:6 which also belongs in this other context (cf. the land of Canaan as in 48:3). The statement in 35:7, which does belong with Gen 28:10ff, speaks neither of a city, nor of Luz. Thus, perhaps 28:19b also enters the text later. It remains to be considered why, according to 28:17, the place of the appearance of God *is* the house of God, while in 28:22 the pillar will *become* a house of God only after Jacob's return. Did 28:12+17 and 28:22 originally exclude one another? If yes, which is older? In context of 28:11+18, the erection of the pillow-stone as a pillar in the morning would be entirely unmotivated without the appearance of God. By contrast, one can understand the vow as an expansion to the text, which attaches to 28:18 while the older text ends with 28:17–19a. The vow arises in a journey setting, and perhaps shifts the event so that the place will become a house of God only after the return. Does 28:20–22 then first enter when the event is situated in the flight from Esau? Do these verses, like the flight journey in 28:10, thus belong to the more extensive Jacob narrative cycle? If so, then there was originally a Jacob story which included 28:11–12, the beginning of 28:16, and 28:17–19a. It told how Jacob discovered in a dream that the place where he spent the night was a holy place, the house of God, and the gate of heaven. Yet he had not known it previously. It was thus a story which let Jacob discover the quality of the cult site of Bethel and a story which traced the pillar there back to him.

- Attempting an explanation based upon these observations, one thus suggests in broad strokes *three presumed developmental stages* for the text:

  1. The individual narrative of Jacob's discovery of the cult site of Bethel.
  2. The incorporation of this story into the Jacob cycle which provides the journey setting and the vow.
  3. The expansion of YHWH's promissory speech together with the limited reaction of Jacob.

- Anyone possessing foreknowledge about the history of religion, or who is informed regarding the archaeological data of Bethel, will not stop with the presumed individual narrative about Jacob. According to both archaeology and the Old Testament, Bethel (*tell beitin*) is a pre-Israelite setting. The *religious conceptions* in the individual narrative are not original components of the patriarchal religion. They are ancient oriental. According to the place name, the divinity is El, which raises a question. Does a Canaanite narrative lie behind the Jacob narrative in which the cult site of Bethel was established by Canaanite worshippers even before the Jacob group?

This is enough of the attempt of a historical perspective based upon aspects of individual imagination! It should be restated for encouragement that these aspects, and others, are completed according to the measure of Old Testament foreknowledge, and by the patience of persistent observations and illustrations. They are completed by working on the text with the help of a reference work and a concordance. They make it possible for the exegete to enter purposefully into the scientific, exegetical, methodological procedures. Instead of consulting secondary literature without one's own opinion, the exegete now approaches it with one's own opinions, impressions, and observations. The exegete also critically examines the exegete's own, as well as other, interpretations in order to understand the text historically. In so doing, however, the exegete continually gives way, in the course of the work, to imaginative phases of historical outlook based on newly emerging exegetical problems and insights.

C. METHODOLOGICALLY DIRECTED PROCEDURES

Between the previously operative observation phase and the phase of the methodologically directed investigation, the following *preliminary actions* are suggested:

1. After one has achieved one's own observations on the given section of the text, it is necessary to attain an initial *overview* and an initial *explanation* of the wider terrain, which will subsequently be treated methodologically. This informative orientation results most readily by gaining insight from introductory sections of commentaries or reference works. The *guiding question* of this orientation is: In which literary, historical, and theological context does the given text stand? The question of the literary context seeks information about the context in which the text stands, about the content and development of the book in which the text is found, and, as necessary, about the layers of development of this book. The question about the historical context seeks orientation about the text's time of development. Finally, the question of the theological context strives for knowledge about the theological conditioning and character of the author or the literary context.

In our particular case it is recommended that one seek insight from the introduction to the Genesis commentary of H. Gunkel (*HK* I 1) or G. v. Rad (*OTL*) or in the paragraphs on the pentateuch in an introduction to the Old Testament (or in *ABD*).

2. *Assembling secondary literature* also belongs to the preparation. For this purpose, we refer to the bibliographical helps mentioned in §2 A. For Gen 28:10–22, in addition to commentaries on Genesis, one should especially consult more recent investigations of the text such as Fohrer, *Exegese*, 180–220; A. de Pury, *Promesse divine et légende cultuelle dans le cycle de Jacob: Genèse 28 et les traditions patriarchales*, I–II, 1975; E. Otto, "Jakob in

Bethel," *ZAW* 88 (1976): 165–190. In the broader realm of new movements in penta-teuchal literary analysis, one should consult works like H.H. Schmid, *Der sogenannte Jahwist*, 1976, and R. Rendtorff, *The Problem of the Process of Transmission in the Pentateuch* (see §4DII). Recently, Rendtorff, "Jakob in Bethel," *ZAW* 94 (1982): 511–523; and very thoroughly, E. Blum, *Die Komposition der Vätergeschichte*, WMANT 57, Neukirchen-Vluyn, 1984, 7–35, have treated this text from the perspective of these new movements. The most recent contributions are: J. Van Seters, *Prologue to History: The Yahwist as Historian in Genesis*, Louisville, 1992, 288–307; and S. McEvenue, "A Return to Sources in Gen 28:10–22?" *ZAW* 106 (1994): 375–389.

3. The fact that one now gathers secondary literature, by no means implies that one begins the various sections of the methodologically directed work with a review of that literature. The theses of this literature would too strongly predispose one's own judgment and hinder the development of one's own view. Rather, it is emphatically recommended that one *proceed as follows*: First, with the help of the methodological instructions, the exegete attempts to produce the necessary clarifications. In a broader step, one then consults literature on the respective methodological question. Finally, in a third step, one forms a reasoned judgment in light of the literature.

I. Text Criticism

According to the procedures which are given above in §3,[221] the process is evident and not difficult to perform in the case of our text. After confirming the condition of the transmitted text in *BHK*, which only offers variants in non-Hebrew versions, examination and decisions are easy. In light of the criteria mentioned, there is no cause to deviate from the MT. Anyone using the *BHS* edition of Genesis, can certainly not create any greater picture of the text transmission, and has nothing to decide text critically. The editor has decided for the exegete and not made known a single variant! Instead, anyone who has a lot of time can decode the marginal notes of the masora which BHS offers in abundance. The exegete may want to discover the exegetical results for himself/herself!

II. The Question of the Text's Development

The exegete is already driven to the question of the text's development in the imaginative phase by one's own observations and attempts at clarification prior to entering the exegetical work.[222] The literary critical, transmission historical, and redaction historical investigation belong to the question of the text's development.[223] Now it is time, with the aid of methodological instruction in this area, to acquire a scientifically grounded judgment, which is demonstrable and achievable.

---

221 See above, page 41ff.
222 See above, §11 B II (p. 175ff).
223 Compare above, §1 C II (p. 15) and §4 A I (p. 47ff).

1. Literary Criticism

In connection with the above mentioned commentaries on approach and method,[224] one should begin with the *question of the literary integrity*, and one should proceed through the text with the given series of criteria. It appears that Gen 28:10ff offers *an abundance of indicators* of literary disunity:

a.   Doublets (e.g. 28:16/17: recognition of the holiness of the place; 28:12/13: two appearances; 28:15/20f: promise/condition of vow).
b.   Double or multiple transmission in Genesis (e.g. the naming of Bethel in 28:19; 35:7; and 35:15).
c.   Secondary parenthetical statements (e.g. 28:21b: equating YHWH and Elohim; See "g" below).
d.   Tensions in vocabulary (e.g. the end of 28:14: position; 28:21b: position and context of the statement).
e.   Differences in manner of speech and style (28:15: protection on principal; 28:20: protection on the way now, Gen 28:22b, 2ms address).
f.   Differences of historical background (possibly: anointed pillar in 28:18 over against the religious qualification of the site differentiated in 28:13,17, but one must examine the contextual possibility religio-historically, based on bible dictionaries, encyclopedias, and concordances, etc.; YHWH speaks in 28:13, which is contrasted with God's appearance in 28:12,17, etc.).
g.   Elements specific to layers or sources (such as J's use of YHWH in 28:13,16; Elohim in 28:12,17,20,22 in the patriarchal time for P [which is excluded here stylistically] or E; the dream in 28:12 for E; Haran in 28:10 according to the context of 27:41ff for J; 28:14 for J according to 12:3, etc.).
h.   Tensions of content (e.g. Bethel is the house of God according to 28:17f; but according to 28:22 the pillar will become the house of God after the return).

These indicators can be *evaluated* in the sense of literary disunity. They can also be presumably substantiated at this point, first by the names of God, according to the usual pentateuchal hypothesis as portions of J and E. This attempt was made already in the phase of historical outlook.[225] Insight gleaned from secondary literature shows that this kind of division of the text by J and E is highly debated today.

According to the *limitations* attached to §4 above,[226] it is actually doubtful whether accepting the conflation of two source texts in the present text provides a completely satisfactory substantiation (compare especially limitations "c" and "f"). Above all, the historical outlook phase already demonstrated the fragmentary character of the presumed J-version and the difficulty of coordinating the individual verses literary critically. If one is moved at all into the field of classical pentateuchal analysis (see also the advance of Rendtorff in light of Gen 28, in *The Problem of Transmission*, 57ff,68ff,108ff,140ff, and *ZAW* 94 [1982]: 511–523; and Blum), then one must choose between a JE connection in Gen 28 or acceptance of a literarily disunified base text which has been expanded by 28:13aβ–15

---

[224] See above, p. 53ff.
[225] See above, p. 180ff.
[226] See above, p. 55ff.

(Rendtorff, Blum) or by further additions (Fohrer, *Exegese*, 182–185). This decision depends upon: 1) which image one makes on the basis of methodological preconceptions about the literary development of the Pentateuch, 2) how, using traditional pentateuchal source theory, one decides about the state, flow, and profile of J and/or E, with respect to the text of Gen 28; or 3) upon the transmission historical investigation which one must first undertake according to the limitations of c) and f) in §4 B II 2 (p. 55ff.).

Because of the confusion which dominates current research regarding point "1," one must abandon a really justified literary categorization in the framework of an individual study of Gen 28:10ff. Since the recent investigations of Rendtorff and Blum establish a literary model of the Pentateuch without the traditional source writings, we will execute the illustration in that which follows under the working hypothesis of classic Pentateuchal analysis, without claiming a decision.

Addition for the American/English Edition

It should be emphasized once again that §11 does not intend to present a new thesis about the origin of Gen 28:10–22. Rather §11 intends to illustrate an exegetical technique with fluid possibilities. A new thesis about this text would have to consider today's more well known difficulties before one could find the classic Pentateuchal sources, Yahwist and Elohist, in this text. The reason is clear since the explanatory model executed in §11 shows that J has been received only fragmentarily, while E dominates, which is an exception to the rule (see below, p. 186). A new investigation of the text might come to a simpler result without presuming the classic sources of the Pentateuch. I am indebted to my assistant, K. Schmid, for the comments which he provided: (1) The beginning of the text's development consists of an independent individual narrative: 28:11f, 16 (the first three words), 17–19a. (2) This individual narrative was then adopted into the Jacob Cycle by 28:20–21a,22a (28:21b,22b are more recent expansions to the Jacob Cycle). (3) Later, in connection to a larger literary work (presentation of the ancestral period or the primal history + the ancestral period, or larger still?), a theological accentuation in the sense of Gen 12:1–3; 13:14–17 was undertaken by Gen 28:13–15,16 (the remaining words).

2. Anticipating the Transmission Historical Approach[227]

a. The Material

The literary critical investigation has not yet decided whether Gen 28:13–*16 (henceforth called the J version) is part of a Yahwistic version along with 28:11–12, the beginning of 16, 17–22 (henceforth preliminarily called version A). For this reason, the transmission historical question should be addressed as necessary to both possibly literarily independent versions. One must also consider the prophetic reference in Hos 12:5,7, as insight from secondary literature or concordance work on Bethel or Jacob indicates. If Hos 12:5,7 is also literarily independent of the Genesis account, then one finds three written references to the same event which are literarily independent of one another. They must go back to a common older transmission.

---

[227] See above, §4 (p. 55f).

The next element is a *comparison*. All three references include the appearance of God to Jacob in Bethel while on a journey that necessitates a return. It is noteworthy, however, that God does not appear in version A, and says nothing. According to the proceedings in 28:12,17f, Jacob makes a vow, and only there does it speak of protection on the journey. In J, by contrast, the protection of Jacob while traveling is the subject of God's promissory speech. Is that an older thread? Everything depends upon Hos 12:5,7. If one glances at the text, commentaries, and secondary literature regarding the *Jacob transmission in Hosea*,[228] shows a text critically problematic passage. In Hos 12:5, if one decides with many for the solution, *'immô*, then Hosea knows a version of the transmission in which God speaks with Jacob in Bethel, as with J. Indeed, the content would agree with J in the assurance that Jacob will surely return with the help of his God (12:7)!

b. Observations and Initial Decisions [229]

The question of how one should evaluate this agreement of J and Hos over against A depends on whether Hos 12:5,7 stems from Hosea (Northern Kingdom), and whether it is independent of the J formulation, or relatedly, independent from the current form of Gen 28:10ff. An excursus into Hosea and the development of the book of Hosea is necessary for clarification. If one decides for Hoseanic origin, then J and Hosea offer *an older thread of transmission* with the promise of a return during the appearance of God. This thread is missing in A, or relatedly, it appears in the vow. What did this transmission thread look like prior to the written versions? Again, individual comparison is necessary. All versions, including the vow in A, have "return" (*šûb*), but they differentiate the goal. J has "in this land" (28:15, cf. 28:13). A has "to the house of my father" (28:21). J and A also share promises of assistance and protection (28:15,20), whereby J is formulated more basically ("wherever you go"). Is this formulation also an older thread? In deciding, two problems come together:

1. Is J formulated on the basis of A? Is it thus, as supposed, an expansion, apart from the promise of the return? If one seeks parallel references to the individual promissory elements in 28:13–15 with the help of concordance work, and then arranges these literary critically and redaction critically according to the source profile, then one discovers extensive J images with the expansive horizon. To this search, one adds simultaneously the literal agreements in the formulations of 28:20–22 under expansion (land instead of father's house) and generalization ("wherever you go"; reason in 28:15b). This observation can suggest the decision that there was not an independent J version. Rather, J presupposes A and enlarges it with 13–*16. However, one must add the limitation that J also found a divine speech in A, which has now been subsumed in 13–*16, and at any rate, A contained a promise of return. Or was there still more?

2. Is J dependent upon A? If so, then the promise of assistance and protection for the return is only given in the reference of 28:20 (A). The problem now is: Did J adopt this promise from version A in 28:20 or did version A already contain this promise in the

---

228 Compare, e.g. J. Jeremias, Der Prophet Hosea, ATD, Göttingen, 1983, p. 148,154; Blum, Die Komposition der Vätergeschichte, p. 18,161ff; H.D. Neef, Die Heilstraditionen Israels in der Verkündigung des Propheten Hosea, BZAW 169, Berlin, 1987.

229 See above, §4 (p. 55f).

divine speech which is now subsumed under 28:13–15? That means: Can the divine speech in version A have contained both the promise of return, assistance, and protection which is present in the appearance of God as well as the formulation of the vow? Here literary criticism and transmission history must incorporate form criticism as a check.[230] What else do the formulations of the vow presuppose? The result (cf. Otto, "Jakob in Bethel," 170ff, with literature): By genre, Gen 28:20-21a,22 is a thoroughgoing vow formulation. However, in parallel instances (e.g. Judg 11; 1 Sam 1; 2 Sam 15), this genre does not presuppose a promise that was taken up in the vow. Thus, version A cannot have contained the divine promise together with the vow in 28:20–22. The possibility of both is excluded! If J only expanded A, then J would have taken the parallel promise from 28:20–22, and arrived at a thread (divine speech with promise) by literary means which is also independently attested in Hosea. That scenario is highly unlikely!

The explanatory attempts employed thus far must be corrected to the degree that one agrees with the expressed understanding of Hos 12:5–7. Since J and Hosea, independently, reflect a promissory divine speech to Jacob in Bethel, it must be an older thread which A expunged in favor of the secondary formulation of a vow. *That means*: J does not depend on the A version. Rather, J *processes an older transmission independently*, even if one can only recognize this transmission as J lying behind 28:10,13–*16 in the present text. According to Hosea, the older transmission contains the promise of return and (because of the independence of A and J) it also contains the promise of assistance and protection. However, this promise was not expanded and generalized as with J, but was related explicitly to the journey as still present in A's secondary version of the vow.

3. Return to the Literary Critical Approach

On the basis of the transmission historical work, the *relationship of both versions* in Gen 28:10ff can now be *decided*. Expectations that J only expanded an older version must be corrected. Both versions are literarily independent of one another.

The *identification* of these versions, as expounded at the conclusion of "I", depends upon preliminary decisions. If one uses the classic pentateuchal analysis as the basis, which admittedly is not an easy task today, then one must certify the condition, the course (the pillar shall become the house of God in 28:22 [E] which anticipates 35:7 [E]), and the profile of J and E. That certification determines that version A belongs to the Elohistic source, and that version J belongs to the Yahwistic source which is here incorporated fragmentarily into the text of Gen 28. The accusation that the assignation of 28:13 and 28:*16 to J was produced formally and preliminarily, based solely on the criterion of the divine name, can be rejected by additional data in the text. One can be of the opinion that, on the one hand, the appearance of YHWH speaking in 28:12–17 excludes the conceptualization of the heavenly ladder with messengers on the other

---

[230] See above, §4, p. 55f.

hand. Either YHWH encounters Jacob directly or the encounter results indirectly through God's messengers at the gate of heaven. However, then the thesis of Blum (p. 11) becomes doubtful, namely that 28:12+13 are formulated as the content of the dream and form a indivisible climax (heavenly ladder, messenger, YHWH's presence, and the same chiastically in 28:16f). Further, the numinous quality of the location was discovered by Jacob. That discovery was reported twice, in 28:16 and 28:17. Once it was a surprising discovery of Jacob, the second time it was a frightening discovery. Is that a climax (Rendtorff, Blum)? It is much more likely a doublet.

This conclusion can be strengthened by incorporating investigations from the secondary literature for the written sources. In so doing, one asks to what degree the versions in Gen 28 agree with the tendencies of the sources stylistically (cf. Fohrer, *Exegese*, 186ff), form critically (note the oracle style of 28:13–15), regarding the tradition historical background, and in respect to the means of processing a transmission and particular tendencies (J expands and generalizes considerably in 28:13–15!). Also, research results concerning the status of the historical identification of the sources should be considered.

4. Transmission Historical Analysis

The work has established, however, using vacillating literary critical premises, that one should proceed from *three* literarily independent *witnesses to the transmission*: version J, version E, Hosea 12.[231] The following decisions have been necessary:

- The older transmission also offered a divine speech within the framework of an appearance of God. E's elimination of the appearance in favor of the formulation of a vow is secondary.
- This divine speech is not identical with 28:13–15 where one encounters J's own formulation (compare, e.g. Otto, "Jakob in Bethel," 178). The pre-literary content of the transmission only included the promise of a return (J,E, Hosea) and the promise of assistance and protection (J+E).

The subsequent transmission historical questions should at least be sketched. The *chief problem* is: What did the pre-literary transmission of the divine speech look like?

The J fragment and Hosea offer no further evidence beyond the journey setting and Bethel as the place of the event. One should note that all three literarily independent examples (Hosea, J, and also E) situate the event in a journey setting for Jacob. This thread must belong to the preliterary stage. From this observation one deduces that the preliterary transmission, "Jacob in Bethel" was not an isolated narrative when it entered the written examples. Rather, it was *part of a larger narrative entity*, a station in the presentation of Jacob's journey. Even this larger entity must be ascertained more closely, principally

---

231 One should of course include Gen 35 in the transmission historical analysis. Compare, de Pury, *Promesse divine*, 528ff; Otto, "Jakob in Bethel," p. 179ff; Blum, *Die Komposition der Väter-geschichte*, p. 7ff,35ff. We cannot treat this problem for reasons of space.

by comparing the Jacob transmission appertaining to the sources (J, E, P, Hosea) as a whole as well as the analytic and synthetic determination of their pre-literary transmission. In practical terms, one would incorporate a critical consideration of the existing research results. One would move toward a pre-literary Jacob-Esau-Laban cycle to which the pre-Israelite transmission of Gen 28 belonged prior to the transcription in sources, or its adoption in a prophetic speech (compare Noth, *Pentateuchal Traditions*, 79ff; de Pury; Otto, "Jakob in Bethel," 182ff; but also the first major section of Blum, *Die Komposition der Vätergeschichte*). The divine speech, with its promises regarding the situation, is apparently connected with this transmission layer and its setting in Jacob's journey.[232]

Is the *oldest transmission stage* thus attained? Has this Jacob-Bethel transmission behind Gen 28 thus always been a component of this cycle (so de Pury; though a glance through the literature shows most researchers differ)? The fact that the text then has two goals (the justification of the holiness and the naming of Bethel as well as the protection of Jacob on his journey) is puzzling. Nevertheless, the answer to this question essentially depends upon whether one can detect the shape of an even older individual story which was independent prior to the incorporation into the cycle. Since J and Hosea offer no additional evidence, one can only concentrate upon the E version in the transmission historical shape for this earlier story. Only a comprehension of the form critical approach can take us further at this essential point. It must provide information as to whether the contour of the genre of an individual narrative is visible.[233]

5. Anticipating the Form Critical Question regarding the Pre-literary Shape of the Transmission of Gen 28:10ff

The subject of the inquiry is the transmission historical form of Gen 28 within the cycle, as ascertained to this point: the situation of Jacob's journey + 28:11–12 + the divine promise + 28:17–19a. Whether the journey setting and the promise related to it belong to an older isolated narrative is questionable since they presuppose the cycle.

If one does not simply infer the answer from secondary literature, *the question regarding the shaping genre of the individual narrative* can be purposefully placed by observing the shape of the designated contents in some circumstances. Thus, one finds: narrative, patriarchal hero, material center in a location which was discovered by the patriarch as a place of divine presence; indicators of the presence (28:12+17); cultic fixtures (pillar); therefore the naming (28:19a). Bible knowledge or concordance work (looking under holy places in Old Testament narrative books) leads to parallel references. Basic knowledge of the Old Testament indicates that these elements concern etiologically shaped sagas about cult establishment. Compare Gunkel, *Einleitung*, §2; Fohrer, *Introduction*, §12,6; W.H. Schmidt, *The Faith of the Old Testament*, p. 22ff, etc.

If one determines the genre at this point by the helps provided above in §7,[234] which cannot be done here for reasons of space, then a comparison with other place name etiologies and cult discovery sagas from the early period of Israel shows the following: In the cycle form of Gen 28, the genre of an individual saga is indeed foundational. Its focal

---

232 The inversion of the promise into a vow in 28:20–22 is first situated in the transmission stage before E or in E itself. Compare Otto's discussion.

233 Compare §7 above.

234 See above, p. 106ff.

points unfold in the appearance of God to the founder of the cult at a supposedly profane location (28:11–12), and the founder's reaction and establishment of the cult (28:
17–18), and the logical naming of the holy location (28:19a). Thus, we encounter here an
older individual narrative associated with Jacob.

6. Return to the Transmission Historical Analysis

The form critical exploration has provided evidence that the cycle
adopted an *older individual narrative* which told how Jacob unexpectedly experienced the appearance of God (28:12) in Bethel (28:11), how he recognized
the quality of the site (28:17), erected the pillar (28:18), and named the location the "house of God"/Bethel because of the appearance (28:19). The
relationships to a journey setting, and perhaps the divine speech associated
with the journey setting as well, probably did not belong to this individual narrative.[235]

> Has the *transmission historical starting point* of Gen 28:10ff now been reached?
> The exegete would perhaps answer the question affirmatively. However, if one re-
> calls the presuppositions from the historical overview, and if one resolved the question
> in the procedural step of the historical setting (§9), then the exegete knows that Bethel
> was a pre-Israelite sanctuary and already existed in the patriarchal period. If one ad-
> dressed tradition history (§8) to this individual narrative, then on the basis of the his-
> tory of religion, one is compelled to conclude that 28:11–12, 28:17–18, and no less so
> the name Beth-el (= house of El) contain pre-Israelite concepts from the ancient orien-
> tal Canaanite realm. The only (proto-)Israelite element in the individual narrative
> appears in the form of Jacob and perhaps the manner of reference to Elohim instead of
> El. These observations suggest the conclusion that the origin of the individual narrative
> was *initially* the *Canaanite cult etiology* for the Canaanite sanctuary of Bethel.
> This narrative may be the transmission historical beginning. However, observations
> from the history of religion in the framework of §8 allow one to consider, along with
> many researchers,[236] whether there is *yet an older concept* associated with Bethel at
> work in the transmission. Tension between statements about the pillar and 28:12+17, as
> well as 28:22, imply the divinity of the place was not thought to dwell in heaven, like the
> Canaanite deity, but in the pillar of Bethel. Gen 28:22 then contained an older reference
> adopted secondarily into the vow.

7. The Transmission Historical Synthesis

Outlining the work for the individual transmission stages, according to
the instructions in §5[237] and the corresponding procedural step in the historical setting, provides the following:

---

[235] For the question of the transmission historical relationship to Gen 35, see the literature
mentioned above in footnote 231.

[236] Cf. V. Maag, "Der Hieros Logos von Beth-El" (1951), in Maag, *Kultur, Kulturkontakt und
Religion*, Göttingen, 1980, p. 29–37; V. Maag, "Syrien-Palästina," in *Kulturgeschichte des Alten Ori-
ents*, H. Schmökel, ed, Stuttgart, 1961, p. 448–605 (especially 563ff); H. Donner, "Zu Gen
28,22," *ZAW* 74 (1962): 68–70; W.H. Schmidt, *Faith of the Old Testament*, p. 24.

[237] See above, p. 69ff.

a. *The oldest traces of the transmission* of Gen 28:10ff possibly point into the *pre-Canaanite megalithic culture* of Palestine (V. Maag). These traces tell about the divinity which was worshipped in Bethel at that time. It was incorporated in the pillar which was erected by an apparently giant person (compare Gen 6:1–4, etc.). One should include information about the pre-Canaanite inhabitants of Palestine and their megalithic culture (catchwords: pillars, dolmen, "giants," inhabitants of Palestine).

b. The narrative attains its *first tangible transmission form* when the sanctuary of Bethel became *cult site of the Canaanites*, who worshipped El of heaven there. They saw in Bethel the place of the association with his messengers for his work on earth. They saw Bethel as the house of El and the gate of heaven. Narrative threads associated with the place from the pre-Canaanite period became integrated. One should include information about the Canaanite settlement of Palestine and about the conceptualizations of Canaanite religion.

c. With its strides into the land west of the Jordan (compare the historical analysis of the Jacob transmission in the secondary literature), the *proto-Israelite Jacob group* also adapted the sanctuary of Bethel.[238] They identified El, who was worshipped there, with their own ancestral god. They incorporated the constituting patriarch of their group as the one who established the cult. In this sense they took over the Canaanite cult etiology as the isolated narrative of Jacob. As a check, one should examine analogous transmission historical processes elsewhere in the Jacob and patriarchal transmissions.

d. According to the examined analysis, the next transmission stage is the *further development until the point of adoption into J, E, and Hosea.*

First, one must determine the shape, position, and function of the individual narrative in the *Jacob-Esau-Laban Cycle*, which itself received various influences over the course of time.[239] This determination is necessary especially since, according to the normal analysis of the Pentateuch, this cycle first entered into complete association with the patriarchal transmissions. With those patriarchal transmissions it also entered into complete association with the transmissions directed to Israel from the patriarchal period to the conquest. In a different form, it was then taken up by J and later E. With considerable certainty, it was during this process that the journey setting came into the narrative, and perhaps also the journey promise in the divine speech. The focal point changes from Bethel to Jacob, and indeed progressively to Jacob as a member of the increasingly narrated salvific history of Israel. It is still another problem whether the replacement of the divine speech by the vow was accomplished in this strand of the transmission process or by E.[240] It is only possible to make this very difficult area more precise, or to reach one's own responsible and considered conclusions, by means of tedious and extensive investigations of the entire Jacob transmission, the transmission history of the Pentateuch, and

---

238 The historical interpretation of the transmission historical relationship to Gen 35 allows one to make these perceptions more precise. See Otto.

239 Compare the extensive investigations of de Pury and Otto about this problem.

240 See above, footnote 232.

the history of Israel. As a rule, the exegete must rely entirely upon the results of secondary literature, and make a reasoned choice when possible. From the most recent literature, one would place de Pury, Otto and McEvenue on one side and Blum, Rendtorff, and Van Seters on the other side.

8. The Redaction Historical Approach

If one directs the synthetic perspective of the development of the transmission onto the realm of written conveyance, then one asks the redaction historical question (§6).[241] According to the literary critical results already ascertained, one should treat the following (under the working hypothesis of classic Pentateuchal Sources). On the one hand, one should treat the *adoption* of the Jacob-Bethel transmission within the Jacob cycle or even within the larger context of the patriarchal period to the conquest *in J and E*. On the other hand, one should achieve redaction historical aspects for Gen 28 from the *subsequent redactional layers* of the literary development of the Pentateuch (JE, JE^{dtr}, JEP), and also situate the additions of 28:19b and 28:21b.

The task appears extensive, but it is considerably reduced in practical terms since this expanded problem would have to take up explanations in the secondary literature. However, widely accepted explanations do not exist. Already with the transmission realm between the individual narrative and the written source, the exegete of the text entered largely uncertain terrain. In the redaction historical realm everything related to E is widely debated. The normal dating (H.H. Schmid, Van Seters) and existence (Rendtorff, Blum) of J has been called into question. Moreover, virtually nothing is known about the material profile and the treatment of the subsequent redactional stages.

The *adoption into E* can only be distinguished with difficulty from the state of the existing transmission available to E. And the research produces very different attempts regarding the flow of the context, the profile of the context, and especially the assignation of the vow in 28:20–22.[242] As a result, the *adoption into J* should be particularly investigated. If one adheres to this written source in the usual manner in spite of the current discussion,[243] then one shows that J indicates a framing function in his narrative text of the Jacob-Bethel scene.[244] Above all, the existing divine promise to Jacob yields information about the great promissory oracle of 28:13–15 in light of its structure. Namely, all of the essential promises to this point in J's presentation of the patriarchal period are here concentrated on Jacob, the father of the twelve tribes, the father of Israel. Here the interest in the sanctuary of Bethel has been completely displaced by a continuing interest: presenting YHWH's designation of Israel. J makes this designation using promissory oracles in the patriarchal story. All of these promissory oracles progress toward 28:13–15 as

---

241 See above, pp. 75ff.

242 Regarding the Jacob story in E, compare the discussions in the recent works of de Pury, *Promesse divine*, p. 519ff; and Otto, "Jakob in Bethel," p. 182ff.

243 Compare Old Testament introductions. Rendtorff arrives at different determinations for the promises of 28:13–15 on the basis of his new methodological thrust. Likewise, Blum does the same.

244 Compare Otto, "Jakob in Bethel," p. 182ff.

the climax of the patriarchal promises in J: the promise of land for Jacob and his descendants (cf. 12:1; 13:15); the promise of increase (cf. 12:2; 13:16); the promise of the means of blessing for all nations (cf. 12:3).[245] The fragmentary condition of J in 28:10ff only allows one to offer suppositions about the complete form of the transmission based upon 28:13–*16 and 28:10.[246]

The *Yehowistic (JE) redaction* would have been an important redaction critical process which decisively shaped the existing form of Gen 28:10–22. In this case, it essentially transmitted the E version (because it was more concrete?). From J, the Yahwistic redaction only included the following: 28:10 as the introduction because of the J context which served as the foundation; the promissory speech which was missing in E; and in 28:16. The fact that these sections were incorporated organically without a violent technique appears to be a process which was historically possible.[247]

The illustrative text of Gen 28:10–22 at this point requires that one be satisfied with suggestions, and causes one to give way to excerpted use of the leading questions developed in §6. The reason: one must have clarity regarding the larger literary context and especially regarding the pre-literary and the literary history of development of the Pentateuch. In the concrete case of a work on this text, one must make a preliminary decision between various models.

III. The Question of the Presuppositions of the Stages of Gen 28:10–22

In §1 it was demonstrated[248] that this related area of questions included three fields of investigation: form criticism (§ 7), tradition history (§8), and the historical setting (§9). Because these procedures presuppose considerably detailed study, the exegete must already form one's own observations and impressions in the imaginative phase at the beginning of one's work, even though less extensively than with the linguistic observations of the text. These questions must be asked for *each* of the text's developmental stages which have been ascertained, to the degree that they are visible in the text. We must here limit ourselves to an *illustrative problem for each approach* which can demonstrate the procedure.

---

[245] One must here exclude the particular problem which the unusual portion of 28:14a presents for transmission history and redaction history.

[246] De Pury, *Promesse divine*, p. 87–344,519ff, offers a thorough investigation of the outline of the Yahwistic transmission.

[247] The observation of the symmetrical correspondence of the narrative elements is apparently important for the growth of the transmission of Gen 28, as already demonstrated in the historical overview (see the chart above, p. 177). This principle of symmetrical shaping, which organically incorporates the changes to the transmission in our case, appears to have been widely practiced in Ancient Israel. For example, it is used in Gen 1 and Isa 1:21-26, texts which are literarily and transmission historically unified.

[248] See above, §1 C (p. 14f; cf. 95ff, 121).

1. The Form Critical Approach

If one looks back at the development of Gen 28:10ff, then the individual story may have already had a fixed linguistic shape that would also have remained fixed in the subsequent stages. Elements from the history of religion and tradition history belonging to this early phase suggest as much. If so, investigation of the *linguistic shape* of the individual transmission stages, the first component question of form criticism (§7),[249] must already begin in the realm of oral transmission.

The *determination of the genre*[250] for each of those transmission stages which were added during the work was already indicated above for the Canaanite narrative and for the individual Jacob narrative.[251] The form critical investigation of the subsequent transmission stages should note that the original dominant genre, "etiological saga of the founding of a cult," is only just a component genre in the continuing transmission. This change corresponds to a displacement in the life setting. Because it entered the Jacob cycle, the independent cult narrative became part of a larger narrative entity which now forms the framing genre. Accordingly, the life setting is no longer a circle of worshippers and the cult in Bethel. Rather, in growing measure, the life-setting is Israel which reaffirms itself from its own history and within this history by the transmission of the patriarch Jacob in Bethel. Correspondingly, the transmission of Jacob in Bethel, which is thus incorporated and evidenced, could be expanded by additional component genres. J does so by the oracle of 28:13-15,[252] while E does so through the vow (28:20,21a,22).

This *vow* can serve as an example of form critical investigation. Transmission history demonstrated that this passage joined the older transmission form and changed it. It is thus an expansion text which presupposed the preceding narrative of Jacob in Bethel.[253] In spite of this insight into the *limits*, the text materially represents a self-enclosed process, which for its part, demands, however, that fulfillment of the vow also be narrated in the continuation. This recognition confirms the transmission historical finding that the passage belongs with the narrative contexts beyond the isolated story.[254] One can clearly recognize three parts regarding the question of the *structure and the structural components*: an introduction which the subsequent process qualifies as a vow (28:20a); a direct speech which the formulation of the vow offers literally in two parts. The first part is a conditional clause with an imperfect verb introduced with 'im. It names the conditions for redemption (28:20b,21a). The second part is a vow promise (28:21) introduced with wĕhāyāh at the beginning of 28:21b.

---

[249] See above, p. 102ff. Extensive investigations of the linguistic shape of Gen 28:10–22 are found in Fohrer, *Exegese*, p. 186ff.

[250] See above, p. 106ff.

[251] See above, p. 188f.

[252] Regarding the genre, see H.-M. Dion, "The Patriarchal Traditions and the Literary form of the »Oracle of Salvation«," *CBQ* 29 (1967): 198–206; de Pury, *Promesse divine*, 209ff.

[253] See above, p. 189, footnote 232, and p. 190f.

[254] See above, p. 190f.

A certain *perspective on the subject* is thereby given. The subject is Jacob's future founding of the sanctuary and practice of tithing. It does not concentrate on the details of the preparation, nor on the immediate circumstances. Rather, it is an important promise associated with a stipulation. The significance of this stipulation underscores the journey of Jacob as the primary interest of the person speaking. Even this journey, however, is not seen comprehensively in all possible aspects (travel route, encounters and adventures on the journey). Rather, the journey is seen from the perspective of the time in sojourn which conceals dangers within it. Therefore, the time of sojourn should be a time of the safekeeping of life and of return: protection, sustenance, clothing.

Is a *genre* present? In this instance, the procedure is simple. The formulation of the introduction of 28:20a shows that one should inquire about vows. Genre parallels are not difficult to find using the concordance under *ndr/nēder* (e.g. Judg 11:30–31; 1 Sam 1:11; 2 Sam 15:7f). They confirm that the observed compositional elements comprise elements of the genre "vow."[255] The stylistic feature of the etymological figure in the introduction is firmly attached to this genre. The genre thus has its *life setting* (compare reference works under "vow") at holy (1 Sam 1) or at profane (2 Sam 15) locations in the mouth of individuals who are in a threatening or dangerous situation. In 28:20–22, the genre is thus used consistently with its life setting. It is also demonstrated that the vow itself belongs with a setting of the exposition of a threatening situation. Thus, Jacob's threatening journey must also have been narrated with the images of 28:20–22. On the other hand, as already evaluated with the approach to the development of Gen 28, it cannot already have had an oracular promise for the same situation.[256]

An investigation of the *genre history* in 28:20–22 could also bring insight into the age of the transmission historical change.

2. The Tradition Historical Approach

The question of the intellectual world of Gen 28:10ff involves a series of aspects, as developed in §8 above.[257] One should ask about the following for each of the text's developmental stages. One should ask about participation in the particular world view with its thought pattern, and, as necessary, where the text currently deviates and transcends that world view. One should ask about the religious and theological convictions; about the processed store of knowledge, awareness, and material; about the impact of terms; and finally about fixed themes and concepts which are adopted. A transmission like Gen 28 which has such a long history of growth certainly also reflects considerable changes in the intellectual world.

Even an initial sweeping overview makes such *changes in world view and religious convictions* quite apparent with perspectives from the history of religion and theology. These perspectives include: a comprehensively simple horizon of the divinity in the holy stone of Bethel; then Bethel as the location of a

---

255 Richter demonstrated this in his investigation mentioned in footnote 219.
256 See above, p. 185ff.
257 See above, p. 185ff.

divine palace related to a God of heaven and earth; God's dwelling in heaven and the mediation of God's work on earth whose background presupposes a comprehensive perspective on the world as well as an architectural standard of diverse temple and palace construction. Further, the perspectives include the more limited relationship of this perspective to the Jacob group. They include the tribes of Israel whose experience of God is simultaneously changing and deepening in the realm of historical experience as typified for Israel by the ancestral religion (significance of God in Bethel for the group and the traveling protection for Jacob). Finally, these perspectives include the universal historical perspective which the divine assertions of J compel. One can recognize these changes in a number of fixed contents in Gen 28, to the degree that one inquires into the co-existing viewpoints, processes, convictions, and conceptualizations, and to the degree that one situates these contents in Israel materially, chronologically, and geographically.[258]

A *specific example:*"House of God" in 28:17 may illustrate the procedure in several outlines of investigations with respect to the history of the term and the concept. A glance in lexica (HAL, THAT, TDOT) provides a wide spectrum of meaning for *bayit*. Nevertheless, the text reference is limited to a place and to the associate with God. By referring to parallels, one limits this spectrum to dwellings, a temple or a palace (if the divinity is presented as a royal god). Parallels also show that these dwellings can lie entirely in heaven (Ps 36:9). They do not have to be visible as a building, but still may be, as even Gen 28:10ff presupposes, since Jacob internalized the holiness of Bethel by discovering this quality in the place.

Bethel thus means house, dwelling, temple, or even palace of god. Which is meant more specifically? What did Canaanite narrators conceptualize who brought this term into the text? And what did they intend as self-evident? One should proceed from the constellations of the text and inquire into them purposefully.

It speaks of the "house" of *Elohim*. Elohim is not very suggestive as the abundance of examples in the concordance demonstrates, but in the context, according to 28:19, the place is named Beth-el, that is house of the God *El!* If one searches the concordance for parallels to this view under Bethel, then one is driven to the more striking reference to "El-Beth-El" in 35:7, which means the god El from Bethel! What concepts are associated with the god El as the god of a Palestinian sanctuary? Consulting Old Testament parallels with the help of the concordance under '*ēl* leads to El as the Canaanite god. By investigating the history of religion ones attains clear precision about the place, dwelling, lordship, court, worship, and the relationship to the local Elim of the god El which were apparently intended as self-evident in the Canaanite cult etiology of Bethel.[259] Even limi-

---

258 Fohrer, *Exegese*, p. 199ff, treats the "the fixed syndrome of significance" in more detail. The E version has: fear in the face of the nearness of the divine (28:17), and the erection of the pillar (28:18). The J version has the self-presentation of YHWH ("I am YHWH" in 28:13a), the different promises and the naming of the location in 28:19. One should also investigate the "gate of the temple" (28:17) and "all the tribes of the earth" (28:14) instead of "all nations."

259 Compare, for example, THAT and TDOT under 'el; *Wörterbuch der Mythologie* (see above, p. 32); Maag, "Syrien-Palästina," (see footnote 236), p. 563ff,570ff; H. Gese, *Die Religionen*

tations become clear. Nothing is adopted for the development of the cult etiology of Bethel from the complicated pantheon of Ugarit or from the problem of the relationship to Baal. Perhaps the El religion still had a simpler form here. In any case, it concerns a religiosity which coalesces with the sedentary, socio-historically different Canaanite culture: Bethel as sanctuary of the neighboring urban culture of the Canaanite city Luz.

What conceptualizations are associated with the *house* of El? Again, one must proceed with the realities presumed in the text. The house is not simply removed into the heavens, but the house is at the cult site of Bethel (28:19). On the other hand, El is not on the earth, he is instead in the heavens (28:12). He acts on the earth through messengers who enter earth from the heavens at the site of Bethel by a giant ladder, and then return. The sanctuary of Bethel is thus the earthly exit of a building conceptualized as extraordinarily high, which reaches into the heavens. The house of El is in this extension of the entire earth and heaven. Thus one conceptualizes that Bethel stands at that spot on the earth where the house of El towers high into the heavens. Bethel stands at the prominent point where the work of El on the earth through his messengers begins. From whence does this concept come? How is it contoured? How is it shaped for the Canaanite cult etiology? The exegete achieves a precise answer by incorporating corresponding texts and meanings (including pictorial representations) in the presentation of Canaanite religion together with its ancient oriental influences (especially those from Mesopotamia). This precision is attained by informing one's self from dictionaries and reference works in the fields of the history of religion and Old Testament theology, looking under El, *bayit*, and temple. If the exegete is familiar with the essay from C. Houtman, "What Did Jacob See in His Dream?" (*VT* 27 [1977]: 337–351), then the necessity of re-examining the tradition historical and the religio-historical background of the text's assertions about the structure becomes clear.

3. Determining the Historical Setting

If tradition history treats the intellectual world of the text in its history, then the historical setting (§9) treats the text's historical world by its realities, its social conditions and the experiences of persons in it. The historical setting treats these experiences to the degree that one can observe and master the correlation to the historical world with its events, social conditioning, tradition historical guidelines, and to the degree that the texts themselves tentatively allow one to determine. The question must be asked for each of the ascertained text stages separately. However, historically *broad questions* are demanded in some circumstances.[260] *Examples* of the sequence of the procedure are suggested briefly.

In the historically broad perspective one should perhaps treat the following: Where is Bethel (ancient site)? What are the archaeological realities and conclusions about Bethel? What does one know about the history of the sanctuary of Bethel? To which po-

---

Altsyriens (see above, p. 32); F. Stolz, *Strukturen und Figuren im Kult von Jerusalem*, BZAW 118, Berlin, 1970, esp. p. 149ff; Schmidt, *Faith of the Old Testament*, p. 138ff. Regarding Bethel in particular, see O. Eißfeldt, "Der Gott Bethel," in *Kleine Schriften*, vol. 1, 1962, p. 206–233.

260 See above, p. 144ff.

litical territory did it belong over the course of the history of Israel? What larger political processes could be important for the horizon of the transmission process? (This question is of significance in light of the long extensive development of the text which reaches into the post-exilic period.) What processes are associated with the place (pre-Israelite, conquest, Jeroboam I, Amos, Josiah)? What socio-historical changes can one note for the sanctuary's circle of worshippers? What (ever expanding) group of persons relates itself to Jacob over the course of time? What is the history of the institution of the vow and the tithe, as well as the cultic object of the pillar (appearance, worship, customs, function)? Relatedly, is it plausible after the time of Josiah that Bethel would have been a cultic center with a pillar (cf. the P version of Gen 35)? Examples for specific clarification: the path from Beersheba to Haran via Bethel (situation of the place, old routes); clarification of *sullām* (ladder, steps, ramp); is the stone pillar as something to lay under a person's head historical understandable as a custom?

An *example* for the historical setting of a *specific transmission stage:* We take the J version contained in 28:10,13–*16.

First, one should collect information about the time, setting, and author of the given transmission stage, which in this case is J. As a rule, this information can be gathered from reference works and Old Testament introductions, which can then be deepened by consulting the corresponding presentations of the time period in text books or monographs about the history of Israel. This consultation is performed in order to attain the most dynamic perspective possible of the time. If one places J in the Davidic-Solomonic period, as was common earlier, then the pertinent historical transmission realm is the fortunate formation of the kingdom from the tribal territories which occurred almost overnight. Characteristics of this historical arena included: the formation of the territorial state threatening the federation of Israel; the enormous social and cultural historical upheavals; mastering the problems of this new entity by connection with the transmission, which lead to unrest and rebellion even in the time of David; the expanded geographical horizon which was observable at that point; the phenomenon of ruling non-Israelite areas and people within one kingdom. In addition, the older transmissions, which were only oriented toward the land of Israel, offered no extensive clarification for this situation.

This entire event could be experienced as inconceivably fortunate. From the relationship of the leading traditions to that point, one would have experienced the unforeseen reality before one's eyes, but also the tension and irritation of that which is new. Questions of the identity of Israel, in the face of the new elements, were certainly not just theoretical. They were problems unavoidably necessitated by the experience of the time.

If one sees the Yahwistic accents in 28:13–15 from this dynamic background, then one can gain intentions related to that time and a profile of the goals of J toward the hearer/reader. Experiencing the present as being a large (meaning powerful) people as the descendants of Jacob in one's own land is not some unintelligible, profane-political effect. Rather, it is the redemption of a promise to the ancestors deriving from the trustworthy God, YHWH. This promise was given particularly to Jacob, the progenitor of the people of the twelve tribes. Israel had its identity from this promise. The generalized promise in 28:15b leads into the present and, for Israel, qualified the time between Jacob and the great kingdom before them as the eminent confirmation of the power of

YHWH in history. The new perspective of other nations inside and outside the kingdom is explained in the promise as the mediation of blessing. Also, the new perspective is given as a value for understanding their history and for orienting political action. When expanded and justified in more detail, these suggested profiles demonstrate the function of determining the historical setting. Still, they belong already to the interpretation.

D. INTERPRETING THE HISTORICALLY DETERMINED MEANING OF GEN 28:10–22 IN ITS VARIOUS STAGES OF GROWTH

Of course, the complete explication of the content presupposes that all the procedures are also carried out, in contrast to the necessarily illustrative sketches in the preceding. This expectation and reasons of space, necessitate that we continue this type of work for §10 only in areas which illustrate its usage: its procedure, its functional connection to the events from the individual methodological procedures, and the directions of its inquiry.[261] As presented, the interpretation should primarily be performed by taking up the impressions from the imaginative phase for each transmission stage separately.[262] Next, one should extend the interpretation to the entire Old Testament development. Then, one should add considerations regarding the meaning of the text in light of our present time. Finally, the entire exegetical work climaxes in an appropriate English translation of the text. We must be satisfied with catchwords. We will note the sections of the workbook in parentheses whose approaches provide the acquisition of those results reached.

I. The Individual Transmission Stages

The formative *Canaanite transmission stage* belongs to the area of Canaanite settlers in Middle Palestine (city of Luz), perhaps in the middle of the second millenium (§§7,8,9). They adopt the existing stone sanctuary at Bethel for the (chief) god, El. They establish this process by taking up older narrative threads concerning this sanctuary. They establish the place name Bethel in a cultic etiology. For the worshippers, this narrative clarified the quality and the equipment of the sanctuary (§7) as the preeminent place which El chose as the place of his work in the earthly realm (§8). The event fundamentally validating the quality of Bethel was narrated as the initial event, as the discovery of the holiness of the place and as the founding of the cult. The strands of El, which were universal and concretely significant for the circle of worshippers, expanded the pre-Canaanite concept of God on the stone of Bethel. These threads articulate the highest quality of the presence of El, like other El sanctuaries in Palestine, each for their respective region. They thereby articulate

261 See above, p. 158ff.
262 See above, p. 175ff.

the cultic accessibility of the highest divine guarantor of all enduring areas of life, perhaps the essential agrarian areas of life, at the holy place (§8).

The Canaanite cultic etiology was (also) taken over by the *Jacob group* who adapted the Bethel sanctuary (§5). This adaptation happened, however, in a changed experiential environment. A previously seminomadic group now became a sedentary group who identified their leading ancestral god with the Canaanite El of that place. By introducing their ancestor Jacob as the discoverer and founder of the cult, they strengthened themselves and legitimated their claims (§9). The experience of God in Bethel changed. El of Bethel was confirmed as the leading god of the Jacob group, to whom they owed their conquest. The universal implications of 28:12 could be condensed, and in some cases reduced, into the group (§8).

The incorporation of the individual Jacob story into a *Jacob cycle* could provide confirmation of this change in the experience of god at Bethel (§§4, 5,7). It could provide confirmation as to how large the Israelite circle of worshippers might have been who increasingly traced themselves to Jacob. The holiness of the place Bethel and the power of the god being worshipped (YHWH) is no longer established by the quality of the place itself mentioned in 28:12,17. Rather, the holiness is provided by the promise from God of protection (§§4,5,7) which Jacob received at this place. By this time, the scene is now a meaningful deepening of the experience that all descendants of Jacob owe their existence and their condition to the fulfillment of this promise to Jacob. The experience of the accompaniment and the leading of their own god reaching into the present time had proven God to be an effectively sympathetic god in Bethel (§§8,9). Even in these contingencies, this God had been proven by the gift of experienced realities in their own life conditions.

We must skip over historical backgrounds and reflections of the experience of God in the various shapes of the Jacob cycle, including the incorporation into the salvation history presentation for all Israel, and for E. Still, we will cast a glance at the Yahwist. As 28:13–*16 demonstrates, the transmission here attains considerably more and new accentuation from the background of the realities of the historical location (§9). Instead of God making himself known at the unknown place, resulting in the holiness of Bethel, Bethel is now just the place where the long recognized YHWH appears. In the patriarchal period, YHWH here concentrates promises for Israel on Jacob, the father of the twelve tribes of Israel. It is essential for Israel, in reference to its own experiential reality, that YHWH unexpectedly appeared to Jacob (28:16). Above all, it is essential to know what YHWH promises, with qualifications and stipulations, for the present experience of Israel in the circle of nations, expanded and made problematic by the new situation of the monarchy.[263]

---

263 See above, p. 192ff.

The interpretation of the redactional stages of transmission (§6) must again be by-passed.[264]

II. The Old Testament Development

An overview of the Old Testament development shows that the original meaning of the transmission (establishing a cultic site in one's own region as the holy place bestowing god's presence) does not continue. The *experience of the presence* from the cult site of Bethel is shifted to the historical condition of Israel by the adoption of the proto-Israelite and the Israelite transmission. Through alternating and internally changing horizons, Gen 28 deepens the current experiential world of Israel as the place of divine closeness. It deepens the event of divine gift and leadership from the small radius of the Jacob group to Israel and its land in the circle of all nations.

Even in times of deprivation, the entire state of the promise in Gen 28 established expectations and legitimated hopes in JE. This expectation and legitimation occurred, for example, in the time of Josiah and since the time of the exile, in complete contrast to the opposite experience which existed. The meaning was no longer mastered inside the narrative of Gen 28 alone, but by its inclusion into the great historical works with the deuteronomistic and priestly accents that reached from the creation to the exile. In all of these transmission stages, the *emphasis providing meaning* to the text lies in the promises (or for a time in a tangential line, the vow). From these promises, later Israel has inferred meaning for establishing its identity, for itself and for YHWH in the experiential realm of Israel.

III. Considering the Text's Movement of Meaning in Light of Our Present Time

Also here just a few remarks. That which in many respects appears obtuse and strange to the modern reader, does not prove to be simply as naive in the historical illumination of the origin and transmission of the text in the Old Testament.[265] Rather, it should be perceived as the articulation of meaning for an experiential world. The claim of the statement, the particular existence, the particular area of life, even the political dimension of life and the historical community life of the people should not be perceived as something which is unquestionably accepted. It should be perceived as the gift of the benevolently giving God working in the present. Through the story one gleans the amazing feature from the miracle, which is not even surrendered in times of deprivation. God turns to the earth, allows himself to be found, and actively sustains

264 However, see "The Old Testament Development" in the following section.
265 See above, §11 B I (p. 174f).

existence. Today, the thoughtlessly self-serving acceptance of life and the given world appear in the mirror of this text. Likewise, the text illuminates how the flight into surrogate areas which replace the holy, now as before, requires places of assurance and encounter. The text shows how Gen 28 in its transmission path protects one from perceiving god as the extrapolation of worldly values. The transmission tendency of displacing the Canaanite threads of the narrative in favor of the historical experiential realm of God, requires no one to adopt these historically conditioned elements no matter how pervasive and powerful their assertions might be as images. Rather, it teaches one to see the *depth of meaning of Gen 28*. For the Christian, this depth is shown in Christ. Gen 28 would teach the Christian to understand Christ as the holy place of God's turning to the world; to understand Christ as a person, as a guarantee of the promise of God's accompaniment and sustenance of life; to understand Christ as the release of meaning for conquering contradictory experiences in the sin, suffering, and death of the individual, and the worldwide threat against humanity; to understand Christ as the guide on a path which does not end in ideals which are realized in an earthly nation, but which lead to God over all the dangerous paths of human existence. "Jesus speaks to Nathaniel: 'Truly, truly, I say to you, you will see the heavens opened and the angels of God ascending and descending on the son of Man.'" (John 1:51)

APPENDIX: LITERATURE ILLUSTRATING THE EXEGETICAL TREATMENT OF A TEXT

H.W. Wolff. Der große Jesreeltag (Hosea 2, 1–3). Methodologische Erwägungen zur Auslegung einer alttestamentlichen Perikope. EvTh 12 (1952/53): 78–104 (also in: Wolff, Gesammelte Studien zum Alten Testament. ThB 22. Munich, ²1973. p. 151–181.

K. Koch. The Growth of the Biblical Tradition. Part II: Selected Examples, p. 111–220.

O.H. Steck. Die Paradieserzählung. Eine Auslegung von Genesis 2,4b–3,24. BSt 60. Neukirchen-Vluyn 1970 (=Steck, Wahrnehmungen Gottes, p. 9–116).

E. Zenger. Ein Beispiel exegetischer Methoden aus dem Alten Testament (Ri 9). In: Schreiner. Einführung. p. 97–148.

G. Fohrer. Exegese. § 12 (Gen 28:10201–22).